The Film Studio

CRITICAL MEDIA STUDIES
INSTITUTIONS, POLITICS, AND CULTURE

Series Editor
Andrew Calabrese, University of Colorado

Advisory Board

Recent Titles in the Series

Changing Concepts of Time
  Harold A. Innis
Mass Communication and American Social Thought: Key Texts, 1919–1968
  Edited by John Durham Peters and Peter Simonson
A Fatal Attraction: Public Television and Politics in Italy
  Cinzia Padovani
Entertaining the Citizen: When Politics and Popular Culture Converge
  Liesbet van Zoonen
Campaign Consultants, Communications, and Corporate Financing
  Gerald Sussman
Contracting Out Hollywood: Runaway Productions and Foreign Location Shooting
  Edited by Mike Gasher and Greg Elmer
The Medium and the Magician: The Radio Legacy of Orson Welles, 1934–1952
  Paul Heyer

Forthcoming

Raymond Williams
  Alan O'Connor
The Blame Game
  Eileen Meehan
A Violent World
  Nitzan Ben-Shaul
Mediated Terrorism
  Edited by Anandam P. Kavoori and Todd Fraley

The Film Studio

Film Production in the Global Economy

Ben Goldsmith and Tom O'Regan

ROWMAN & LITTLEFIELD PUBLISHERS, INC.
Lanham • Boulder • New York • Toronto • Oxford

ROWMAN & LITTLEFIELD PUBLISHERS, INC.

Published in the United States of America
by Rowman & Littlefield Publishers, Inc.
A wholly owned subsidary of The Rowman & Littlefield Publishing Group, Inc.
4501 Forbes Boulevard, Suite 200, Lanham, MD 20706
www.rowmanlittlefield.com

P.O. Box 317, Oxford OX2 9RU, UK

British Library Cataloguing in Publication Information Available

Library of Congress Cataloging-in-Publication Data

Goldsmith, Ben, 1967–
  The film studio : film production in the global economy / Ben Goldsmith and
Tom O'Regan.
    p. cm. — (Critical media studies)
  Includes bibliographical references and index.
  ISBN 0-7425-3680-7 (alk. paper) — ISBN 0-7425-3681-5 (pbk. : alk. paper)
  1. Motion picture industry. 2. Motion picture studios. 3. Industrial location. I.
O'Regan, Tom. II. Title. III. Series.
PN1993.5.A1G634 2005
384'.4—dc22

                                                                          2004024349

Printed in the United States of America

∞™ The paper used in this publication meets the minimum requirements of
American National Standard for Information Sciences—Permanence of Paper for
Printed Library Materials, ANSI/NISO Z39.48-1992.

This book is dedicated to Elizabeth Mitchell, Eloise and Sam Goldsmith, and Dominic and Joseph O'Regan.

Contents

Acknowledgments

This book would not have been possible without the assistance and support of a large number of people. Our sincere thanks go to all those who agreed to be interviewed for the project that became this book between 2001 and 2004. In particular, we would like to thank Daniel Dark, Michael Grade, Dina Iordanova, Ann Nolan, Jeremy Pelzer, Nick Smith, Naoise Barry, Jane Boushell, Ned Dowd, Moira Horgan, Vinnie McCabe, Padraig Murray, Morgan O'Sullivan, Rod Stoneman, Henning Molfenter, Matous Forbelsky, Tomas Krejci, Lynne Benzie, Louisa Coppel, John Cox, Elle Croxford, Dale Duguid, Lynn Gailey, Barbara Gibbs, Carol Hughes, Terry Jackman, Robin James, Vic Kasper, Gary Keir, John Lee, Garry Macdonald, Murray Pope, Veronica Sive, Henry Tefay, Marc van Buuren, and Kim Williams.

We also wish to acknowledge the Australian Film Commission, especially Catherine Griff and Kim Ireland, who supported this project in its early stages.

Particular thanks go to our research assistants and associates: Susan Ward, Mark Ryan, Kitty van Vuuren, and Tiziana Ferrero-Regis.

We also wish to thank Allen J. Scott for generously making available to us, prepublication, his book *On Hollywood*.

At Rowman & Littlefield, we would like to thank Andrew Calabrese, Erica Fast, Brenda Hadenfeldt, and Jeska Horgan-Kobelski for assistance in preparing and editing the manuscript.

Ben Goldsmith would like to acknowledge the support of the Australian Research Council Postdoctoral Fellowship scheme, Griffith University, and the Australian Film, Television, and Radio School. He dedicates this book to his wife, Elizabeth Mitchell, and their children, Eloise and Sam Goldsmith.

Tom O'Regan would like to acknowledge the support of the Australian Research Council Discovery Grant scheme and the University of Queensland. He dedicates this book to his twin sons, Dominic and Joseph O'Regan.

Introduction

A *studio* is generally defined as a workshop for artists and photographers, or a workshop or rehearsal space for dancers or actors. In relation to film, the workshop or building for cinematographic, sound, or music recording is generally referred to as a *stage*, and the term *studio* or *studios* generally means "all the buildings on a film [or television] company's site, whatever their function."[1] A studio or studio complex may include some or all of the following: silent- and soundstages, set preparation workshops, stores and lockups, makeup salons and dressing rooms, wardrobe rooms and laundry, production and administration offices, editing suites, processing laboratories, sound mixing studios, audio suites, scoring or orchestral stage, library, special effects and model workshops, backlot, water tank, preview screening room, and commissary. Stages usually incorporate "specific design structures that make [them] ideal for production: high ceilings, insulated walls, lighting grids and additional power considerations."[2]

Studio is also widely used to refer to a commercial film production company which may or may not own and occupy a "studio"—that is, a physical site of production. The most obvious examples of this are the Hollywood studios, often referred to simply as "the majors"—Twentieth Century–Fox, Warner Bros., Sony Pictures Entertainment, Universal Studios, the Walt Disney Company, MGM, and Dreamworks SKG.

In this book, we use the term *studio* or *film studio* to denote the physical infrastructure used for the production of feature films and television programs. This book is about the contemporary enthusiasm in various parts of the world to build, renovate, or redevelop large-scale studios capable of hosting high-budget, often special effects–driven English-language feature films. This is happening in existing production epicenters—Los Angeles, Rome, Prague, Berlin, London, New York, Toronto, Sydney—and in places that have not previously had an extensive connection with Hollywood or international film and television production more generally. This enthusiasm has been fostered by producers—including the Hollywood majors—seeking to take advantage of the enhanced mobility and flexibility of audiovisual production enabled by technological developments and globalization.

The promise of international production—to build local capacity and skills, to make a significant contribution to the local economy, to raise the profile and image of a place—generates in turn local enthusiasm critical to the development of infrastructure necessary to service this production, including, most importantly, studios. Historically this was the case for Florida, Vancouver, the Gold Coast (Australia), and Bucharest in the late 1980s and early 1990s, but it is also now the case for Cape Town, the Isle of Man, Melbourne, and Alicante. Studios and places are now competing against each other on the basis of their ability to provide a range of generic skills, services, and expertise to individual films, augmented by what are claimed to be unique or compelling local advantages—the availability of state-of-the-art studio infrastructure, particular creative individuals or firms, and the proximity to specific locations.

In this book, we use the film studio to investigate this competition among places to attract film production, concentrating both on its effects in particular places and on global film production dynamics. We will examine both film- and non-film-related rationales behind this global "serial reproduction" of studio complexes. The book begins from the recognition that studio complexes are simultaneously part of the larger international audiovisual production economy and part of localized film, cultural and creative economies, and policy frameworks. In its analysis of the film- and non-film-related work of film studios and the rhetorics deployed around them—what they do and what they enable—the book explores the broad global and particular local dynamics driving the dispersal of English-language feature film production in particular, and the consequences of and responses to that dispersal. Through the optic of the film studio, this study argues that this global dispersal of production is best understood as an unstable and unequal partnership between a footloose international production economy and situated local actors and intermediaries. We identify the various types of film studios and examine the consequences of these developments for "Hollywood," for international film production, and for the places hosting these studio complexes.

Most of the literature about how international production is changing overlooks the development of studio complexes and concentrates instead on what is driving this global dispersion of production. As a result, locations appear to be more or less interchangeable. By contrast, our focus on a vital piece of production infrastructure—the film studio—not only illuminates these "push" dynamics by anchoring them to place and space but also, importantly, allows for the consideration of the "pull" factors drawing production to particular places. In doing so, it makes visible the important and ongoing role of place, local intermediaries, and physical infrastructure in the global dispersal of production.

By taking studios in general and places in particular as its focal points, this book aims to throw a new light on the dynamics of international production and changing film policy formations in an era of globally dispersed and networked production. It also makes a significant contribution to current debates in critical media studies on the commoditization of culture, the political economy of the entertainment industries, the business strategies of multinational corporations and the responses of local actors, and cultural aspects of globalization.

Notes

1. *The Focal Encyclopedia of Film and Television Techniques*, (London: Focal, 1969), 785.

2. Steven E. Browne, *Film-Video Terms and Concepts* (Stoneham, Mass.: Focal, 1992), 156–57.

CHAPTER ONE

International Production and Globalization

The hypermobility of contemporary feature film production has sparked a global explosion of interest in building and renovating production infrastructure to service and anchor this production to place. Older studio complexes have been renovated in traditional production locations like Rome, Berlin, London, New York, and Los Angeles. New complexes have been built in traditional centers, as well as in a variety of nontraditional locations, including Vancouver, Bucharest, Cape Town, Wilmington, and Wellington. These studio complexes and accompanying production infrastructure are some of the "boring institutions" that "cool projects" rely on.[1] They respond to the circumstances and logic of a global industry and particularly of blockbuster production—what director Sir David Lean described as the "last of the great travelling circuses."[2] This is a beautifully pregnant metaphor, alluding to the illusion and wonder of film, to the size and hyperreality of its production, and also to the nomadism of its practitioners decamping from place to place in the hope of drawing a crowd. Lean's comment catches the intrinsically individualized project-based and -managed quality of these large-scale, sometimes peripatetic productions. They typically use a variety of natural, found, and purpose-built locations around the world. The metaphor also hints at the logistics, scale, complexity, and impact of the staging of these productions both on the places in which they are shot (the location) and from which they are derived and often postproduced (the design center).

One of the major differences between the contemporary production environment and that in which Lean worked is that more places are equipped with the requisite infrastructure necessary to sustain the circus, minimizing the costs of trekking in equipment, supplies, and people from Los Angeles or London or another major filmmaking center. In this chapter, we explore the emergence and intersection of these location and design interests identifying the role of infrastructure and location and a project-based orientation in organizing the material conditions of international production.

Location and Design Interests

The hypermobility of blockbuster and other international productions and the availability of globally dispersed infrastructure are core aspects of the "colossal transformation" of the contemporary international landscape and ecology of film production.[3] Both are products of the same production system—the global Hollywood of Miller et al.'s formulation.[4] While they are clearly closely linked, each serves discrete—sometimes contiguous, sometimes disaggregated—interests. Blockbuster production is driven by the peripatetic "design interest" of the international producers, sometimes including the Hollywood majors, and employs (short-term) project-based thinking, while infrastructure provision is driven by "location interest" and employs longer-term "located thinking," where the primary concern is to maintain a permanent production presence in a particular location.

The two interests converge when extensive infrastructure is created to serve the needs of particular films. Often this infrastructure is "struck" or dismantled at the end of the shoot, like the elaborate, windswept town of Edoras in *The Two Towers*, or the freeway "studio" built for the second and third parts of the *Matrix* trilogy at Alameda Naval Air Station in California.[5] Sometimes the infrastructure remains available for other projects and productions for a limited period, as did the hangars and acreage of Hatfield aerodrome in the United Kingdom that served initially as a location for *Saving Private Ryan*, before becoming the principal location and site of eleven European villages for the HBO series *Band of Brothers*. Occasionally the infrastructure becomes a permanent fixture, as did the Fox Baja studios built around enormous water tanks that had been created especially for *Titanic*. According to producer Jon Landau, this facility was created because

> [n]o single existing site in the world could contain the scale of our production and the attendant facilities that were required to film the scenes that Jim Cameron envisaged. . . . In order to support the scope of the film and to be able to facilitate both interior and exterior production it was more efficient to custom build it all in one place.[6]

Another example of permanent infrastructure is Leavesden Studios, which were created initially for the James Bond film *GoldenEye* and used subsequently for *Star Wars: Episode I—The Phantom Menace* and for the Harry Potter series. In each case, a blockbuster created spaces for filmmaking that replicate either together or separately the stages and backlot of the traditional film studio. Here we can see plainly played out what Susan Christopherson identifies as the important "role of transnational firms" like the Hollywood majors "in fostering production networks, including territorial production complexes, while retaining centralized control of production and distribution."[7] These firms may retain an interest in the infrastructure, as Fox does in Baja, but they may withdraw after the conclusion of a particular shoot and leave the infrastructure as a local issue.

Unsurprisingly, the sheer cost of developing these spaces has also led Hollywood majors to seek partners to help them build and pay for infrastructure. While temporary and semipermanent infrastructures require the care and attention of local agents, the more permanent infrastructure demands much greater care and attention from local agents. At one end of the scale, the *one-off production*, which utilizes demountable infrastructure and perhaps flies in all or most of the cast and crew, is a particular kind of major event for the location. It may have been bound to place through local initiative and through the potential of a cinematically unexplored location. The *one-off, fly-in production* requires a range of ancillary services from the *region* in which the shoot is located including hotels and transport, and it will often require casual short-term manual labor and sometimes local extras. With more permanent infrastructure, the local investment may be much greater, as the producers seek a variety of incentives and local contributions to share and minimize their risks and costs in return for choosing a particular location. Alternatively, the prospect of getting international productions regularly to particular localities—particularly high-budget blockbuster productions—has led actors other than the Hollywood majors to develop infrastructure in a location to help secure these productions. Examples here would be the Serenity Cove Studios in Sydney, the Prague Studios in the Czech Republic, and mooted developments in Cape Town and Toronto. In these cases, the aim is to be competitive enough to attract the "travelling circus" of international producers and production to that location, and to obtain as big a return as possible in the way of the employment of locally situated film services companies, local cast and crew, facilities, and a wide range of ancillary services. Governments at national and subnational levels are inevitably required to provide assistance in order to gain a local advantage in what is an increasingly competitive marketplace.

While technological and communications developments may have freed film production from the need for long shoots in studios through long hours in postproduction, in fact, this production infrastructure remains critical to the making of the modern blockbuster. It is also critical to a place's chances of hosting filmmaking on a regular basis. This realization has led a variety of public and private sector agents to finance the construction or renovation of studio space. While the Hollywood majors retain interests in some facilities around the world, the job of promoting these facilities and ensuring that they are regularly used tends to fall to local partners—film commissions and other government agencies, and consortia of production service companies working collaboratively to win work. Efforts to attract international production typically involve subnational or regional governments and organizations, thus illustrating the ways in which blockbuster production reaches beneath the plane of the national. This kind of "located thinking," however, has also contributed to reassessment of national film policies to incorporate the servicing of international production alongside support for lower-budgeted domestic initiatives. New partnerships have been established between film agencies and investment, immigration, and trade and arts agencies. These linkages are clearly evident in New Zealand around the making of *Lord of the Rings*.[8]

The local interest in marketing the range of infrastructure and services in a location inevitably makes studio complexes part of a larger package of infrastructure designed to deliver and develop local capacity to handle large-scale international production. This capacity is built not only by constructing physical infrastructure like studio complexes but also by strengthening and coordinating the clustering of film-related companies and qualified personnel in preproduction, production, and postproduction services. Ideally, the needs of peripatetic international producers would then be able to be served in a one-stop shop. This focus on production spaces and capabilities has been accompanied by a parallel governmental and corporate attention, first, to unlock the "locations" and so make the natural and built environments of a place available on favorable terms to international producers and, second, to build the liaison networks critical to facilitating the "travelling circus" and ensuring repeat performances. Such networks assist in securing permits for location shooting, organizing work permits for personnel coming from overseas, and providing local expertise particularly in location management to scout locations and coordinate with local owners, authorities, and film service providers. These "infrastructures" ensure that there are no unexpected elements that might significantly add to the costs of production and so increase the risks in shooting films in a location—and consequently jeopardize future production in a place.

This concern to smooth the way for production has led to the development of film commissions and film offices capable of providing these liaison services and ensuring a "film-friendly" environment for production.[9] Low-cost labor is no longer enough; the price of attracting blockbusters now typically includes taxation incentives and other measures to facilitate the production of these international feature films and television programs in particular territories. This kind of coordinated effort to attract Hollywood production was first systematized in U.S. states outside Los Angeles, but it has recently become a feature of an increasing number of places—cities, states, and nations globally—including now Los Angeles itself. The result is a potent mix of push and pull between international producer and locality that, although it had its origins in the initiatives and production processes of the Hollywood majors themselves, has acquired something of a life of its own as various places compete to establish circuits of production linking them to Hollywood and the international market.

Both the push of Hollywood to find and, if necessary, build the best location to deliver a "quality" blockbuster project and the pull of agents representing potential film locations have resulted in a reconfiguration of production circuits. Local agents often undertake extensive "previsualization" work and identify available infrastructure including purpose-built filmmaking facilities and various built and natural environments. Studio complexes equipped for Hollywood-standard production have been built around the world as entrepreneurs, governments at various levels, and film service companies seek to provide the total package increasingly demanded for blockbuster production. This has in its turn increased the competition for work while simultaneously reinforcing the international market for production.

Here the geographic dispersal of Hollywood and international production more generally is integrally tied up with the new geography of studio complexes and natural and built environments. Increasingly production is taking place where the studios are located. This helps explain why places with established and extensive film production and service infrastructure such as Toronto have become so interested in developing large-scale, state-of-the-art studio complexes to complement the many soundstages, facilities, and services already available in that city. Building studios is here a means of continuing to be one of the premier sites outside Los Angeles for the production of international film and television.

Intense competition also explains the attention in location marketing to small nonfilm differences that might swing a production to one location rather than another. Hotels, restaurants, and cultural amenities underpin the attraction of shooting in London, Toronto, Sydney, or New York, while the absence of five-star accommodation was seen as a critical missing element for Prague in the early 1990s and a problem in Eastern Europe more generally today. The lack of restaurants and other diversions of an adequate standard for Hollywood stars was touted as a reason for a major production not coming to the Australian Gold Coast in 2002. The availability of creature comforts for actors and filmmakers is an old theme certainly not confined to the present. Through the 1950s and 1960s, London proved to be a very attractive domicile for a number of Hollywood producers who split their time between Los Angeles and London (and also took advantage of the favorable tax treatments they received there for a time as foreigners).

Here we hypothesize that the contemporary growth and character of infrastructure are consequences of two related things. First, the character and circumstance of location production has changed with the emergence of an identifiable "location interest" in which locally situated companies, agencies, and infrastructure providers promote a place as a filmmaking venue. Location production now means extensive or complete packages of facilities, services, and natural and built environments rather than simply being the obverse of studio-based production. Second, the project-based,[10] one-off production that Janet Staiger[11] identifies as becoming the dominant production system in Hollywood by the mid-1950s has evolved and matured. What Staiger calls the "package-unit system" is a mode of production common to the entertainment business generally. As Allen Scott notes, production in this business "breaks down into a multitude of detailed tasks carried out by specialized firms and subcontractors," with individual projects bringing these "specialized producers . . . together in intricate networks of deals, projects, and tie-ins that link them together in ever changing collaborative arrangements and joint ventures."[12] These networks, collaborative arrangements, and joint ventures comprise the "design interest." In this context, infrastructure creation may be thought as simply a response to the new organizational and institutional form and opportunities that have been generated in a project-based production system where the advantage enjoyed by particular locations is increasingly figured as a combination of purpose-built and enhanced and found natural and built environments.

Importantly, these two dynamics of location and one-off production hold for both the current geographic dispersal of production and studio development and the continuing importance of Los Angeles as both the preeminent site for production and the "command and control" center of the international film industry. In circumstances where international producers routinely decide among a number of competing locations for a film, including Los Angeles itself, Los Angeles is just another possible (albeit very advantaged) production site. This is further underscored by the fact that securing Hollywood productions for Los Angeles and California more generally has become a priority of private consortia, labor, city, and state governments alike, just as it has in Vancouver, London, New York, Sydney, and Berlin. Consequently, any explanation of the geographic dispersal of production based on project and location dynamics should also hold for Los Angeles.

Location Is Everything

Locations are fungible and malleable infrastructures of various kinds for film production. Film shoots use a variety of physical sites including studio stages, backlots, purpose-built structures, and existing natural and built environments. From a production management point of view, the studio is simply one of the locations to be managed, shaped. and bent toward the film's art direction and vision alongside, for instance, the beach, the rain forest, and the skyscraper. The studio is in this context just another location for production. At the same time, digitization is blurring the never hard-and-fast distinction between purpose-built and existing natural and built environments and the lines between reality, artificiality, superficiality, and verisimilitude.

The contemporary conjunction of studio and location cuts across two traditions of thinking about cinema, one as a medium of illusion and artifice and the other as a medium of verisimilitude and realism. These traditions, dating back to Méliès and the Lumières brothers, counterpose the created world of the studio set to the "authentic" background and locale of the found location. The distinction between the studio and the location was reinforced in the move in the 1950s of some Hollywood producers and production away from studio-based production and toward shooting on location. This produced a sharp contrast, particularly an ideological contrast, between films made on location and films made in the studios as the package-unit system was replacing the producer unit system.[13] Here *location* referred to the "found" place that was then to be more or less faithfully rendered on screen. The found place conferred integrity as an authentic background and locale rather than being manufactured in the studio. Location production secured the exotic, the unique, and the authentic. Hence the tendency for producers to go to the locations in the storyline rather than reproduce these locations in a (usually Hollywood) studio backlot.

The contemporary market for locations presents us with a very different scenario. Now the "artifice" of the studio and the "reality" of the location are not counterposed. Rather, there is a fundamental continuity between them as physical sites of production for both illusionist and realist filmmaking.

Now the location has become the totality of what is available in a place, from studio stages and backlots to natural and built environments, from the range, skill, and depth of film service providers and crews to the liaison services available for production. Here the built and natural environments of a place are valued as much for what they can stand in for, what they can be bent/reshaped to represent, as they are valued for themselves. So Prague's natural and built environment makes it an ideal setting for medieval Europe (*A Knight's Tale*), the eighteenth century (*The Scarlet Pimpernel, Plunkett & Macleane*), Victorian London (*From Hell, Oliver Twist*) and mid-twentieth-century Europe (*Anne Frank*), while its studios house entire other worlds (*Children of Dune, Alien vs. Predator*) and supercharged parallel universes (*The League of Extraordinary Gentlemen*). Aida Hozic notes how Cincinatti's film commission offers "everything from an urban tenement area that has doubled for Harlem in the 1950s, Manhattan and Queens in the 1940s, Chicago in the late 1910s and the present-day New Jersey, to sprawling rural farmland and estates."[14] In both cases, the natural and built environment has become ever more superficial and cinematic—that is, more like the studio backlot in terms of potential for shooting and presentation.

Producers may be drawn to any number of elements making up the particular location, depending on the requirements of the project. From the perspective of local agents, the capacity to supply most or all of the potential elements that producers may require will enhance the prospect of retaining as much of the production as possible and perhaps seed future projects. Sometimes places do have natural advantages where there are personal ties to a place, so that it was not simply serendipitous that *Peter Pan* was shot in the director's hometown (Gold Coast, Australia). Sometimes locations have cinematic advantages: Martin Scorsese cited the opportunity to work on Federico Fellini's soundstage as a reason to make *Gangs of New York* at Cinecittà in Rome, although the film arguably might have been made in Scorsese's hometown, New York, had a decision on the renovation of the Brooklyn Navy Yard as a studio facility gone the way of the producers.[15]

It would be tempting to conclude that with growing numbers of film commissions representing particular regions on the basis of being both somewhere and anywhere, the path toward participation in global cultural production seems to depend "on the ability of places to successfully suppress their uniqueness and painlessly transform themselves into *whoever, whatever, whenever* sites."[16] That is, their attraction has become dependent on their capacity to be "bent" or "reshaped" for a variety of creative or narrative purposes. This is the Australian state of Queensland-as-anywhere setting of international production from the films *Scooby-Doo, Fortress,* or *Peter Pan* to the *Mission: Impossible* television series in which the locale is disguised by the matte of international production leading to the claim that "no aspect of Queensland culture [is] involved."[17] This claim may arguably be true of the production process, but once finished and made available for distribution across multiple platforms and channels, these productions invariably become part of the imagination, memory, and history of the location, and sometimes become part of its reputation as well. A place, like a studio, can build the critical industrial commodities of reputation and trust by virtue of its capacity to be remade convincingly as somewhere other than it is, but the studio does not exist "anywhere." It relies on the "location interest," the availability of surrounding infrastructure and proximity to diverse environments to add "cinematic value" just as the place relies on the studio to add economic and cinematic value.

What we are seeing here is the transformation of the logic of location production that pertained in the 1950s and 1960s, as places are increasingly serving and explicitly being designed to service the project needs of international blockbusters. A place may still "play itself" and be a central feature of a major film, as when Savannah featured in *Midnight in the Garden of Good and Evil* or Prague and Sydney featured in, respectively, *Mission: Impossible 1* and *2*. But it is as likely to be a stand-in for somewhere else.

In this context, it is worth revisiting the trajectory of Hollywood's own location thinking. Hozic notes how in Hollywood's first half century the major studios "shot most of their films in their studios themselves or on ranches that they had purchased in the vicinity of Hollywood."[18] This meant that the studios, backlots, and aspects of the built and natural environment of Los Angeles stood in for anywhere and everywhere. As Jeremy Tunstall and David Walker observe:

> California looks like everywhere for a simple reason. The state's landscapes have doubled for all regions of the world. Like an infinitely versatile extra, California's topography has had a walk-on role in countless productions. The Ojai Valley played Shangri-La in the movie *Lost Horizon*; the Mojave Desert has been the Sahara; Camp Pendleton, on the coast between Los Angeles and San Diego, was once Iwo Jima; the Santa Monica Mountains, Korea. China Lake, its expanse fittingly lunar, was once the moon. California's landscape is a universal backdrop against which any story can play.[19]

In this case, representing somewhere else—another time, another continent, another culture—was integral to the development of Los Angeles. So the capacity of a location to *have meaning* even when it is representing something or somewhere else should never be underestimated. The contemporary logic of dispersed location production is in this light simply a variant of long-standing Hollywood practice. Cincinnati, Vancouver, Sydney, or Prague can now do what Los Angeles and California have done for so long: stand in for somewhere else. Just as Hollywood began by consistently representing somewhere other than its actual location, so, too, many of these places are yet to represent themselves. Will they, like Hollywood, become places with signifying and representational power, albeit perhaps with many fewer layers? The *Lord of the Rings* cycle has created a "Frodo economy" for New Zealand, based on increases in tourist numbers and interest from international producers that reaches down into all sectors of the economy and remakes them in its image.[20] The unasked question here, though, is how sustainable is the *Lord of the Rings* boom in tourism, screen production, and ancillary services in New Zealand?

What prevented other places from securing productions and presenting themselves in a similar light at an earlier stage? A couple of different answers to this question are possible. First, going on location was not generally a preferred option in classical Hollywood for several reasons: Location shooting was costly and there were risks in "production away from home." Hozic lists these as higher wages for location shooting as productions could not afford to ignore labor demands on location in ways they could in a studio; and the pressure cooker environment of a location shoot in combination with the low boredom thresholds or high libidinal drives of stars that "brought to the surface personal conflicts and attractions among the actors, making it difficult for producers and directors to supervise their interactions," while "extraneous factors such as weather or noise could easily ruin numerous hours and sometimes days of shooting."[21] Second, very few places had the level of facilities, crew skills, capacity, and sophistication to handle Hollywood productions with any regularity. Production then tended to concentrate in the larger filmmaking centers of the major European countries (the United Kingdom, France, Germany, Italy, and Spain). This increased the risks associated with location production.

We can see that the recent moves to reproduce Hollywood-standard infrastructure and to develop production services and liaison networks have led to the significant reduction of risks involved in location production and expanded the range of places offering infrastructure of the requisite standard. Location production no longer necessarily entails higher costs; depressed labor costs and conditions are one of the claimed comparative advantages of a number of locations, including the "right to work" states in the United States but also Vancouver and Prague. There is clear evidence that a New International Division of Cultural Labour (NICL) is emerging, attended by a "race to the bottom" in areas such as labor costs and conditions as production costs are squeezed.[22] But while cost is a keen issue for block-busters, they have other, more creative drives. And they have a range of place-bound effects including a legacy of infrastructure and transformation that may be lost sight of through the lens of totalizing theories like that of the NICL.

In the 1950s and 1960s, "going on location" (or location thinking) offered the promise of creative and financial freedom afforded by distance from Hollywood. Tax advantages were available to above-the-line workers. The availability of the actual location rather than a set built in a studio conferred authenticity and realism, while simultaneously providing a solution to the problem of accessing funds frozen in many countries after World War II. But even though many factors favored locations playing themselves, some emerged to stand in for somewhere else. The western genre was, after all, invigorated in the 1960s and early 1970s by Italian and Spanish locations—and arguably a European sensibility and take on the "West"—in the spaghetti western.[23] So even at the high point of location production where places "played themselves," a substantial element of Hollywood was in the work being done in these locations—locations that often included substantial studio complexes modeled, as were Cinecittà and Pinewood, on their Hollywood counterparts.

This kind of "runaway production" generated considerable complaint in California in the early 1960s, just as it has in the early 2000s. Then as now, there was concern about the outflow of production from Hollywood to elsewhere in America and abroad; similar evidence of a rise in levels of international production from a low base (claims of it having tripled from 1940 to 1960);[24] similar calls for subsidies and concessions and favorable tax treatment to match foreign subsidies, concessions, and tax regimes; and similar suggestions—this time from MPAA president Eric Johnston—that overseas production was "supplemental international production" that "provided additional income and jobs in the US."[25]

But, as Hozic points out, this earlier high point of location production had significant problems that could outweigh the benefits, as evidenced by the significant decline in international production from the high points of the 1960s. Distance meant there was not the same capacity to control the production and the expenditures being incurred. So despite the "obvious cost-advantages of filming abroad, the average cost of films produced outside of the US turned out to be higher than the cost of films produced in Hollywood."[26] While there were savings to be had on below-the-line costs of crew, set designers, and other workers, significant costs were associated with paying the travel, accommodation, and living costs of the above-the-line workers—principal actors, producer, director, and others—that could outweigh the advantages of lower costs for below-the-line workers. Hozic additionally notes that the combination of frozen funds and local subsidies led producers to spend freely while on location, leading many films to go over budget and lose money.[27] Going on location also made sense in the 1950s and 1960s because the "foreign market" was that much more important to Hollywood's bottom line than it became in the decade from the mid-1970s to the mid- to late 1980s. Cinema-going levels held up much longer in Europe than they did in the United States owing to the more limited scale of television where multichannel marketplaces and commercial television took some time to develop. Foreign markets also offered sources of funding and partnerships, as they still do.

Obviously the resurgence of "runaway production" in the 1990s and 2000s is somewhat different from that of the earlier period. Greater control at a distance, courtesy of telecommunications and digitization, is now possible, making for better and more effective management of production and control of costs. Money flows freely across borders, and there is considerably more experience in managing and coordinating increasingly complex productions. Decisions on location are now part of the "project" orientation as every production becomes an individual project that is managed accordingly. The "design interest" of each project will require decisions to be made about locations, and each project will need to decide whether to use a studio and, if so, which one to use. Producers are able to approach location production with a greater sense of security than previously, owing to improved communications and local infrastructure. Various local agents from film commissions to location managers work hard to create the conditions that will satisfy hypermobile producers.

But while producers' risks may have been reduced, the risks and vulnerabilities do not leave the location or stop being issues for place-bound workers when the production wraps. The lulls in international feature production experienced in Australia in 2003 and the United Kingdom in 1998 are constantly feared everywhere.[28] These lulls have spurred efforts in these locations to coordinate offerings, to form and pursue a "location interest."

In this context, studios are not in opposition to locations; they are part of locations. This means that in order to think about studios and their global dispersal, we need to consider how such studios are on a continuum with each other and with the natural and built environments within which they are situated. So films that might have been shot on a Los Angeles backlot are now being done wherever. And other places are standing in for the traditional production centers of Los Angeles, New York, and London: Los Angeles is re-created in New York for *Hollywood Ending*, New York is re-created in Rome for *Gangs of New York*, and London is re-created in Berlin for *Around the World in Eighty Days*.

Globally dispersed production and Los Angeles–domiciled production are governed by the same project logic. The project-based character of high-budget feature films ensures that location decisions are one-off decisions. Indeed, the one-off, packaged character of production provides encouragement to a variety of local agents to pitch for these productions, in the process creating an international market for high-budget international feature film and television production locations. In this context, the meaning of "going on location" has been transformed such that it now includes natural and built environments, studios, facilities, and service providers. Here the very meaning of *location* has changed. Managing passage backward and forward along the continuum of Hollywood-domiciled and international production requires careful attention to the "location interest." Its counterpart, the "design interest," is the view from Hollywood, the view that the project form of organization—a form of organization filmmaking is increasingly sharing with other industries—offers the best means to exploit the advantages of globally dispersed production and situated liaison networks. We will now elaborate the development of this thinking in order to determine its points of coincidence with and divergence from the location interest.

The Logic of the Project

Globally dispersed production is a response to the organizational and institutional form and opportunities that have been generated in a project-based production system. The system, which was dominant in Hollywood by the mid-1950s, works "because of four factors: flexible delivery of services by specialized companies; intense interaction between small units that are part of a dynamic global industrial sector; highly diverse and skilful labour; and institutional infrastructure."[29]

This system, which Staiger calls the "package-unit" system, was predicated on the need "to seek out, negotiate, and plan every project."[30] Staiger advances a number of reasons for the shift toward the package-unit system. Initially, prosperity, particularly for those producing "A" films, and new U.S. tax laws encouraged well-placed individuals to leave studio employment and set up their own independent production companies.[31] A range of other factors were at work in dispersing this system around the world in the period after World War II: postwar reconstruction measures adopted in Europe like freezing the assets of American producers and distributors and restricting the outflow of U.S. currency, which prompted a wave of production in Britain, France, and Italy in particular; the dark period of blacklisting in Hollywood, which drove many filmmakers away from southern California; changes to the U.S. tax system; technological change; and the activity of United Artists from the 1950s.

The history of United Artists is well documented by Tino Balio in his book *United Artists: The Company That Changed the Film Industry*. Balio notes that in the 1950s, "in return for distribution rights, United Artists [UA] would offer talent complete production financing, creative control over their work, and a share of the profits. . . . Since UA owned no studio, a producer could make his picture anywhere in the world to suit the needs of the story or the economics of the venture."[32] UA's producers were well placed to establish themselves anywhere in the world and take advantage of the common features of the production environment particularly in Europe in the decades after World War II: subsidies, quotas, frozen funds, and tax benefits arising from incorporating abroad. United Artists worked with British, French, and Italian filmmakers in those countries and others to produce films such as *Tom Jones*, *A Fistful of Dollars*, and *Viva Maria*, directed by Louis Malle, starring Brigitte Bardot and Jeanne Moreau, and shot in Mexico. These films were green-lit in large part on the basis of their international appeal, rather than their prospects for success in the United States, and consequently their international box office takings often outstripped their U.S. grosses. This is also a feature of many of the contemporary films and television programs classed as "runaway" by the U.S. Commerce Department.[33]

The Paramount antitrust decrees of 1948 that ordered the separation of exhibition holdings from production-distribution sectors further encouraged the shift to the package-unit system by allowing firms to "concentrate on making fewer, specialized projects and financing or buying the more desirable independent films." In this context, the package-unit system fitted emerging distribution strategies (which were themselves products of changing consumption patterns and new methods of understanding and mobilizing audiences) in which the "industry concentrated even more on a highly differentiated film" aimed "primarily at first-run audiences only."[34]

Its key feature in comparison to the previous system where a slate of six or seven films was common was its transitory character as components of film production were put together on a short-term basis. With the package-unit system and its short-term film-by-film arrangements, "the self-contained studio" disappeared as employment came to be based on the film and not the firm.[35] Labor, services, and materials were no longer the preserve of a single company but rather the "entire industry," which could now act as a talent and service provider pool.[36] Characteristically:

> A producer organised a film project: he or she secured financing and combined the necessary labourers (whose role had previously been defined by the standardised production structure and subdivision of work categories) and the means of production (the narrative "property," the equipment, and the physical sites of production).[37]

In circumstances of one-off productions of limited duration, leasing or purchasing of the various elements of the production became the norm. This "component packaging" in its turn supported the development of an array of support firms to provide specialized services—anything from costumes and props, camera, lighting, and recording equipment to special effects technology and postproduction. It also ensured that a much more extensive rental market in studio stages developed as one-off productions looked to secure space at the right time, in the right place, and on the most favorable terms.

In the old system, the "studio resource . . . was a key element in the competition among, and collective market power of, the Hollywood majors,"[38] reinforcing their control over sources of supply (including in the 1920s and 1930s supply of equipment).[39] The majors' interest in studio resources sometimes spurred and sometimes was a response to the significant geographic concentration or agglomeration of production infrastructure, services, and expertise in a particular region.[40] As a U.S. Department of Commerce report put it, "facilities were geographically fixed due to the complex construction and infrastructure necessary to connect all of the disparate pieces of specialized equipment that were configured to perform certain processes."[41] Before the coming of sound, the Hollywood studios invested in production and infrastructure in New York (Paramount) and in Europe. Paramount, Warner Bros., and Fox all had studio facilities in London in the 1920s, and Paramount also operated the Joinville studio in Paris at this time as well as having a coproduction deal with the major German film company Ufa, which then owned the Babelsberg Studios.

Such a situation suited what was a horizontally and vertically integrated industry, with predictable and straightforward distribution and production pathways through film theaters associated with the majors and exhibition chains internationally through output deals. The scale and extent of studios in Los Angeles as elsewhere in turn depended on the size, financial muscle, and depth of *local* film production capacity. As the U.S. Department of Commerce put it, there needed to be "a sufficient amount of local film production to support the substantial capital investment in their plant and equipment."[42] In practice, this message meant that the existence of purpose-built studio complexes depended in part on the capacity of a local production industry to sustain them until the production dynamics began to shift from the 1950s, and nonlocal production became the desired object in many places. Before the 1950s, film output was dominated by the major film studios, which tended to use their own stages, facilities, and staff on productions; further production capacity in these locations was provided by smaller independent companies that might only make a few films a year. Although these companies could not afford to "own or even have entire studios for the filming of their pictures," they nonetheless could rely on rental studios and some of the larger Hollywood studios like Universal who were prepared to rent studio space and labor support to independent producers.[43]

These several elements created significant barriers to entry not only for new players but also for players in smaller countries who were able to draw on limited local infrastructure. Extensive purpose-built studios therefore tended to develop in the larger European countries on the periphery of major metropolitan centers—and these studio locations in London, Rome, Paris, Prague, and Berlin attracted international productions. For their part, indigenous production companies in smaller countries such as Australia and Canada worked from smaller studio facilities in one or two locations. Soviet bloc countries such as Bulgaria, Romania, Yugoslavia, and East Germany were able to build or refurbish large and integrated studio complexes after World War II because of the communist command-and-control system that centralized almost all screen production in particular locations as an organizing surveillance and efficiency principle.

This project-based form of organization opened the way for the development of a more extensive film service provider market, a competitive labor market of skilled workers, competition between facilities providers for work, and the development of mechanisms to facilitate short-term collaboration among service companies and facilities that encouraged their clustering into particular locations and precincts to better facilitate collaboration. For Staiger, this represented an "industrial shift away from mass production" toward the "film-by-film financing and planning" characteristic of a project-based industrial system.[44]

Then as now, Hollywood production relies on an army of small to medium-sized businesses that provide contracted services to the production industry, which has proved an ideal form to manage the "growing risk associated with an increasingly segmented market in which different products competed for the consumer's entertainment expenditures."[45] With increased uncertainty and a multitude of pathways for audiovisual product, the contemporary entertainment industry adopted an increasingly flexible and specialized shape, looking to independent producers to "develop these differentiated film products."[46] In this sense, our contemporary period is an intensification of a dynamic begun with the package-unit system of the 1950s and a more developed response to ever-proliferating audiovisual outlets. Then as now, film and television markets are subject to rapid changes in consumer tastes and fashions, with many productions losing money and a few hit productions covering this slate.[47]

While everything seems the same, all has in a sense significantly changed. These similarities in physical form and function belie the substantially different place and function of these studios in contemporary ecologies of local and international production. These studios are not as important under a contemporary "knowledge resource" system based on one-off production as they were in a "control of (physical) resource" system with its portfolio of productions and manufacturing model. They are, however, important to various locations, locales, and situated film services companies, film commissions, and the governments they enlist as vehicles for the development of "clusters" and production networks. They are therefore central to the formation and promotion of the location interest.

The default position of the contemporary studio complex is that it is assumed to be servicing *parts* of production rather than the "whole" productions, as was often the case in the classical era from the 1920s to 1940s. This has had the consequence of making the studio just another location (for production) alongside natural and built environments in a locale. The studio is part of the imitable and purchasable infrastructure of a location to be packaged into a high-budget Hollywood feature production. The way this global market for infrastructure has developed to serve the needs of individual projects means that even in cases where the majors have an interest in infrastructure and so might be thought likely at least to be sympathetic to the located interest (e.g., Warner Bros. in Germany and Australia, and Fox in Australia and Mexico), project-level decisions remain paramount. This means that a major may not send its most prized projects to particular facilities simply to keep them turning over; sometimes this will only happen after considerable lobbying by located interests (as in Queensland to secure the Warner Bros.–Village Roadshow joint venture *House of Wax 3D* for the Warner Roadshow Studios in 2004 after the facility had stood empty for almost a year).

The blockbuster film project exists at the interface between the adaptive and outsourced regime of the project form (flexible specialization in an independent production system) and the permanent organization of the Hollywood majors. Through their involvement in initiating, develop-ing, coordinating, and distributing either their own or nonaffiliated proj-ects, the majors continue to exercise market power and influence. The Hollywood majors and independent production companies become in this project-based environment "incubators" and "sponsors" of projects."[48] Pro-jects in this context are brought into being from "a platform of delibera-tion, preparation and pre-selection" that is often provided by the majors and independent production companies.[49]

For Gernot Grabher, projects have not so much replaced more traditional and permanent forms of organization as created "interdependencies between projects and the firms, networks, localities and institutions that feed vital sources of information, legitimization, reputation and trust that provide the very preconditions for the 'projectification.'"[50] But the sheer size of these projects in terms of their cost, timing, and special resources required makes "boring institutions" all the more vital. This is particularly so in the area of coordination and control.[51] Saskia Sassen puts this most appositely for our purposes here, when she suggests that the dispersal of economic activity that is so much a characteristic of the global financial and producers services in-dustries "brings about new requirements for centralized management and control."[52] The result is another seeming paradox that she expresses as the interdependent and mutually defining relationship between "geographic dis-persal" and "locational concentration"—and that here can be expressed as the dispersal of production and production capacity internationally requiring an intense concentration of activity and controlling and coordinating func-tions in Los Angeles. This is what Christopher Thornberg, a senior econo-mist with UCLA Anderson Forecast, described as the city's evolution from a "production center to a design center."[53] There can be little doubt that Hol-lywood remains the vortex, the point in the circuit through which every project must pass on its path to global audiences, and where every project, however subtly, is transformed.

Paradoxically, the peripatetic blockbuster and its accompanying globally dispersed production system support the continuing agglomeration and con-centration of production in Los Angeles. Not only do solely Hollywood-domiciled blockbusters continue to feature on production slates but globally dispersed production invariably carries out only part of *the total production* on location, with the remainder of the production, particularly postproduction, being based mostly in southern California. By way of example, the second and third *Matrix* films were filmed in both Australia and California, and *Star Wars: Episode III* was shot in Sydney in 2003, but the postproduction work for all these films was largely carried out in California.

Conclusion

As of December 2004, eight of the worldwide top ten highest-grossing films of all time[54] were largely or completely shot outside the mainland United States, although most returned to California for postproduction. *Titanic* was shot at Fox Baja Studios, Mexico; *The Lord of the Rings* trilogy was shot in New Zealand; the two Harry Potter films—*Chamber of Secrets* and *Sorcerer's Stone*—and *Star Wars: Episode I—The Phantom Menace* were shot in a London studio; *Jurassic Park* in Hawaii. Only *Finding Nemo* and *Shrek 2* (numbers eight and ten on the list) were largely or completely made in the mainland United States. Whatever the value of such a list, it nonetheless draws our attention to the way that globally dispersed production has become an intrinsic and routine trait of both the contemporary Hollywood blockbuster and of feature film production more generally.

This global dispersal is itself a product of three interrelated factors. First, the further development of the blockbuster as a project-based system of production has allowed diverse inputs from a more globally defined industry than has been hitherto possible. Second, a larger number of locations have been able to form and pursue a location interest and provide the package of studios, other facilities, services, and natural and built environments necessary for blockbuster production. This availability in its turn has created an organized global market in locations for blockbuster production that has benefited Hollywood producers while increasing the vulnerability of filmmaking locations to production downturns. Third, the combination of the design interest of the Hollywood majors in developing projects and the location interest of places in securing projects has given rise to interrelated dynamics of global geographic dispersal at the level of the production shoot and concentration in Los Angeles at the level of production design (and, to a great extent, postproduction). The system of location production characteristic of the contemporary blockbuster supports *both* global production and L.A. centricity. Indeed, the task facing the Hollywood majors, independent producers, and the various facilities, film commissions, and film service providers located around the world is to transform one-off, itinerant blockbuster projects into something more permanent through developing or securing a portfolio of projects or undertaking numbers of unrelated projects. The design and location interests therefore coincide in their mutual aim to transform "episodic project collaboration" into "more enduring project networks."[55]

Habits of thinking that counterpose studio to location, artifice to realism and authenticity—even Hollywood-based to runaway production—do not adequately capture the entailments of this contemporary production environment. The gap between what is possible in studio production, on one hand, and in natural and built environments, on the other, has reduced significantly. The very meaning of *location* has changed. Location production is no longer the obverse of studio-based production. The location is now the bundle of physical sites and services available in a place for filmmaking. Los Angeles will continue to be the vortex, the design center, and the venue for considerable amounts of production and postproduction, but it is also, now, just another location.

Notes

1. Gernot Grabher, "Cool Projects, Boring Institutions: Temporary Collaboration in Social Context," *Regional Studies* 36, no. 3 (2002): 205–14.

2. Cited in Sir Alan Parker, "Building a Sustainable UK Film Industry: A Presentation to the UK Film Industry," UK Film Council, 5 November 2003, 13; available at www.ukfilmcouncil.org.uk/usr/downloads/BaSFI.pdf (20 February 2004).

3. Parker, "Building a Sustainable UK Film Industry," 10.

4. See Toby Miller, Nitin Govil, John McMurria, and Richard Maxwell, *Global Hollywood* (London: British Film Institute, 2001).

5. Edoras is now available only to the imagination of intrepid tourists. Ninety-five percent of the timber, steel, concrete, fiberglass, and polystyrene used in sets built at Alameda, including the freeway, was recycled, with some of the timber transported to Mexico and used to build low-income housing. "Movie Makers Create Environmental Ending," *In Business* 24, no. 2 (2002): 4.

6. Cited in "The Fox Baja Studios," available at www.titanicmovie.com/present/mi_prodnote_6.html (15 December 2003).

7. Susan Christopherson, "The Limits to 'New Regionalism': (Re)Learning from the Media Industries," *GeoForum* 34, no. 4 (2003): 415.

8. See "New Zealand Home of Middle-earth: Services and Partners," available at www.filmnz.com/middleearth/partners/index.html (20 February 2004).

9. For a discussion of the role of film offices and location expos, see Aida Hozic, *Hollyworld: Space, Power and Fantasy in American Cinema* (Ithaca, N.Y.: Cornell University Press, 2001), 87–88; Mike Gasher, *Hollywood North: The Feature Film Industry in British Columbia* (Vancouver: University of British Columbia Press, 2002), passim.

10. Grabher, "Cool Projects," provides a useful synoptic overview of the evolution and character of the "project" as a particular form of institutional organization from the late 1940s to the present.

11. Janet Staiger, "The Hollywood Mode of Production, 1930–60," in *The Classical Hollywood Cinema: Film Style and Model of Production to 1960*, 2d ed., ed. David Bordwell, Janet Staiger, and Kristin Thompson (London: Routledge, 1985), 330.

12. Allen J. Scott, *The Cultural Economy of Cities: Essays on the Geography of Image-Producing Industries* (London: Sage, 2000), 181.

13. These terms are borrowed from Staiger, "The Hollywood Mode of Production."

14. Hozic, *Hollyworld*, 88.

15. Had the producers of *Gangs of New York* been successful in their tender for the conversion of the Brooklyn Navy Yard into a studio facility in 1999, the film may well have been made in New York. See Jill Goldsmith, "Ahoy, Busy Producers," *Variety*, 26 January–1 February 2004, 9.

16. Hozic, *Hollyworld*, 88–99. Gasher, *Hollywood North*, makes this point with respect to Vancouver and British Columbia, while Hozic sees it as a more general point.

17. Toby Miller, *Technologies of Truth: Cultural Citizenship and the Popular Media* (Minneapolis: University of Minnesota Press, 1998), 163.

18. Hozic, *Hollyworld*, 92.

19. Jeremy Tunstall and David Walker, *Media Made in California: Hollywood, Politics and the News* (New York: Oxford University Press, 1981), 13.

20. See "Frodo Economy rings up the dollars for New Zealand," *ABC Online*, 30 November 2003, available at www.abc.net.au/news/newsitems/200311/s1000231.htm (23 February 2004). An estimated 10 percent of the two million people visiting New Zealand in 2003 were apparently influenced to come to New Zealand by the scenery depicted in the movie.

21. Hozic, *Hollyworld*, 92–93.

22. See Miller et al., *Global Hollywood*.

23. See Christopher Frayling, *The Spaghetti Western: Cowboys and Europeans from Karl May to Sergio Leone* (London: Routledge & Kegan Paul, 1981).

24. Hozic, *Hollyworld*, 96. The 1940 starting point is, of course, a problematic one in that it is in the midst of World War II, when Hollywood's European production ambitions were substantially curtailed.

25. Hozic, *Hollyworld*, 96–97.

26. Hozic, *Hollyworld*, 97.

27. Indeed, Hozic points out that Hollywood's major financial disasters—from *Ben Hur* (1925) to the more recent *Waterworld* (1995)—were shot on location.

28. For Australia, see Australian Film Commission, *National Survey of Feature Film and TV Drama Production 2002/2003* (Sydney: Author, 2004). For Britain, see Alice Rawsthorn, "Film Industry Searches for a Second Take on Success: The Sector May Face Trouble If Another Blockbuster Is Not Found," *Financial Times*, 27 August 1998, 7.

29. Miller et al., *Global Hollywood*, 55.

30. Staiger, "The Hollywood Mode of Production," 337.

31. Staiger, "The Hollywood Mode of Production," 331.

32. Tino Balio, *United Artists: The Company That Changed the Film Industry* (Madison: University of Wisconsin Press, 1987), 42.

33. United States International Trade Administration, *The Migration of US Film and Television Production: Impact of "Runaways" on Workers and Small Business in the US Film Industry* (Washington, D.C.: U.S. Department of Commerce, 2001).

34. Staiger, "Hollywood Mode of Production," 333.

35. Staiger, "Hollywood Mode of Production," 330.

36. Staiger, "Hollywood Mode of Production," 330.

37. Staiger, "Hollywood Mode of Production," 330.

38. Danny Miller and Jamal Shamsie, "The Resource-Based View of the Film in Two Environments: The Hollywood Film Studios from 1936 to 1965," *Academy of Management Journal* 39, no. 3 (1996): 9–10.

39. This also included cinema projection and camera equipment. On the problem facing a Canadian filmmaker purchasing camera equipment in the teens and twenties of the twentieth century, see Gasher, *Hollywood North*, 28.

40. At this point, it is worth noting that already by the 1920s, a well-established facilities rental market existed in southern California, as there was in Florida and Arizona. See Gene Fernett, *American Film Studios: An Historical Encyclopedia* (Jefferson, N.C.: McFarland, 1988).

41. United States International Trade Administration, *Migration of US Film and Television Production*, 66.

42. United States International Trade Administration, *Migration of US Film and Television Production*, 66.

43. Staiger, "Hollywood Mode of Production," 318.

44. Staiger, "Hollywood Mode of Production," 332.

45. Susan Christopherson and Michael Storper, "The City as Studio, the World as Backlot: The Impact of Vertical Disintegration on the Location of the Motion Picture Industry," *Environment and Planning D: Society and Space* 4 (1986): 308.

46. Michael Storper, "The Transition to Flexible Specialization in the US Film Industry: External Economies, the Division of Labor, and the Crossing of Industrial Divides," *Cambridge Journal of Economics* 13 (1989): 281.

47. Scott, *Cultural Economy of Cities*, 174.

48. Grabher, "Cool Projects," 206.

49. Grabher, "Cool Projects," 211.

50. Grabher, "Cool Projects," 206.

51. Grabher, "Cool Projects," 207.

52. Saskia Sassen, *The Global City: New York, London, Tokyo* (Princeton, N.J.: Princeton University Press, 2001), 36.

53. The evidence for this is seen in the rising proportion of management and administration jobs in the production industry in southern California. UCLA Anderson School of Management, "UCLA's Anderson Forecast Conference Examines the Forces Altering the Business of Hollywood," available at www.anderson.ucla.edu/x4495.xml (25 February 2004).

54. The figures are taken from the Internet Movie Database, include only theatrical box office, and are unadjusted for inflation. "World All-Time Box Office Chart," Internet Movie Database, 24 February 2004; available at www.imdb.com/Charts/worldtopmovies (accessed 24 February 2004).

55. Grabher, "Cool Projects," 210.

CHAPTER TWO

Types of Studio

In the previous chapter, we outlined some of the features of contemporary international film production and the general place of studios within this environment. In this chapter, we will focus on the studio itself and begin to explore the diversity among studios, what differentiates them from each other, and what common features they share, as a means to work toward a typology of studio developments. We do not explore the question of the extent to which a particular studio has a recognizable "style"; rather, we are interested here in how the size and location of a studio affects its capacity to host production, whether patterns of ownership and management have an influence on production, how infrastructure within a studio and its links to institutions within the film and television industries and beyond impact on the types of production it is able to attract, what balance of production a studio maintains, how the time of the initial construction and use of a studio affects its output, and how the functional profile of a studio and the spatial concentration or clustering of production activities and services within it limit or enable production.

Size and Location

To a great extent, the size of a studio—how much physical space it can occupy and what opportunities may exist for future expansion or renovation—is determined by its location. Studios comprising multiple stages, a backlot, offices, workshops, and other buildings can require considerable space and are not typically best accommodated in urban or heavily populated areas. Many of the large studios built in Europe before or soon after World War II—Elstree, Shepperton, and Pinewood in the United Kingdom, Cinecittà in Italy, Babelsberg in Germany, Barrandov in (what was then) Czechoslovakia, Ardmore in Ireland—were "edge city" developments, situated on the outskirts of major cities (usually the national capital) where land was freely available and relatively cheap, but still accessible from the metropolitan center.[1] The first studios in Hollywood were also located in what at the time was an undeveloped suburb "separated by eight miles of rough country road"[2] from Los Angeles—and over three hundred miles from the major metropolis on the Pacific coast at that time, San Francisco. A number of the most famous early studios were built in other fringe areas—Universal City in the San Fernando Valley, First National in Burbank, and the Ince Studios (later the headquarters of MGM) in Culver City. More recent developments including Leavesden Studios in the United Kingdom and Prague Studios in the Czech Republic also follow this pattern of edge city development, although both of these studios are renovated aircraft manufacturing plants rather than custom-built facilities as those in earlier periods tended to be.

In recent years, two trends have emerged for studio developments, however, that are not on the edge of a city. The first trend involves the development of a number of large studios in inner-urban areas, including Fox Studios Australia in Sydney, Central City Studios in Melbourne, and Three Mills Studios in London. The proposed major new studio in Toronto is also planned for an inner-urban site, in the Portlands district of the city close to the downtown area. All of these studio developments involve the transformation of sites formerly used for other purposes—docklands in Melbourne and Toronto, distillery and bottling plant in London, and showgrounds in Sydney. As we discuss in more detail in chapter 4, the Toronto, Melbourne, and Sydney studio developments were from the outset driven by regional government agencies and situated within broader urban regeneration strategies. The involvement of government agencies in these three developments—and in the Three Mills Studios in London following its purchase in mid-2004 by an agency of the Greater London Council—was motivated in part by a sense of the symbolic contribution each development could make to place marketing, and by the boost that the studio could give to media and creative industries in each city. But inner-urban studios may be restricted from expansion by their location. For example, Ealing Studios in London, which claims to be the oldest film studio in the world and was first used for filmmaking in 1902, is now surrounded by urban development and cannot expand beyond its current site. Fox Studios

Australia in Sydney was only able to create additional stages and production spaces following the closure of the public studio tour.

The second trend has seen the development of studios in regional or rural locations some distance from major metropolitan areas and existing media infrastructure. Examples here include Island Studios on the Isle of Man in the United Kingdom; South West Studios in Cornwall, United Kingdom; Warner Roadshow Studios on the Gold Coast, Australia; Fox Studios Baja in Rosarito, Mexico; and the proposed developments in Cape Town, South Africa, and Alicante, Spain. As we discuss in more detail in chapter 5, these are to some extent "extreme" developments requiring often substantial investment and entailing considerable risk for developers and local government. In most cases, these studio developments have been motivated by a "location interest" desire to capitalize on existing, often small-scale and sporadic production that has been drawn to a place because of the quality of its natural or built environment or for cost reasons, although the principal production office may be located somewhere else. The absence of a permanent studio facility limits the ability of these places to attract and retain whole productions. The aim in building such a facility is then to attract a greater volume of production and to retain as much production as possible within the region, as well as to build local capacity, create jobs, and generate flow-on effects in other sectors of the economy. The studio is then conceived as a vehicle for the diversification of the region's economic base and is valued by local government and other representatives of the location interest for the intangible or symbolic benefits that it is hoped will result from the development.

It is worth remembering that this trend is not without historical precedent—the establishment of studios in Hollywood and elsewhere around Los Angeles in the 1900s and 1910s was driven in part by a desire for distance from New York and the "Trust"—the Motion Picture Patents Company—which towered over the film industry at this time. Peter Hall summarizes the reasons for the move to California: "Los Angeles offered an ideal combination of cheap land and property, a cooperative Chamber of Commerce, sun, diverse landscape, and remoteness from New York, plus nearness to the Mexican border," beyond which the tentacles of the Trust and the long arm of the law could not reach.[3]

The Warner Roadshow Studios on the Australian Gold Coast was initially developed in circumstances where the surrounding region had the potential to attract location production but was not at the time a major production destination. This studio development is a good example of an attempt to diversify the regional economic base, to create film industry infrastructure where previously there had been none of significant scale, and to contribute to the promotion of the region as a tourism, leisure, and entertainment center. The location of a theme park, Warner's Movie World, next to the studio exemplifies this logic.[4] Other recent studio developments incorporate a theme park element for precisely these reasons. Fox Studios Baja in Mexico, for example, has clear synergies with efforts to build on the tourism potential of the Baja California region, which is acknowledged in the development of the "Foxploration" studio tour. The Rosarito site was chosen primarily for its geographic location—close to the southern California epicenter of English-language audiovisual production—but also perhaps to take best advantage of incentives and advantages to locate in Mexico under North American trade rules.[5]

The size of a studio, particularly the number of stages it contains and their dimensions (height, width, and length), is an important determinant of the kind and variety of work it is capable of hosting. Many studios have been proposed or developed in recent years with an eye to the blockbuster market, but many do not have enough large stages to accommodate the needs of a big, high-budget production that may require multiple stages and construction workshops. And efforts to host the biggest productions (which are attractive for financial reasons because they may hire several stages and ancillary buildings or occupy a whole studio for months at a time, and also desirable for the prestige they can bestow on a studio) may compromise other production possibilities or arrangements. For example, when *Scooby-Doo* was made at the Warner Roadshow Studios in 2000–2001, no other simultaneous production was possible, and one of the studio's long-standing "anchor tenants," the production company Coote/Hayes, was forced to relocate its production elsewhere. Two new soundstages were added to the Warner Roadshow Studios in 2002 in an effort to capitalize on the prestige and "blockbuster effect" of *Scooby-Doo*, but while the additional infrastructure helped the studio to win the right to host the production of *Peter Pan* in 2003, when that production finished, the studio lay idle for a year as Coote/Hayes, which makes movies of the week and television series including *Beastmaster* principally for the American market, moved its operations to Melbourne.

As the Warner Roadshow Studios example shows, the size of a studio determines not only the total amount of production that can be hosted but also the amount of simultaneous production that a studio is able to service. Cinecittà's twenty-two soundstages, permanent sets, and large backlot make possible the simultaneous production of a number of projects across the different genres that in theory, at least, makes the likelihood of long lulls in production much less likely.

Patterns of Ownership and Management

There is no one common pattern of ownership and management for contemporary studios. They can, however, be grouped together on the basis of the balance and share of public and private interest in the parent company; the extent of their direct links with multinational media conglomerates; and the organization and level of "exclusivity" in their service provision arrangements—that is, whether the studio has a commercial interest in on-site service providers and the extent to which the studio determines the mix of service companies operating on the site.

Many studios are fully privately owned, some in whole or in part by Hollywood majors or other major multinational media conglomerates, some by smaller media companies, and some by companies whose principal business lies outside the media sector. Examples of the first group include Fox Studios Baja and Fox Studios Australia, both owned by News Corporation; Warner Roadshow Studios on Australia's Gold Coast; and, until recently, Studio Babelsberg, which was owned by Vivendi from 1992 to 2004. Examples of the second include Lions Gate Studios in Vancouver, owned by Lions Gate Entertainment; Media Pro Studio in Bucharest, owned by Central European Media Enterprises; Ciné Cité Montreal, owned by the Comweb Group; and Shepperton and Pinewood, owned by the Pinewood-Shepperton Group. Studios owned by nonmedia companies include Barrandov, owned by the utility company Moravia Steel, and Vancouver Film Studios, owned by the property development and management company McLean Group. Studios owned or partly owned by governments—national, state (provincial), or local government authorities—include The Bridge in Vancouver, run by a Crown-owned enterprise of the provincial government; Elstree in the United Kingdom, which is owned by its local borough council; Central City Studios in Melbourne, in which the Victorian state government has a major interest; Three Mills Studios in London, which is owned by the London Development Agency; and Cinecittà in Rome in which the Italian government has a stake through the Department for Arts and Cultural Activity's shareholding in the studio's parent company, Cinecittà Holding.

But what does this diversity in ownership tell us about how studios are developed and how they are run? The establishment of a studio entails a complicated and lengthy deal-making process that requires the coordination of governments, investors, production service companies, property developers, architects, and publics. The success of the proposal will depend on certain attributes of the company or consortium proposing the studio to have certain attributes. First, the company or consortium must have credibility within the local and international film and television production industry—or employ people who are known and trusted within the industry—in order to attract both service companies and ongoing production when the studio finally opens. Second, the company or consortium must be politically well connected in order to negotiate the various bureaucratic and political hurdles that must be overcome before construction of a new facility (or renovation of another site) can begin. Third, the company or consortium must inspire the confidence of investors in their abilities to manage the development of the property into a film studio. Fourth, the company or consortium needs to be able to mobilize public opinion favorably on behalf of the development and counter any criticism that may arise. Finally, the company or consortium must have skills in project management in order to operate the studio effectively (and profitably).

Given the financial investment and extent to which such enterprises must comply with legal requirements and regulations, it is perhaps unsurprising that public-private partnerships have been particularly important in the development of some studios. For example, the partnership between the Queensland state government and the commercial operators developing what is now the Warner Roadshow Studios included a package of soft loans, the leasing of land on long-term and favorable rates, and assistance in attracting tenant service companies. This partnership is a continuing one, with the state government providing a low-interest loan of AU$8 million to the studios in 2002 to finance the construction of two new soundstages. The Bridge Studios in Vancouver, a Crown-owned enterprise, partnered with MGM in 1997 to build a soundstage, with the aid of a C$3.5 million investment from the British Columbia government.[6] In most cases, governments take a back seat in any partnership, facilitating the private ownership of these facilities by providing tangible and intangible support to the owners at critical points in the design, approval, and construction phases. Sometimes, however, in the absence of private investment (as was the case in the original development of The Bridge Studios in Vancouver) or when there is a hitch and institutional investment is not immediately forthcoming (as was the case for the original Studio City proposal for Melbourne's Docklands), governments can take a more prominent role.

In terms of service provision, some studios such as Studio Babelsberg and Cinecittà offer what is called "full service" because they have sole or substantial control over the on-site service providers and are therefore able to offer some or all of these services as a package to reduce production costs as an incentive to producers. Other studios may advertise themselves as a "one-stop shop," meaning that all the services necessary for production and postproduction are available on-site, but some or all of these services may be provided by independent companies. Some studios such as Warner Roadshow Studios have contractual agreements with on-site tenant companies that, in return for a commitment to rent space or offices on-site for a set period, guarantee that there will be no other companies within the studios offering directly comparable services. There is no guarantee that incoming productions will use these on-site service companies. Moreover, in most countries it is illegal for a studio to require producers to use particular companies simply because they are situated on-site, but often the proximity and convenience of such service companies will generate some work on incoming productions. Some studios provide only certain services themselves, while others are "dry-hire" or "four-wall rental" spaces, meaning that the empty soundstages are rented, and all equipment necessary for filming must be brought in or rented from companies either on- or off-site.

The rental of stage space alone is not particularly profitable, and studios usually augment their revenue from a number of sources. This may include the provision of film services (e.g., equipment hire, props, and wardrobe hire) and the rental of office space to media companies. It may involve the creation of public entertainment areas such as theme parks, studio tours, cinemas, restaurants, and shops. A number of studios are owned and managed by property development groups, and the studio may form part of a larger business park development. In some cases the studio may be colocated with residential, retail, and hospitality development.

In relation to the work that goes on in a studio, it might be assumed that ownership by a major media corporation would lead to use of the studio by productions associated with that corporation. However, the disaggregated nature of contemporary international production provides no guarantee that any of the major media corporation's production work will be put through its own studio facility. So although we can identify a group of studios that are owned or partly owned by international media conglomerates, productions financed or partly financed by these same conglomerates are as likely to be made in independent studios as inside their own studios. For example, the three *Matrix* films coproduced by Warner Bros. and Village Roadshow were made at Fox Studios Australia in Sydney, while 20th Century Fox and Disney Television have both made a number of movies of the week at the Warner Roadshow Studios in Queensland.

The *name* of a studio can have a bearing on the volume and type of work attracted there. For example, while the Warner Roadshow Studios is much more closely associated with the Village Roadshow group of companies than with Warner Bros. and its affiliates (Village Roadshow Production Management has

offices on the site, and more Village Roadshow productions have used the studio than Warner Bros. productions or joint Warner Bros.–Village Roadshow
productions), the studio is called Warner Roadshow Studios because the name
Warner is more instantly recognizable to international producers and connotes
familiarity, credibility, and prestige.

In general terms, though, the ability of a studio to attract international
work may have less to do with their ownership by major corporations and
more to do with a range of other factors, including currency exchange rates,
levels of incentives available in a territory, the "film friendliness" of local authorities, the pool of local talent, the degree to which the studio and related
on-site businesses are plugged into international networks, and so on.

The professional and industry networks of the studio management team—
and in some cases those of the owners—are an important factor in the type
and volume of production that flows through a studio, but one that is difficult
to quantify. For example, Rainer Schaper's professional connections while
head of Studio Babelsberg were important in reestablishing the studio as a site
of international production, with *Enemy at the Gates* and *The Pianist* both
coming to Babelsberg through his connections. Michael Lake has similarly
been a key figure in the history of the Warner Roadshow studio. Lake facilitated the migration of a number of former colleagues from the Melbourne-
based production house Crawfords to Queensland in the early 1990s to establish a production presence on the Gold Coast. More recently through his base
in Los Angeles, he has been instrumental in marketing the studio and famil-
iarizing powerful industry players with what it has to offer.

Quality of Infrastructure and Institutional Connections

The quality of infrastructure within a studio is the principal point of distinction between a temporary facility (such as a converted warehouse) and a
permanent studio.

The infrastructure within the studio will typically include stages of various sizes that are adequately soundproofed, powered, often air-conditioned,
and serviced by adjacent production offices and construction workshops.
The load-bearing capacity of the roof of a stage is also important and will
sometimes advantage purpose-built studios over converted spaces since not
all warehouses or factories will have roofs strong enough to bear the load of
lighting and other necessary equipment. The availability of specialized craft
and production workers on-site, together with associated services including
set decoration, equipment hire, film processing, and postproduction services, is essential for a studio to offer full service or to claim that it is a one-

stop shop facility. The presence of special features such as internal and external water tanks, permanent sets such as interiors of aircraft, and mockups of city streets and other building facades all add to the attraction of particular studios.

In order to be competitive for high-budget feature film in particular but also for television production, studios are now expected to be equipped to service the needs of digital production and postproduction. Digital readiness has become a benchmark against which studios are measured and market themselves. This will likely include the availability of high-speed fiber optic networks to enable digital transmission between service providers both within the studio and outside. The growing interconnection between production and postproduction—for example, the incorporation of visual and sound effects planning at earlier stages in the production process or the use of digital intermediate masters to enable image manipulation during the production process—increases the importance of the controlled environments offered by studios, but it also places new requirements on them.

The capacity of studios and service providers to meet the digital needs of producers is an increasingly important factor in the marketing of particular locations. Cinecittà, Ealing Studios, and Studio Babelsberg, for example, tout their state-of-the-art digital facilities alongside their skilled artisans and permanent backlots as primary reasons to film there. All of these studios have been extensively and expensively refurbished in recent years to enable them to offer state-of-the-art digital facilities. As the owners of these studios well know, digital readiness comes at considerable cost even for those studios able to incorporate a digital plan from inception. For example, a proposed facility for Tokyo will cost an estimated U.S.$1 billion.

The quality of a studio's infrastructure and its attractiveness to producers are not limited to the facilities within the studio. Just as important is related infrastructure outside the studio gates. This will include, first, the pool of talent—principally but not solely below-the-line talent—in the surrounding area and the availability of experienced crew. Many productions will bring in their own crew, often for key positions, and employ local workers in a more junior capacity, with the extent of this practice depending on local labor agreements, immigration regulations, and the needs of the particular production. The evolution of Vancouver into a major production center over the last two decades owes much to the willingness of local film unions to accommodate the demands of international producers.

Second, the extent of facilities and skilled services able to be drawn on over the course of a production can enhance the attractiveness of particular studios and locations. Studios in places with extensive and long-standing media sectors such as Sydney, London, Rome, and Berlin can have an edge over studios in places with less developed surrounding media infrastructure, although the availability of tax breaks and other financial incentives in the latter places can erase the advantage of established centers.

Third, the reputation of a particular place as a site of film production, film culture, and broader creative activity may significantly increase its prospects of attracting large-scale and ongoing production. For example, the *Lord of the Rings* trilogy has showcased the versatility of New Zealand locations, the skills of New Zealand craft workers and postproduction facilities, and the creativity of its above-the-line crew so that New Zealand is now firmly on the horizon of international producers as a production destination.

Fourth, the natural and built environment surrounding a studio will often be the principal draw for production, but studios may also be attractive because of their proximity to particular locations. The popularity of Barrandov Studios as a production location in recent years is due in no small part to Prague's capacity to double as a variety of European cities at different moments in history.

Fifth, a studio will usually need to be close to a major urban center that can provide quality accommodation, restaurants, and additional entertainment for cast and crew, as well as access to international flight and other transport connections. In the past, it has been suggested that one of the reasons why Eastern Europe did not host a large amount of international production was the standard of hotel and transport infrastructure. These concerns are now being addressed in many countries, and they may in turn be factors in the growth of international production in, for example, the Czech Republic and Romania. Conversely, the Warner Roadshow Studios in Australia was helped in its first years by its accessibility and the proximity of relatively cheap, quality, seaside hotels and apartments that could accommodate crews flown in from other centers initially for short periods to work on individual productions.

Sixth, the film-friendliness of local and national authorities and the role of film commissions and agencies can aid a studio's efforts to attract production, as we will discuss in more detail in the next chapter. Local authorities act as gatekeepers providing access to public land and facilities, and the permits necessary and charges levied on productions for the use of locations and the mobilization of ancillary services—police, fire brigade, rail—can act as a disincentive for production. National immigration regulations and procedures for importing film equipment can also either ease or hinder the production process. Film commissions, agencies, and local service companies also play a part in guiding producers through local regulations and helping them access ancillary services, production incentives, and tax breaks. The level of incentives and tax breaks offered by national and subnational authorities is, of course, a factor in many decisions about the location of production.

One of the distinguishing features of Studio Babelsberg is the presence in the adjacent Media City (Medienstadt) of the offices of Medienboard Berlin-Brandenburg and the Berlin-Brandenburg Film Commission, two agencies whose role is to encourage film production in the region, and the Konrad Wolf Film and Television Academy, which moved to the Media City in 2000. In 1998, Studio Babelsberg in partnership with the German regional investment bank Investitions Bank des Landes Brandenburg (ILB) established a film production finance and management company, Studio Babelsberg Independents (SBI), specifically to invest DM50 million annually in production by small and medium-sized production companies in the Berlin-Brandenburg region.[7] Studio Babelsberg has also benefited from the availability of funding from the European Union in developing and refurbishing the site. In March 2001, a studio spokesman estimated that European Union sources and national subsidies had provided half of the nearly DM1 billion investment in the site to upgrade basic infrastructure including roads, sanitation, and electricity as well as production infrastructure over the previous decade.[8] The recent accession of the Czech Republic to the European Union means that studios in that country may have access to a range of European Union funding programs. Most studios, however, do not have this same range of institutional connections.

Another set of institutional connections is provided by the relationship some studios have with local television broadcasters. This may sometimes appear to be a marriage of convenience and sometimes part of an explicit strategy of centralizing production in a studio to create a production epicenter. The latter is certainly the case for Cinecittà—literally translated as "cinema city"—and Studio Babelsberg, with its adjacent Media City. At other times the relationship may be part of corporate logic and design, where broadcasting operations are subsidiaries of the studio operator's parent company. So the program production needs of channels carried on the Australian pay TV network Foxtel can be partially met on the Fox Studios site.

The Balance of Work

While high-budget international feature production is literally "the big picture" for many of the studios under discussion here, most studios will actually host a mix of feature films, TV series, movies of the week, TV commercial

(TVC) production, and music video production rather than exclusively host-ing features. High-budget feature films are the mainstay for some of the larger studio, including Fox Studios Australia, Fox Studios Baja in Mexico, Pinewood-Shepperton and Leavesden in the United Kingdom, and Barran-dov in the Czech Republic. Other usually smaller studios host mainly movie-of-the-week and television series production, which generally requires less stage space and ancillary services than the high-budget features. Studios that host broadcast television production require stages with flat, usually con-crete, floors to enable television cameras to glide across them; stages for fea-ture film production often have wooden floors to enable sets to be fixed tem-porarily to them. Most studios host a variety of production work.

The balance of work at a studio may change quite dramatically over time. The Warner Roadshow Studios was best known until recently for its televi-sion series, movie-of-the-week, and TVC production work. But since *Scooby-Doo* occupied the studio in 2000–2001, its focus has moved to high-budget features. As we discussed earlier in this chapter, however, while this change in focus may offer the opportunity to enhance the studio's reputation, it may also entail costs. Hosting the *Scooby-Doo* shoot required the displacement of the movie-of-the-week and television series production that had sustained the studio for a number of years.

Barrandov Studios is another example of the changing balance of work over time. Until the end of the communist regime in the late 1980s, Barran-dov had been the epicenter of the local feature film production industry. While a number of high-budget international feature films were made there in the 1990s, most notably *Mission: Impossible*, Barrandov was sustained through much of the decade by TVC production, which accounted for up to 40 percent of production. In the years since 1999–2000, high-budget inter-national features have again become dominant.

As we will discuss in more detail later in this chapter, studios often enable other forms of media work by virtue of the central position they occupy in new media precincts such as those established at Studio Babelsberg and Fox Studios Australia and those proposed for Leavesden, Ealing, and Melbourne.

When Studios Were Built

The period in which a studio was built matters in terms of the kinds of in-frastructure it maintains and, just as important, the expectations it generates among the film community, policymakers, governments, and the public. Stu-dios created in the heyday of the "national film studio" idea, roughly from the 1920s to the 1950s—Cinecittà, Studio Babelsberg, Barrandov, Ardmore—

were designed with varying degrees of success to be national production epicenters. They typically employed large numbers of film workers across a variety of functions and services and commanded significant public investment
and attention. The legacy of their having been "national film studios" is evident in the continuing sense of public ownership of them by the local filmmaking community, publics, and governments. There is a corresponding interest in and expectation about the kinds of productions undertaken within
them and the character of their refurbishment to meet changing production
circumstances and an ongoing expectation—not always realized—that these
studios continue to influence the shape and character of local production.

In the same period as national film studios were being established in Europe, studios were developed in the United Kingdom but without the same
imperative to rationalize and centralize production through a single dominant studio. British studios were typically developed either by British cinema
entrepreneurs—J. Arthur Rank and Alexander Korda, for example—who desired to become "majors" in their own right, or by Hollywood majors. For
American companies, the development of studios in the United Kingdom
had three motivations. First, the purchase or establishment of studios in the
United Kingdom provided an opportunity to make films that met British and
British Empire quota regulations. Second, the studios enhanced Hollywood's
permanent production presence in one of the most important markets for
American films. And third, the studios made British stories, locations, personnel, and the creative culture of London more accessible. Consequently,
the major British studios—Elstree, Shepperton, Denham, Shepherd's Bush,
Pinewood—were founded with a more commercial mandate and were more
internationally oriented than the majority of their European counterparts.

Like their "national" and Hollywood counterparts, the British studios
have been forced to adapt to the changing international production environment. Pinewood, for instance, was initially modeled on Hollywood studio practice and relied in Rank's heyday in the 1940s and 1950s on a large
number of its own productions going on at the same time. But, as international production dynamics changed, there was no longer the same guarantee of continuity of production, and decisions on production location
tended to be made on a project-by-project basis. The studio became a rental
facility providing soundstages and production services to the international
production industry rather than producing its own films. The recent merger
of the Pinewood and Shepperton studios enables the use of production
space in both studios to be synchronized in order to maximize occupancy
and returns and to accommodate as much production as possible. Pinewood
has also recently reequipped two of its stages for television production by

adding state-of-the-art digital production equipment. Like the merger, this development broadens the range of work Pinewood is able to service and enhances its position as a multifaceted media hub or "media city."

Other large studios have transformed themselves through the addition of digital postproduction facilities and other new media capacities to become multifaceted media hubs and remain epicenters of production in their respective regions. The clusters of audiovisual production activity that have built up over time in the vicinity of these studios have facilitated this transformation. Since the early 1990s, this media city model has become one of the preferred strategies for renovating existing large studios as it offers the prospect of diversifying the revenue base and capitalizing on the existing media cluster. A number of former national film studios and various U.K. studios either have been or are currently in the process of being renovated as media hubs. This kind of renovation is designed to retain their competitive advantage in the market for international production and to ensure they are well placed to service the future needs of old and new, local and international media production. The media city model is also apparent in a number of new studio developments, particularly those in centers that did not previously have internationally oriented studios such as Fox Studios Australia, Central City Studios (Melbourne), and the studios proposed for Alicante and Toronto.

The period from the 1960s to the present day has witnessed the emergence of another type of studio that is principally oriented toward international production. As we discuss in more detail in chapter 5, many of these new developments are located outside core film and television production locations, including studios built in Malta in the 1960s, Vancouver in Canada and Wilmington in North Carolina in the early 1980s, the Gold Coast in the late 1980s, Romania in 1992, Mexico in 1996, and Isle of Man in 2002. These studios are often on a smaller scale than those developed in the earlier period such as Pinewood, Cinecittà, and Studio Babelsberg and often contain fewer soundstages than these larger, older studios. This is in part because they are not intended to fill the same comprehensive function as the earlier studios or act as a national production epicenter. Rather, they are principally designed to service the particular—one-off—needs of the contemporary international production industry, where decisions about the location of the shoot are made film by film, and all studios that are not producing their own films compete for individual projects. Studios are also extremely costly developments: the larger they are, the more expensive they are to equip and maintain, and the harder it is to ensure continuity of production.

Over time, a studio of this type may expand, with stages added as a studio's reputation and volume of work grow. This growth may in turn attract a greater range and depth of locally available ancillary services. Governments and other representatives of the location interest tend to pay increasing attention to the fortunes and needs of a studio as its growth enhances the profile of a place as a venue for international production in a particular location. This may involve direct or indirect financial assistance to aid expansion and the provision of international production incentives. Vancouver is the paradigmatic case of this expansion of film studios with accompanying governmental support.

Some of these studios have specialized in particular types or forms of production through catering a number of productions with similar needs. In the case of Fox Studios Baja, which was built around the water tanks created for *Titanic*, the resulting specialization has been embodied in the physical plant. The success of international TV series and MOWs (movies of the week) made at Warner Roadshow Studios during the 1990s gained the studio a reputation for this kind of work, which in turn attracted more of the same and encouraged the development of related specialized skills in the region.

Functional Profile and Spatial Concentration

Studios are notable for the extent and type of production work they undertake and for the degree to which they enable concentration of this work in a single place. They have always clustered production and postproduction services in one location but have done so in different ways. Currently, we can identify three different models of functional profile and spatial concentration of production activities and services:

- The *production precinct*, which services production but does not have extensive postproduction facilities and services
- The *cinema city*, which is oriented toward film and television drama work and usually contains the range of production and postproduction services necessary to provide full service
- The *media city*, which contains all of the features of the cinema city but which may also include a greater range of television broadcasting production facilities, other new media services, training facilities, and non-media-related creative industries

While the lines between these three types of studio are permeable, they represent three identifiably different logics of both studio development and of production and postproduction clustering.

Production precincts focus solely on the production shoot. Studios of this type comprise one or more stages, workshops, production offices, and perhaps a backlot and fixed sets, but they offer a limited range of production services and little or no postproduction services or capacity. Typical examples are the Toronto Film Studios, Prague Studios, and Leavesden Studios. Producers rent all or part of the studio and then hire in production service companies as required.

In the cinema city, the cluster is organized to provide production and postproduction services to feature films, movies of the week, and international television series. Some of these studios offer the full range of production and postproduction services themselves, although most rely on a range of tenant companies to provide the one-stop shop. Warner Roadshow Studios in Australia, and MediaPro and Castel in Romania exemplify this model. The business model of cinema cities is focused on attracting and retaining as much high-budget feature, movie-of-the-week, and international television series production as possible via the provision of a suite of facilities and services on-site.

In the media city, a much larger cluster of tenants is likely to include information and communication technology (ICT) companies with a predominant media production focus, film and broadcasting-related companies, and, often, training facilities. Most media cities will have an on-site television broadcaster. The range and type of production and postproduction services available is much broader than in the cinema city and may include digital animation production in addition to feature film and the full spectrum of television production including news, infotainment, live audience programs, special events (including concerts), as well as drama. Where a typical cinema city like Warner Roadshow Studios might have 11 tenants onsite, the prototypical media city, Studio Babelsberg, is home to more than 130 media-related companies. Media cities are fully digitally capable with a high-speed network backbone.

The presence of so many companies offering a diverse range of services has a number of benefits for the owners of media cities. First, revenue from the lease of office space provides long-term, defined income. Second, the studio is able to service a broad range of productions both on- and off-site simultaneously. Third, the existence of this extensive range of facilities and services can be a powerful draw for incoming production. The business model of the media city is consequently more complex than that of the cinema city. Not only does it seek to attract and retain high-budget features, movies of the week, and television series production through providing a range of facilities and services on-site, but the presence of so many tenant companies means the studio is recast as a form of commercial property/industrial park development. While their primary function is still to service film and television production, media cities characteristically have a number of other public functions. Many media cities include extensive public areas comprising cinemas, concert halls, restaurants, function and conference centers, retail areas, theme parks, and studio tours. Such leisure and entertainment facilities serve to further diversify the revenue base, augment the studio's public profile, and reposition it at the center of a broader media, leisure, and entertainment and retail cluster. The incorporation of these features has been a means to either develop sites that had not been previously used for film production, such as Fox Studios Australia in Sydney, or to transform and renovate existing studios such as Cinecittà, Pinewood, Studio Babelsberg, and Barrandov.

The Ealing Studios redevelopment, with its focus on new media and creative industries, represents a new variation of the media city model. This redevelopment shares many of the characteristics of the media city in that it is oriented to feature film and television production and promises to service a variety of firms and activities. But it also foregrounds Ealing's new media outlook and includes, in a more central way than in other media cities, non-media-related "creative industries" such as design, fashion, and architectural services as well as IT companies that have no or only a minor media focus.

Conclusion

In this chapter, we have sought to capture the diversity and scope of the contemporary studio. By using a number of variables, we have been able to group together and differentiate between studios on the basis of their size and location, ownership, their age, the balance of the production work they undertake, the quality of their infrastructure and institutional connections, their functional profile, and the concentration of services, facilities, and companies within the studio. All of these variables determine, to a greater or lesser extent, how these studios participate in the international production ecology and how they are related to local production ecologies. They are also factors determining the circumstances under which new studios have been developed and existing ones renovated.

Studios are increasingly being recognized as engines of the wider creative economy and anchor elements in creative industry and new media cluster development. Cluster analysis has become an important part of assessing the economic viability of particular areas and the potential of particular regions, and has spawned a range of studies. Allen J. Scott's study of the Los Angeles and Paris film industries and Krätke's study of the Potsdam-Babelsberg film industry[9] identify place-specific characteristics, the quality and depth of local and international networks, the extent of interfirm collaboration, and synergies with related industries as critical determinants of the success or failure of particular cultural product/creative industries clusters. The recognition that studios are at the center of regional transaction networks and drive much creative and related activity in a particular region is informing the contemporary enthusiasm of many public authorities for the construction or refurbishment of studios. Their aim is to use the studio to create in Scott's words "dense networks of specialized but complementary producers clustered together in industrial districts" and to replicate the "transactions-intensive agglomerations of specialized firms" characteristic of Los Angeles film, television, recording, and multimedia industries.[10] It is now the policy of a number of agencies around the world—from local government authorities to regional and national development agencies—to develop and enhance their clusters of creative industries through studio developments. In the following chapter, we will investigate the role of government and the policy environment of the contemporary studio in more detail.

Notes

1. Peter Hall, "The Future of Cities," *Computers, Environments and Urban Systems* 23 (1999): 173–85.

2. Peter Hall, *Cities in Civilization* (London: Weidenfeld & Nicolson, 1998), 521.

3. Hall, *Cities in Civilization*, 534.

4. It should be noted that the theme park was the "hook" for Warner Bros. to enter the studio deal, with film production capacity and income from soundstage rental lesser considerations.

5. The border regions of Tijuana, Mexicali, and Ciudad Juárez have become centers of electronics manufacturing, particularly of television sets, as a result of transnational corporation investment over the 1990s drawn by regional comparative advantages: "geographic closeness to the United States; political and labor stability as well as labor force flexibility, availability and cost," but also because of "open trade policies, deregulation of this sector and intense promotion of FDI." See Jorge Carrillo, "Foreign Direct Investment and Local Linkages: Experiences and the Role of Policies: The Case of the Mexican Television Industry in Tijuana," paper presented at XV World Congress of Sociology, Brisbane, Australia, July 2002.

6. Neil M. Coe, "A Hybrid Agglomeration? The Development of a Satellite-Marshallian Industrial District in Vancouver's Film Industry," *Urban Studies* 38, no. 10 (2001): 1753–76.

7. "German Studio Launches Production Outfit," *Screen Digest* (October 1998): 218.

8. Mark R. Johnson and Vanessa Liertz, "German Studio Transforms Itself into a Co-producer," *Asian Wall Street Journal*, 21 March 2001, N5.

9. Stefan Krätke, "Network Analysis of Production Clusters: The Potsdam/Babelsberg Film Industry as an Example," *European Planning Studies* 10, no. 1 (2002): 27–54.

10. Allen J. Scott, *The Cultural Economy of Cities: Essays on the Geography of Image-Producing Industries* (London: Sage, 2000), 205.

CHAPTER THREE

※

Studios, the "Location Interest," and Policy

The most successful of the places competing for international production rely on a combination of built and natural environments, film services infrastructure including studios, and a strong "location interest" underwritten by a supportive policy and regulatory framework. This combination of elements not only plays an important role in influencing producers' decisions about where to locate individual productions but is perhaps more importantly critical to a place's chances of attracting production on a regular, ongoing basis. Reputable film service companies and qualified, experienced personnel provide a necessary "quality assurance" and reduce the risks associated with that production. Studios provide the option of a controlled production environment that complements surrounding built and natural environments. And a film-friendly milieu not only allows producers to plan with confidence but also provides incentives for them to base production in a particular place.

Studios—both purpose-built or redeveloped production facilities—are critical elements of this portfolio. The availability of a studio opens up storytelling possibilities in a place, nurtures the development of associated services and infrastructure for both local and high-budget international production, and permits the optimal use of the natural and built environment. The studio strengthens the competitive advantage of places in the marketplace for international production (which is largely a marketplace for *parts* of feature film or television productions). In this *disaggregated* production system (a characteristic of Hollywood and cultural product industries more generally),[1] studios compete for production, although service companies within a studio such as visual effects companies or film-processing laboratories may independently bid for and work on parts of productions not shot on the studio's stages.

Studios also provide an opportunity for a place to win as much of a production as possible by offering a range of production and postproduction services in one location and minimizing the perceived risks for producers. These risks include productions being forced to use substandard crews and film services; lack of access to required locations and appropriate policing and control services; costly production delays resulting from immigration issues or procedures to obtain permits for filming in certain locations; the imposition of unforeseen levies and costs during production that may blow out the production budget; poor ancillary services such as accommodation and catering that may affect the well-being of cast and crew. Studios can then be vehicles for the *reaggregation* of production in one place and the limiting of risk.

If studio complexes, the range of associated film services, and locations are three pillars of the location interest, a fourth pillar is the range of *measures* many governments and private agencies undertake to pitch for and secure a share of this international production. These may include a variety of tax concessions, in some cases direct subsidies to production, assistance to producers to ease the path of production through necessary legalities including obtaining relevant permits, permissions, and visas, as well as support for the development or renovation of production infrastructure, including studios. These measures are part of an overall package designed to market a place, construct or renovate a film milieu, and promote the use of local film services.

The restless mobility of international production is a combination of "push" and "pull" factors or, in our terms, a combination of the design interest and the location interest. To date, most academic work and commentary on the film industry in the United States in the form of reports by government agencies and trade bodies have focused on the design interest perspective— that is, on how international production benefits from and chooses between the packages of financial incentives, labor costs, and assistance on offer in different places, and how the availability of these incentives has affected film production in the United States.[2] By contrast, less attention has been paid to the location interest—that is, not only to what is on offer in particular places, but why local agents and entities are now collaborating to attract production, and how film policy has changed with a new emphasis on film services and the potential of film production to reinforce broader policy ambitions in areas such as urban regeneration, the development of information and communication technology industries, the fostering of creative industries, tourism marketing, and the promotion of a city, region, or nation as a competitive and attractive place for investment, work, and leisure.

In this chapter, we investigate how and why it has become common for film policy at national, regional, and local or municipal levels to include the active promotion, development, and financial support for studios and other infrastructure alongside initiatives to support film training, production, script development, and marketing of films by local filmmakers. We will discuss the continuities and disjunctions between these and previous policies. The chapter concludes with an assessment of the logic of studio developments as part of emerging film services policy frameworks.

The Spread of Studios

For a time it seemed as though large cities and places that aspired to attract the lucrative business of film production could meet the spatial needs of producers with limited temporary or permanent studios fashioned from converted warehouses, factories, aircraft hangars, or bus depots (such as The Bridge Studios in Vancouver, Canada). Where there was an existing production industry, many if not all services required by international production could be obtained in the city or region around such sound stages. But in recent times, to maintain or grow their share of international production, these centers have needed to develop integrated production spaces that allow for the collocation of a variety of services. As a consequence, something of a recent vogue internationally has been to build large-scale studios to enable considerable amounts of work on a project to be conducted on a single site. Studios with multiple soundstages capable of meeting the production needs of high-budget and blockbuster production while simultaneously servicing movie-of-the-week, television series, or advertising production are springing up or being talked up around the globe. Existing facilities are undergoing extensive and often extremely costly refurbishments to remain technologically competent and internationally competitive.

International film and television production is acquiring the same spatially dispersed yet globally integrated form of organization of economic activity Saskia Sassen finds characteristic of the world economy.[3] With statistical data on the volume and total production spend of international film and television production indicating that such production has become an integral part of film economies from Vancouver to Prague, London to Cape Town, policy makers and film service providers alike are increasingly concerned with attracting and maintaining their jurisdiction and their company's share of film production. The sense of common purpose among policy makers and service providers has been a powerful motivation behind the development of the location interest in particular places.

Along with tax and investment incentive schemes, favorable foreign currency exchange rates, and a pool of highly skilled personnel, studios are core components of the production infrastructure necessary to attract and generate ongoing work. As such, studios "play a structuring role" as focal points and key indicators of the health of production in a place.[4] Increasingly, it seems, they require ongoing support in the form of periodic injections of public funds or largesse to remain competitive and on the technological cutting edge.

Vancouver has become a leading production center over the last fifteen years due in no small part to the efforts of the provincial government, which owns one of the three major studios in the city. Montreal also has two major studio complexes, and in 2002 two purpose-built studios were announced for Toronto, to be built with considerable assistance from the city and the provincial government on land earmarked for the city's failed bid for the 2008 Olympic Games. As we discuss in more detail in chapter 4, neither went ahead as planned. And in Australia, new film studio complexes have been built over the past decade on the Gold Coast, in Sydney, and in Melbourne, all with substantial state and/or federal government assistance, both direct and indirect.

Studios are attractive to governments because of the economic and employment effects they have both within and beyond the film and television production industries. Audiovisual production has been described as a "locomotive" industry because "the number of production workers directly working in the industry belies the true impact of the industry on the economy because so many upstream, downstream, and peripheral industries depend on the primary production plant."[5] Other locomotive effects include the concentration of production in a place and growth in the total amount of that production. This is clear in the case of New South Wales and Fox Studios Australia. In the early 1990s, prior to the establishment of the studio, New South Wales hosted around 40 percent of total (both local and international) film and television production in Australia.[6] In the three years between 1998–1999 and 2000–2001—after Fox Studios Australia had opened—New South Wales attracted almost 54 percent of total production and almost 68 percent of feature film production.[7] By contrast, production figures for Victoria—which had been roughly equal to those for New South Wales in the years prior to the opening of Fox Studios Australia—decreased. This loss of market share was a principal reason behind the establishment of the Central City Studios that opened in Melbourne in 2004, although it remains to be seen if the new studio will have the desired effects of drawing large-scale production back to Victoria.

Governments at national, state, and local levels have also played key roles in the renovation and refurbishment of existing studios. Elstree Film Studios in London where Alfred Hitchcock made some of his early films, and more recently where the first three *Star Wars* films were produced, is owned by the Hertsmere Borough Council, which has invested over £10 million in the complex, including refurbishing two enormous soundstages. Cinecittà, the famous studio in Rome, was partially privatized in 1998 after being state owned since the late 1930s. Studio Babelsberg, formerly the home of the East German film industry, received approximately €500 million in assistance from the European Union, from the German federal government, and from the Brandenburg state government after privatization in 1992.

Government involvement is common because of the scale, cost, and high-profile character of studio developments and because of the often lengthy bureaucratic processes such as obtaining planning approval and undertaking environmental and heritage assessments that must be negotiated prior to construction or major renovation. Governments will often support these projects by investment (as in Melbourne and Vancouver), providing loans (as on the Gold Coast), or making available public land on favorable terms (as in Toronto and Brooklyn) because of the prestige and symbolic importance attaching to studios. Studios are attractive to governments because they are perceived as important generators of employment in both the film industry and related service industries, as export-oriented developments, and as more environmentally friendly than many other manufacturing industry developments. As we discuss in the next chapter, studio developments can provide productive and effective means of cleaning up problem, polluted areas and function as vehicles for the transformation of the industrial base of a place and spatial use in urban areas. For its part, the international production industry has come to depend on this "friendliness" of governments to facilitate the development of production infrastructure.

The development and implementation of policies to attract international production are closely linked to policies designed to assist or enable studio development, and this is true for the places within the United States as outside. Policy makers around the world are responding both to the same long-term trends in the screen industries toward internationalization and globalization and toward "vertical disintegration" of production, or what Susan Christopherson calls "virtual integration."[8] In Allen J. Scott's words, "the production of films, television shows, musical recordings and multimedia products breaks down into a multitude of detailed tasks carried out by specialized firms and subcontractors," with these "specialized producers" being "brought together in intricate networks of deals, projects, and tie-ins that link them together in ever changing collaborative arrangements and joint ventures."[9] Once production becomes disaggregated in this way, it becomes possible for parts of production to be carried out not only by different firms in the one city located in different parts of the city but in other cities and countries.

Governments, infrastructure providers, and service companies in production and design epicenters like Los Angeles, London, and New York have had to develop and pursue a location interest in order to maintain their lead status, just as other cities—whether Miami or Chicago, Sydney or Toronto—need to pursue their own location interest and find ways to exploit this disaggregated production system in order to maintain, modernize, and extend their production infrastructure. The studio is a vital piece of this infrastructure, and so it is perhaps unsurprising that similar rationales are advanced within the United States and internationally to convince city politicians and regional policy makers of the merits of supporting studio developments. Similar estimations and projections of benefit accruing from international production and studio complex investment are advanced, and similar measures from frameworks to agencies—film commissions and film offices—are put in place by local and state authorities to attract production and advance the location interest. Outside the United States, support for studios and efforts to attract international production sit side by side with often long-standing film policies that are intended to benefit and often subsidize local production and official coproductions, and that are designed to connect local films and filmmakers into international production, distribution, and exhibition circuits in the name of the national cultural patrimony.

The contemporary enthusiasm for international production and studio development raises some important policy questions. How does the often quite intensive investment and support that governments are providing to international producers fit with existing film policy logics? How do contemporary developments relate to past periods of studio activity and construction, and how do contemporary studio models differ from previous models? Do the objectives of film policy change when a studio and international production become part of the policy mix? How is the relation between local/national and international production affected by this twin trajectory of film policy development? Is support for the studio a new turn in film policy making or an incremental development? What is the relation between filmic and extrafilmic considerations driving studio developments and policy making? How, in the face of the very substantial activity studio complexes generate, do policy makers go about maintaining and developing their local studio complexes?

In light of the sheer scale of contemporary international film and television production and the attention studios command, it would be tempting to see support for studios as a new policy development that alters the very terms of film support. From this perspective, the focus on studios indicates a policy hierarchy in which policies for industrial development take precedence over cultural policies. Global economic integration is prioritized over local production ecologies. Infrastructure support becomes as important as, if not more important than, the promotion and facilitation of local production. Employment generation is foregrounded over previous priorities for cultural identity and development. Cross-sectoral partnerships are favored over partnerships within a narrowly bounded film milieu. The policy focus is now on information and communication technology capacity development, informed by thinking about the clustering of firms, and value chains of media content rather than on support for individual productions in certain forms of film and television content (feature films, documentaries, experimental production, television drama, and children's programs).

From this perspective, policy support for studios and international production replaces both the rationales for and the mechanisms of traditional film support and represents a profound subversion of existing policy instruments. This has been an underlying fear for many individuals, firms, and agencies geared to local production, and the worry of many film critics and sometimes union and production industry representatives. This fear has been compounded as studios seek to attract international productions to generate revenue through price scales that often appear prohibitive for local producers. Policy making involving studios seems to confront long-standing priorities for dreaming the dreams of a place and showing its stories to the world. Cultural development appears to be eclipsed by a more economic rationalist focus on industry development.

We would argue that this is at best only part of the story. In *policy* terms, support for studio developments and international production has augmented rather than supplanted local production support mechanisms (indeed, the contemporary policy problem is more one of encouraging *both* local and international production and managing the relations between them). There is also not so great a distance between the focus on studio development and international production and previous governmental attentions to film and television as might be claimed.

We need to be cautious for a number of reasons in discussing studios and support for international production as radically different or new departures in film policy or public policy more generally. Governmental support for the development of studio complexes is not new. There is a long history of infrastructure provision in film policy making and urban development with which studio complexes connect. Public and private partnerships are neither new for governments nor unfamiliar in film policy and other public policy making. The idea of developing value-adding clusters and precincts has extensive governmental precedents in the cultural sector and is a centerpiece of knowledge-economy thinking. By the same token, the concern to connect national production capacity to international production and financing implicit in studio development is a long-standing one—the variation lies in the instruments used.

Government Support for Studios

Ardmore in Ireland, Cinecittà in Italy, Babelsberg in Germany, and Barrandov in the Czech Republic have all been supported by their national governments over several decades. In British Columbia, the provincial government has played a prominent role in facilitating the construction of studios, and it controls one of the largest studios in Vancouver, The Bridge Studios, through the British Columbia Pavilion Corporation. Indeed, this public support—whether it be by way of public contribution in cash or kind, loans on favorable terms, or ownership or part ownership by governments (national, state or provincial, or local government authorities), as with The Bridge or Elstree—can be traced in previous screen-policy initiatives.

These kinds of government support are not confined to centers outside the United States. In 1999, New York's Kaufman Astoria Studios, founded in 1920 as a production center for Famous Players/Lasky, announced a U.S.$8.3 million expansion of its film production facility including the construction of a seventh soundstage. In an example of cross-sectoral partnerships at work in the United States, initial funding of U.S.$2.5 million for the expansion came from the New York City Council; the New York state government provided U.S.$1.7 million in grants and loans through its Empire State Development Corporation; the borough of Queens contributed financial assistance in the form of a U.S.$125,000 grant from the borough president's office; and the New York City Economic Development Corporation, which is leasing the land for the expansion on a long-term basis, also made available a U.S.$1.2 million loan.[10]

British, Canadian, and Australian governments have, in the past, financed the construction of broadcasting and film studio infrastructure through support given to public service broadcasters—the BBC, CBC, and ABC—and documentary film agencies such as the Canadian National Film Board and Film Australia. There is also a long history of film policy support of various kinds for the development of studios. When the South Australian Film Corporation (SAFC) was established in the early 1970s, a small-scale studio facility to attract film and television production to the state was an integral feature of the package of film support.[11] The provincial government initiatives to build studio complexes in Vancouver, British Columbia, in the early 1980s and Gold Coast, Queensland, in the late 1980s and early 1990s provide additional examples.

Clear continuities in policy making are evident, then, from earlier periods to today, but there are also some important differences. Previous Australian, Canadian, and British support for studios was couched in terms of support for public service broadcasting and the "national interest program" of documentary film agencies. State-run studios in Italy, Germany, and the former Czechoslovakia were likewise designed as "national" flagship institutions through which local production could be controlled and centralized with varying kinds of public service–style remits. This kind of infrastructure support differs from the support for contemporary studios in several ways. First, public broadcasting entities, inasmuch as they are opening themselves up to independent production, are doing so as a means of meeting public service broadcasting programming and policy requirements—these requirements are generally not part of the business model of these new and revamped studios (although Studio Babelsberg is home to the local regional public broadcaster). Second, the principal business of public broadcasters is their own production rather than earning revenue from opening their studios to all comers on a competitive basis, as the commercial studios must. Today's governmental support is for a studio that is not intended principally for government-assisted production but rather is open to all types of production on a competitive basis.

The development of a studio in South Australia was motivated by the state film corporation's remit to facilitate production in a state without significant existing infrastructure. Government control over the studio through the SAFC created tension between the potentially contradictory policy objectives of keeping the studio occupied and creating the conditions under which independent film and television production could flourish. By contrast, there is a formal separation between Queensland's film agency, the Pacific Film and Television Commission (PFTC), and the Warner Roadshow Studios. The PFTC's brief is to enable both local and international production in Queensland, which often involves the agency in promoting the studio as part of its attention to the location interest, but often it will not involve the studio at all. The studio also has its own agents pursuing its interests in Australia and Los Angeles independent of the PFTC.

Public and Private Partnerships

Public-private partnerships are not new in the film industry. Film financing models in Western Europe, Canada, Australia, and New Zealand in which the film agency provides part of the funding for production with private funding making up the remainder is one example. In the Australian case, for instance, private investment triggers public monies through the Film Finance Corporation. We contend that the large studios are built on new alliances between the public and private sectors—in this case, between media production companies, studio infrastructure providers, real estate developers, and governments. These alliances are characteristic of broader trends in cultural policy making and urban planning that stress partnerships between government and private enterprise. Studios are also part of the "major projects" thinking and mind-set of governments. They are big-ticket items that often require considerable public assistance to become established. In 2003, the Victorian State Government estimated that it would outlay AU$40.2 million over twenty years on the studio development at Docklands in central Melbourne (although it now appears the figure may be much higher), while the Victorian State Department of Innovation, Industry and Regional Development estimates total returns to the state will amount to AU$43.9 million.[12]

Just as governments competitively bid for and provide sweeteners to secure the branches of the Guggenheim Museum or Disney theme parks, so, too, governments work hard not only to secure private investment in construction and studio management but also to attract core or anchor tenants, large and small productions, production services, and postproduction companies. The public contribution may be financial (in the form of tax incentives or subsidies) and may include improvements to transport or utility infrastructure (sewage lines, road or rail connections). But as Hannigan[13] and others have argued, the partnership may not be an equal one in terms of the returns to the public purse measured against the costs in terms of subsidy or tax income forgone through subsidies resulting from the partnership, although it is often claimed that the hard-to-measure intangible benefits generated by the development—particularly in terms of city branding and marketing—more than compensate for actual financial losses. We will discuss these issues in more detail in the following chapter.

Value-Adding Clusters and Precincts

Early on in the development of the Warner Roadshow Studios in Australia, concerted efforts were made by representatives of an emerging location interest to secure a range of tenants with sufficient expertise to enable the studio to function as a one-stop shop, where all production and postproduction needs could be met in the one place. A large number of individuals and companies relocated to Queensland from Sydney and Melbourne to work in or close to the studio.

This early development of a creative cluster was focused solely on the studio complex and film or television production that might be carried out there. Now, increasingly, it is being recognized that studio complexes seed innovation and enable a range of creative work above and beyond what might go on in the complex itself. Recent studies[14] illustrate the central place that studios occupy in production networks. Film workers are attracted to the area to be close to the action. But a range of other creatives—games designers, software developers, musicians, model makers—are also drawn there. This kind of clustering can have what Scott terms "emergent effects,"[15] or the creation of synergies between businesses that will seed innovation. Such synergies are fundamental to the business models and strategies of a number of studios, including Ealing Studios in the United Kingdom.

Over the past five years, these characteristics of studios, what they enable as well as what they do, have been more widely recognized. In part this is due to the ways studio complexes are now articulated in policy discourse to a variety of new economy goals: building knowledge, fostering innovation, allowing creativity to bloom. Studio complexes are integral parts of what are variously called creative, cultural, or "copyright" industries, and they are therefore central components of new service industry–based economic strategies.

The idea of developing value-adding clusters and precincts has extensive precedents in urban planning, particularly planning for cultural facilities and precincts. A considerable body of work on creative clusters sees the clustering of activity as critically central to creativity (which is seen to proceed from clustering), to cycles of innovation, and to growth in the creative sector in a particular location—particularly of the commercial cultural product industries.[16] A virtuous circle is now entertained in which governments can promote the creative industries while continuing to seize on the direct and indirect value and potential of film and television production to drive employment and economic growth. This has fueled government interest in studios, among other things. Such services can be either aggregated together as when colocated film service companies (processing laboratories, production companies, sound and visual effects companies) all work on the same film, but they can also be disaggregated, as when the same companies work on different productions. The advantage to policy makers of thinking in terms of precincts and clusters is that such thinking allows an intervention that is not targeted at one particular cultural form but several, purposefully fosters a culture of innovation, builds relationships and connections, and develops a milieu—for example, companies around the studio as innovative companies. And it powerfully refocuses our attention to film and television production, making us think about its research and development (R&D) aspects. From a clustering perspective, innovation is no longer in the individual film but more in the *processes*, the *ensemble of technologies and practices*. Innovation is therefore as likely to be found in the *services* provided to the filmmaking process, whether in the combination of services or the transactions and interactions between firms, or even in the groups of interests in the field.

Rethinking the Relationship between Local and International Production

Studios can be conceived in much the same way as Sassen describes the global city: "as strategic spaces where global processes materialize in national territories and global dynamics run through national institutional arrangements."[17] Studios oriented primarily to international production are parts of a mobile, fluid, slippery international production ecology shaped by broader industrial trends: international production levels; the relative importance of particular markets; the prominence of coproduction as an industrial norm, the tendency toward agglomeration and the creation of multinational megamedia corporations at one end of the scale and their interaction with a growing number of small firms at the other; and the adjusted role and objectives of state and national government and of media policies.

In many cases, new and refurbished studios are evidence of the globalization of Hollywood, since many are used or partly owned by the same multinational media companies that own the major Hollywood studios. As a 2002 article in *Newsweek International* argues, Hollywood is no longer a place—it's a state of mind.[18] The article painted a picture of the major studios roaming the earth in search of the new magic formula. Four of the Hollywood majors—Sony, Disney, Fox, and Warner Bros.—have begun making films and remaking American films in languages other than English, and they have recently established new production units in a number of countries, including Spain, Brazil, and China. In 2002, Columbia distributed a Chinese-language comedy called *Big Shot's Funeral* costarring Donald Sutherland, which became the highest-grossing Chinese-language film to date. Meanwhile, Warner Bros., the longtime partner of Australian media giant Village Roadshow, is focusing on local-language productions in a number of territories to drive the corporation's global growth. The company recently produced a ten-film series, *Swordsmen of the Passes*, in China and established an office of its Warner Bros. Pictures International division in Shanghai in June 2003 to co-ordinate acquisitions and production work in the greater China region.[19]

But the studios where much of this production takes place are also parts of a local, regional, or national production ecology or cultural sector, rooted or embedded in a place, featuring as employers or workplaces, as physical presences or landmarks in the built environment, as well as economic drivers. While we can trace the expansion of a competitive market for international production, we must acknowledge that it is always to some degree linked to the *local* production ecology of particular cities, regions, and countries. Studios seem to encourage the simultaneous existence of parallel and convergent dynamics. We can see this in Italy where Martin Scorsese made *Gangs of New York* on part of the Cinecittà lot, while Italian film and television production continued on other stages. We can see it in Sydney, where television production for Foxtel channels coexisted with the production of *Star Wars*, or where Animal Logic, one of the tenant service companies based at Fox Studios Australia, worked simultaneously on, for example, postproduction of *Moulin Rouge* and the low-budget Australian feature *Mullet*. While some infrastructure developments such as the studios built around water tanks in Malta and Mexico do focus exclusively on international production, understanding the contemporary studio complex as a part of film policy involves seeing it as a vehicle with the potential to bring the local and the international into a productive relationship. Indeed, there is an implicit and sometimes explicit assumption that "international production" will "cross-subsidize" domestic capacity in some way, through technological renovation, skills development, or some other mechanism.

As noted earlier, local, state, and national governments provide a range of incentives to encourage film production activity in their jurisdiction, including, now, the state of California. Most are directly related to the development of the extensive market for international production, which has also prompted the renovation and construction of production infrastructure, usually with substantial assistance from public authorities. But this international orientation of film policy is a variation on an old theme, albeit one that is now on a more organized and systematized scale. After all, coproduction treaties have long provided an instrument for bringing together local and international production. Continuities have also always been sought between domestic and international production through encouraging patterns of international investment in local film and television productions.

What may be new here is not the support for international involvement in the financing of local productions, but support for international production as such as part of the business model for studios. Governments around the world are busily developing direct or indirect assistance packages to offer to production companies in a bid to construct and maintain competitive studios, maximize opportunities for international production, and promote the location interest. Some of these studios are partly or fully owned by one of the major Hollywood studios or an associated company, just as were many earlier studio complex developments.

Production and investment by Hollywood studios in Europe grew in the late 1940s and 1950s principally as a result of postwar currency controls and other reconstruction measures. But it is important to remember that both international production and international studio investment were not new developments for the majors at this time, either. In the 1920s, Paramount, Warner Bros., and Fox had all invested in studio facilities in London. In addition to the American interests in Britain, the French company Pathé opened studios at Alexandra Palace in north London in 1913. Paramount also operated the Joinville studio in Paris and had a coproduction deal in the 1920s with the major German film company Ufa, which owned the Babelsberg Studios near Berlin.[20]

The factors driving production away from the United States in the period after World War II are still very much evident today: producers' desires to reduce costs, particularly labor costs; less prohibitive union work rules and rates; access to tax shelters; currency fluctuations; a desire for "authentic" or exotic locations; and the generation of additional international market appeal through the use of foreign talent and locations. But the trend is cyclical, depending in particular on the strength or weakness of the U.S. dollar and perhaps on the balance between box office earnings in America and internationally of films produced or distributed by the Hollywood majors: When international box office earnings are high, production will tend to flow offshore. Whereas in Europe after the World War II infrastructure investment by international companies was an indirect result of measures to reconstruct domestic economies, including restrictions on the expatriation of American dollars, now it is a specific policy objective to attract international production and develop studios.

Studios help establish and maintain the presence of international production, but this often operates in parallel to the local production industry. Studios can provide opportunities for constructing convergences and connections between the different sectors (e.g., through crew mobility). They also create a new problem: how to develop convergent and productive relations between the international and the domestic industry.

Toward a Film Services Framework

The resurgence of interest in the studio and international production among policymakers around the world is part of emerging *film services* approaches to policy development and support. In these approaches, the target of intervention is not the film product but the variety of intermediate inputs, organizational arrangements, and expertise associated with the processes involved in developing film projects. In this sense, film services approaches are fundamentally concerned with the capabilities—skills, infrastructures, and networks—that underwrite the capacity of a film industry in a region or locality to create and innovate. Government agencies in the thrall of film services frameworks worry not so much about film projects as about the skills-, infrastructure-, and network-base-supplying transient projects. That is, they pursue a location interest rather than a design interest. They stress the importance of various film services providers in growing and managing the industry. They foreground the existence and extent of facilities in a location, the capacity of its film milieu, its technological competitiveness, and its robustness. Theirs is a concern for the optimal functioning and development of facilities, capacities, and technological infrastructure.

Film services approaches have come to serve a family of governmental purposes. First, these approaches succinctly express and provide a vehicle for the location interests of particular places promoting locally the tasks of international film services provision. They assist in pitching for international projects by foregrounding the provision of services by a range of providers to footloose international production. In emphasizing the services—from location services to below-the-line film workers, from equipment suppliers to facilities providers—required by international production, these approaches encourage systematic thinking on behalf of the situated location interest about international production industry needs. Such an orientation helps local actors to identify key strengths and weaknesses in their capabilities to pitch for and supply plug-in film services. In this context, film services frameworks direct attention toward creating the right settings, including incentives for film services companies to prosper. This attention considers the health, character, and skills development of the film services themselves irrespective of whether these skills and technologies are exercised in local or international productions.

Second, a film services perspective implies an orientation toward servicing an increasingly differentiated and fragmented film and television market. It encourages the identification of identifiably different market segments or niches and therefore focuses attention on (1) where gaps exist, (2) the ways such services can productively supply both international and local production, and (3) how supplying for these different market segments might be better facilitated through connections between the different production sectors.

Third, the film services orientation encourages government and industry to see the various "inputs" into production as having their own trajectories, deficits, and opportunities. Film service frameworks have provided useful recognition of the creativity and innovation of diverse production inputs that would otherwise go without acknowledgment were the focus to be on the individual production and consequently on its content, director, writer, producer, and actors. Intermediate inputs in set design and construction, production design, location management and line producing, special effects, and postproduction can be likewise recognized as valued creative inputs. But this also allows that there might be a mismatch between sectors, that each may have different speeds of development, that each may provide different opportunities for growth and expansion, and that each may be addressed differently. In the context of international production, film services frameworks encourage the envisaging of partial rather than complete industries in particular places. With a focus on the "component" rather than "total product," location interests become oriented not toward the whole film but toward the piecework involved in producing screen production for an increasingly globalized production system.

Fourth, film services approaches allow governments and interest groups to promote the film industry on the basis of the services provided through production and infrastructures to other industries and sectors of society. Here the film industry becomes the provider of valued inputs into other creative industries, the service sector, and ICT industries—variously urban entertainment businesses such as theme parks, digital content and applications industries, games industry, tourism, and even real estate and place marketing. In this way, the film industry is being directly joined up to other—often more compelling—governmental and public priorities. So those involved in seeking to promote and develop policy for the ICT industries get interested in the film industry (meaning the locally and internationally oriented components of it) as a vehicle for generating high-technology products, applications, and processes for uptake in local and international production settings. While this makes the film industry at the service of other industries and values it for the service it provides, it nonetheless permits recognition of the diverse interests in film and television production and consumption. Film becomes important here not in its own right but for its potential to enhance, enable, and innovate not only adjacent creative industries but also broader service sectors and even cities and regions.

Fifth, film services approaches provide belated policy recognition of the structural organization of the cultural economy into networks of small to medium-sized companies supplying disaggregated inputs into transient film projects. In doing so, it provides scope for the development of actions capable of enhancing and facilitating interfirm interaction and collaboration. Film services thinking lends itself to policy intervention to secure viable, healthy, and outwardly oriented creative clusters, precincts, and networks. With its concern for the various inputs into production, the sustainability, skills development, creativity, and growth potential of each input is potentially a priority. This shifts the focus to some extent away from facilitating creative processes and film milieu through the funding of individual projects to facilitating the organizational arrangements, capabilities, and technological infrastructure of the film services sector. There is a tendency to conceive of inputs as clusters of related small to medium-sized businesses requiring coordination and connection. This is film industry development through firm and facilities development, and it assumes that government facilitation, clustering, and interfirm collaboration will generate work by pulling in the demand for services. Governmental support for studio complexes, an interest in infrastructure provision, and the transformative effects of studio complexes, evolving forms of public-private partnership, a developing focus on clusters and creative industries, and consideration of the relationship between international and local production are all sensible within this kind of film services framework.

Sixth, film services frameworks are friendly to emerging creative industries policies concerned with coordinating, integrating, and facilitating connections among the different parts of the film industry and other arts-related industries. In emphasizing inputs and interrelatedness, they permit the boundaries between industries to be crossed, allowing film and television production to be placed alongside related cultural product and entertainment industries like music, games, and multimedia on the one hand and information and communication technology on the other.[21]

Finally, film services frameworks rethink the relationship between the local and international industries. The international industry is seen to be attracted to and involved with a particular region because of the state and character of the local industry and the professionalism of the services, including support services, that are available. International producers are therefore interested in making films and television programs around the world in part because of the state, nature, character, and creativity of the local industry, which may have been principally but not exclusively developed in local productions but now has an international component. This means that the state of international interest is partly dependent on the existing local industry and that there is as a consequence a dynamic relationship between the two industries. So to support and continue to secure international production, local actors need to pay attention to the character of support for the local industry and its capacity and not just the international industry.

In Australia, this logic is writ large in the Victorian government strategy committing Central City Studios to an active integration of local and international production. Attention then needs to be paid to specifying the existing character and nature of the intersection of local and international production, and finding ways in which this intersection could become more productive and mutually advantageous—in short, synergized as a matter of active policy. As a consequence, supplying services in the market for local film and television domestically and internationally becomes more seamlessly situated on a continuum with supplying typically disaggregated film services for an offshore production industry.

Emerging film policy frameworks are friendly to the development of studio infrastructure. The very scale of governmental commitment to and investment in studio infrastructure development "locks in" a film services orientation on the part of government as studio infrastructure provides an added range and depth to the film services able to be supplied in a particular location. Studios also act as powerful cluster- and precinct-generating devices. And the film service interest in a postindustrial workforce made up of contractors and small businesses providing film-related services supports the fundamental paradox of the contemporary film studio in that while such studios compete for parts of feature film or television production in an increasingly disaggregated production environment, they are also vehicles for aggregating production in the one place. Obviously, stressing the services studios provide to other industries, sectors, and the regional social and symbolic economy provide arguments for studios on the grounds of the benefits they confer on the broader cultural-product industries rather than on the film industry per se. This argument thus also contributes to building a case for public-private partnerships in such studios.

Studio developments are being shaped by emerging government priorities in which film and interactive media are valued not so much in themselves as for their larger consequences—the creative industries as locomotive industries. Here attention is given to studio developments as part of an ensemble of services and infrastructure in the film, television, and interactive media areas in a particular region and nation. The priority is placed on film and television as cultural-product industries produced in particular regional agglomerations by interlocking firms ranging from the small to medium-sized enterprise to multinational corporations, all of which are linked to intersecting local and international networks. In circumstances where, as Phil Cooke observes, "policy is moving toward a notion of the region as an important level at which strategic innovation support is appropriate," studios become significant advantages for a region's innovation system.[22] This attention is helped by the increasing role played by regional authorities and local governments in film policy.

While this more infrastructure-oriented support still sits alongside support for individual productions and particular production companies in Australia, Canada, the United Kingdom, and Italy, some evidence indicates that film services frameworks are coming to supplant mechanisms for the support of individual production. There is a clear trend among provincial film agencies in Canada to move away from direct production funding of local production and instead funnel money into film services–oriented enhanced tax credits. The problem with this is that the benefits only "kick in after a production is completed."[23] When the Ontario Media Development Corporation cut its domestic production funding, the number of domestic feature films produced in that province declined. This arguably represents an increasing trend toward seeing the film industry as a plug-in service industry for a global production system creating significant problems for domestic production as a viable option. With studio complexes being seen as an important infrastructure enabling films services to operate at new levels, the studio complex is here afforded significant policy attention. Film service–friendly initiatives are being privileged at the expense of other initiatives, and policy making is becoming less animated by cultural policy concerns.

Conclusion

In this chapter, we have sought to indicate the diverse strands of policy that govern the interest in studios and international production, and that undergird the location interest. The studio has been shown to serve a variety of policy ends—from a signature development in urban entertainment infrastructure to creative precinct development. It serves the imperatives of information and communication technology, creative industries, and film services policy making. It is not easily subsumed under any of these but is rather a nodal point for these intersecting policy frameworks. Under closer inspection, the circumstances in which places attract international production turn on larger policy and urban dynamics to do with how cities, regions, and indeed countries are reshaping themselves and their infrastructure in the light of the new economy and globalizing dynamics. That is, their success will depend to a great extent on how well organized and coordinated are the elements of the location interest.

The criticism of these developments is as varied as are the many different strands involved in policy making for them. We will conclude this chapter by focusing on the problems with international film services. This turns on the *scope*, *character*, and *volatility* of the creative opportunities able to be provided locally in a vertically disintegrated production system whose design—command and control center—is located elsewhere. As Sassen points out, "the more dispersed a firm's operations across different countries, the more complex and strategic its central functions—that is, the work of managing, coordinating, servicing and financing a firm's operations."[24] In these circumstances, the central functions (distribution, financing, preproduction) and key creative positions (producers, directors, editors, lead cast) are often not available to locals. At the same time, servicing international production precisely because it is "the big end of town" in terms of money, employment, and services generated will inevitably get priority in practical and eventually policy terms, displacing local production.

But perhaps the most significant criticism turns on the volatility of international film services in circumstances where production can easily bypass a place because better opportunities have arisen elsewhere, and so leave infrastructure idle and cast and crew without work. Miller, Govil, McMurria, and Maxwell have argued very forcefully that this system is a film version of the new international division of labor that has seen manufacturing relocated to low-cost countries and then relocated again in something of a zero-sum game.[25] While this is perhaps an overstatement given the sophisticated infrastructures and production required by international production, it does point to the "competitive" game being played, particularly in first world countries, where cities and regions inside and outside the United States compete with each other for the right to service international production through their partnerships with firms in the building of studio complexes and the measures they adopt to encourage production. If this competition seems very much in the producer's favor, it is sensible within national, city, and regional development policy contexts centered on enterprise—the "generation of growth-promoting activities by almost any means" and "urban revitalization."[26]

The story of studio development and international production seems to turn on a complex interplay of the local and the global, push and pull factors. To explain these developments, we need to look further afield than the film industry, further even than the "content," creative, and information and communication technology industries of which film is but a part. We need to grasp wider dynamics of urban regeneration and revitalization through infrastructure development; the new economy priorities of governments with their enthusiasm for creative clusters, precincts, and converging services; and the character, planning, and operation of multinational media firms responding to a global economy by incorporating cities and regions into their various networks (and the actions of those cities and regions to become part of these global networks). In the next chapter, we will examine in more detail the relationships between studios and urban regeneration, place marketing, and city branding.

Notes

1. See Allen J. Scott, *The Cultural Economy of Cities* (London: Sage, 2000).

2. See Toby Miller, Nitin Govil, John McMurria, and Richard Maxwell, *Global Hollywood* (London: British Film Institute, 2001); Gerald Sussman and John A. Lent, eds., *Global Productions: Labor in the Making of the "Information Society"* (Cresskill, N.J.: Hampton, 1998); Stephen Katz, *The Migration of Feature Film Production from the US to Canada and Beyond: Year 2001 Production Report* (Los Angeles: Center for Entertainment Industry Data and Research [CEIDR], 2002); United States International Trade Administration, *The Migration of US Film and Television Production: Impact of "Runaways" on Workers and Small Business in the US Film Industry* (Washington, D.C.: U.S. Department of Commerce, 2001); Martha Jones, *Motion Picture Production in California* (Los Angeles: California Research Bureau, 2002).

3. Saskia Sassen, *The Global City: New York, London, Tokyo* (Princeton, N.J.: Princeton University Press, 2001), 3.

4. David Hancock, *Film Production in Europe: A Comparative Study of Film Production Costs in Five European Territories: France, Germany, Italy, Spain, UK* (Strasbourg: European Audiovisual Observatory, 1999).

5. United States Trade Administration, *The Migration of US Film and Television Production*, 5.

6. Australian Film Commission, *Get the Picture: Essential Data on Australian Film, Television, Video and New Media*, 4th ed. (Sydney: Australian Film Commission, 1996), 55.

7. Australian Film Commission, "Value and Share of All Drama Production Activity (Feature Films and TV Drama; Australian, Co-production and Foreign) by Location of Spending in Australia, 1994/95–2002/03," *Get the Picture Online*, 2004, available at www.afc.gov.au/gtp/mpvaluexspending.html (21 September 2004).

8. Susan Christopherson, "Flexibility and Integration in Industrial Relations: The Exceptional Case of the US Media Entertainment Industries," in *Under the Stars: Essays on Labor Relations in the Arts and Entertainment*, ed. Lois S. Gray and Ronald L. Seeber (Ithaca, N.Y.: ILR Press/Cornell University Press, 1996), 91.

9. Scott, *Cultural Economy of Cities*, 181.

10. Charles V. Bagli, "A New Idea of 'Get Me the Coast': Hollywood's Major Competition is Western Queens," *New York Times*, 5 August 1999, B1; John Toscano, "Astoria Studios to Build 7th Sound Stage," *Western Queens Gazette*, 11 August 1999, available at www.qgazette.com/NEWS/1999/0811/Front_Page_Folder/ (21 September 2004).

11. Albert Moran, "A State Government Business Venture: The South Australian Film Corporation," in *An Australian Film Reader*, ed. Albert Moran and Tom O'Regan (Sydney: Currency Press, 1985), 252–63.

12. See Auditor-General Victoria, *Report on Public Sector Agencies* (Melbourne: Auditor-General Victoria, 2003), 186.

13. John Hannigan, "Cities as the Physical Site of the Global Entertainment Economy," in *Global Media Policy in the New Millennium*, ed. Marc Raboy (Luton: University of Luton Press, 2002), 181–95.

14. Stefan Krätke, "Network Analysis of Production Clusters: The Potsdam/Babelsberg Film Industry as an Example," *European Planning Studies* 10, no. 1 (2002): 27–54; Neil M. Coe, "A Hybrid Agglomeration? The Development of a Satellite-Marshallian Industrial District in Vancouver's Film Industry," *Urban Studies* 38, no. 10 (2001): 1753–75.

15. Scott, *Cultural Economy of Cities*.

16. See Scott, *Cultural Economy of Cities*; Department of Communications, Information Technology and the Arts (DCITA), Australia, *Creative Industries Cluster Study: Stage One Report* (Canberra: DCITA, 2002).

17. Sassen, *The Global City*, 347.

18. Rana Foroohar, Alexandra Seno, and Stefan Theil, "Hurray for Globowood: As Motion-Picture Funding, Talent and Audiences Go Global, Hollywood Is No Longer a Place, but a State of Mind," *Newsweek International*, 27 May 2002, 51.

19. Jeremy Kay, "Eliasoph Named Head of New Warner China," *Screen Daily*, 24 June 2003, available at www.screendaily.com (15 July 2003); Foroohar et al., "Hurray for Globowood."

20. Robert Murphy, "Under the Shadow of Hollywood," in *All Our Yesterdays: 90 Years of British Cinema*, ed. Charles Barr (London: British Film Institute, 1986), 47–71.

21. House of Representatives Standing Committee on Communications, Information Technology and the Arts, *From Reel to Unreal: Future Opportunities for Australia's Film, Animation, Special Effects and Electronic Games Industries: Inquiry into the Future Opportunities for Australia's Film, Animation, Special Effects and Electronic Games Industries* (Canberra: Commonwealth of Australia, 2004), available at www.aph.gov.au/house/committee/cita/film/report.htm (20 August 2004).

22. Phil Cooke, "New Media and New Economy Cluster Dynamics," in *The Handbook of New Media*, ed. Leah Lievrouw and Sonia Livingstone (London: Sage, 2002), 294.

23. Alexandra Gill, "End of BC Film Seed Money Decried," *The Globe and Mail*, 7 April 2004, R2.

24. Sassen, *Global City*, xx.

25. Miller, Govil, McMurria, and Maxwell, *Global Hollywood*.

26. Peter Hall, *Cities of Tomorrow*, 3d ed. (Oxford: Blackwell, 2002), 383.

CHAPTER FOUR

❧

Studios, Stargates, and Urban Reimagining

In the previous chapter, we described a number of ways in which studio developments have been attractive to governments and how studios are often considered to complement and further a variety of policy objectives. In this chapter we will discuss in more detail the series of transformations that studios enable, and in particular how a number of recent studio developments have featured in broader local agendas relating to urban regeneration and the reimagining of place. We will examine some of the non-film-related commercial and policy rationales for building and operating studios in particular places and interrogate some of the hopes and expectations for these studios and what they enable. As we began to explore in the previous chapter, analysis of the rationales for studio development indicates common expectations that they will have "locomotive" economic effects and occasion a variety of transformations—what we have elsewhere termed the "stargate" factor.[1] But each of the rationales also plays down the risks and vulnerabilities inherent in providing services to a highly mobile international industry. While each welcomes some of the transformative effects of studios, where the stargate factor works to transform places into somewhere other than they actually are, it may have unforeseen and potentially unmanageable effects on the image of a place and its marketing, and on community identity.

Studios as Stargates

The term *stargate* in the 1994 film of the same name and subsequent television series (*Stargate SG-1* and *Stargate Atlantis*) refers to an interstellar portal or wormhole—a gateway connecting stars or planets across time—that enables the juxtaposition of radically different worlds and environments. The term is pertinent to a discussion of studios and international production because in 1996, MGM Worldwide Television in partnership with the British Columbia provincial government, built a new soundstage at The Bridge Studios in Vancouver especially for the production of *Stargate SG-1*, which to date has run for eight seasons. The series has used many locations in and around Vancouver to stand in for various other worlds, and the stage is available for other projects when *Stargate* is not being filmed there.

Stargate captures some of the characteristics of the studio itself as a portal enabling transformation. It can refer to the studio as a point through which (film) stars pass and thus connote the glamour and celebrity attaching to film production that has proven so attractive to politicians and other agents of the location interest. The studio is also the place at which an idea is transformed into a film, and one space—the stage—is transformed into any other, real or imagined. It is then, in Michel Foucault's terms, a "heterotopia." In his article "Of Other Spaces," Foucault described a *heterotopia* as a single real place in which "several sites that are in themselves incompatible" are juxtaposed. Among the examples he uses, Foucault includes the cinema, but he may just as well have referred to the studio or soundstage on which several *sets* that may in themselves be incompatible can be placed next to each other in preparation for filming. This sense of the studio as heterotopia was captured by Siegfried Kracauer in his description of the work of set builders and designers at what was then the Ufa Studios at Neubabelsberg in 1926:

> The ruins of the universe are stored in warehouses for sets, representative samples of all periods, peoples, and styles. Near Japanese cherry trees, which shine through the corridors of dark scenery, arches the monstrous dragon from the *Nibelungen* [sic], devoid of the diluvial terror it exudes on the screen. Next to the mockup of a commercial building, which needs only to be cranked by the camera in order to outdo any skyscraper, are layers of coffins which themselves have died because they do not contain any dead. When, in the midst of all this, one stumbles upon Empire furniture in its natural size, one is hard pressed to believe it is authentic. The old and the new, copies and originals, are piled up in a disorganized heap like bones in catacombs. Only the property man knows where everything is.[2]

Paralleling these dramatic transformations within the studio is a set of external transformations enabled by the studio. Here the industrial base of a place may be transformed with the addition of a studio, while the ceiling of its ambition in terms of the kinds of production it can hope to host on a regular basis may be raised. These were the arguments used in Melbourne where the lack of an international-standard studio complex was identified both by an industry taskforce and by independent consultants as an impediment to the city's capacity to attract international production.[3] A new studio, it was reasoned, would create opportunities for the existing production industry in the city just as Fox Studios Australia has changed the prospects and focus of Sydney's producers and service providers. An equivalent facility in Melbourne would, it was argued, also assist in stemming the temporary and permanent talent drain to studio-based productions in Sydney and the Gold Coast.

But the Melbourne studio saga reveals some of the unforeseen problems that can arise when the stargate is opened. Despite financial support and other assistance from the Victorian state government, the consortium—composed of Viacom Inc., production company Crawfords Australia, Australian regional television network WIN Television, and Thorney Holdings, which made the original proposal to build a film studio as part of an eighty-nine-acre entertainment precinct that would also include a theme park, a multiplex cinema, and a themed hotel—was bitterly opposed by other industry players led by Village Roadshow (joint owner of the Warner Roadshow Studios on the Gold Coast). Plans for a public float were dropped in 2000 due to a lack of institutional investor interest in the development. As we describe later, the state government continued to pursue the studio development in part because it formed a major part of plans to redevelop the inner-city Docklands precinct, but the revised studio development has also not been without controversy.

The construction of studios also transforms the built environment. This is obvious in the case of new, purpose-built facilities constructed on previously vacant land, but there are also more subtle variations. Existing buildings may be renovated. For cost and space reasons, warehouses, factories, power stations, and aerodromes have been converted into audiovisual production facilities in different parts of the world. The Bridge Studios, the first studio complex in Vancouver, was previously a steel-making plant and a bus depot. In England, the Harry Potter cycle of films are being made at a former Rolls-Royce aircraft factory and aerodrome at Leavesden in Hertfordshire. Here the studio facility will be the centerpiece of a business park and media village. In the Czech Republic, an aircraft factory has been converted into three soundstages in order to service the growing volume of international production initially attracted to Prague by the presence of the historic Barrandov Studios. And in Melbourne, a former Nestlé canning factory on the city's outskirts was temporarily converted to service international production while the permanent, purpose-built Central City Studios was built.

One of the most dramatic transformations of the built environment enabled by a studio—albeit indirectly—occurred prior to the filming of Roman Polanski's *The Pianist* in Germany. After scouting around Europe for an appropriate site for a sequence in which the main character hides in the ruins of a city, the filmmakers were directed by German representatives of the location interest to the town of Jüterbog. The filmmakers were shown the town as part of the package of locations and services on offer to them in and around Berlin, including Studio Babelsberg where parts of the film were shot. Jüterbog had been a military base for much of the twentieth century and at various times for several hundred years previously. The former East German town had housed up to seventy thousand Soviet troops in the decades after World War II. Some of the "brownfields" sites—former military sites, which cover about 60 percent of the town's area—have been transformed into nature reserves, parks, and housing, although supply has consistently outstripped demand. After the Russians left, the town, like much of East Germany, experienced a devastating loss of industry and employment. Jüterbog lost much of its earlier status as a regional political center. The town is heavily polluted by unexploded munitions and other noxious waste left over from its former use. The filmmakers were granted permission to create ruins from some of the remaining barracks, which were due to be demolished anyway. This crafting of the ruins is a story about the vision and skill of production designer Allan Starski and his team, but it is also a story about the transformation of the built environment of a place through film production. This transformation would perhaps not have happened had the studio not been available and had there not been a concerted effort among agents of the location interest to win the production for the studio and the region.

Studios, Urban Regeneration, and the Reimagining of Cities

In contrast with the Jüterbog story of creative destruction, a number of recent studio developments could be described as "creative constructions" in that they have involved the remediation of former heavy industrial areas or problem sites in areas close to the center of major cities. These developments are notable, first, because they form parts of entrepreneurial or "enterprise city" regeneration schemes that are designed to transform urban economies from a previous base in traditional manufacturing and heavy industry toward service industries, information and communication technologies, creative industries, entertainment, and tourism. Second, and relatedly, the studios and the international production they are expected to attract are notable for the ambiguous contribution they make to the "reimagining" or "brand identity" of the host city and its pretensions to global city status.

Studios in Sydney, Melbourne, Toronto, London, and even New York have been built or planned as vehicles for the transformation of sites whose former uses no longer fit with the image, ambition, or planning focus of the modern city. They are symbolic developments and physical manifestations of "entrepreneurial city"[4] or "city of enterprise"[5] planning frameworks that conceive of the cities as "economic and cultural entities which need to undertake entrepreneurial activities in order to enhance their competitiveness."[6] As David Harvey describes, the object of the economic and infrastructural restructuring that lies at the heart of urban entrepreneurialism is to capture "the key control and command functions in high finance, government, or information gathering and processing (including the media)."[7] Studios that host high-budget film production require exactly these functions and "act as lures to draw in investment and expertise and ideally initiate permanent arrangements (i.e., meaning long-term, multi-project investment or co-production agreements between international financiers and locally based production entities) and the establishment of branches of major multinational production companies."[8]

The Fox Studios Australia development in Sydney is one such example of the studio functioning to draw in a major multinational company and simultaneously transforming a problem site close to the center of the city. For more than a hundred years, the site on which Fox Studios Australia now stands was the home of the Royal Agricultural Society. The site, which is located in a band of heritage-listed public parklands, required substantial remediation work to remove asbestos from some of the heritage-listed buildings and upgrade water, sewerage, and electrical services. The agreement to establish the studio was struck at a meeting between Prime Minister Paul Keating and Rupert Murdoch; it was simultaneously announced in October 1994 by the prime minister as part of the long-awaited national "Creative Nation" cultural policy statement and by Murdoch to the annual general meeting of News Corporation. The deal provided a "big picture" centerpiece to the cultural policy statement and met Murdoch's desire to establish a public face for his corporation in its home territory. In addition, the deal solved a problem for the New South Wales state government in deciding what to do with the Showgrounds site after the relocation to Homebush Bay of the

Royal Agricultural Society. As we discuss, this deal, like those in Melbourne, Toronto, and New York, was not greeted with universal acclaim, with the state auditor-general producing a highly critical report that concluded that proper tendering processes had not been followed in approving the News Corporation proposal.[9]

Melbourne's studio forms part of a larger redevelopment of the city's main port district. The studio forms one part of the regeneration of Melbourne's Docklands that envisages a number of residential, commercial, retail, and entertainment precincts replacing the now-disused waterfront site. The Docklands redevelopment follows the pattern of port cities that transformed their waterfront areas in the 1980s and 1990s as part of "place-marketing strategies designed to increase local tourism." Such redevelopments typically involve "dramatic makeovers of urban sites which either efface their former uses, remodel them for recreational purposes or alter them for consumption by tourists as nostalgic or romanticised places."[10] Like the Fox Studios Australia development in Sydney, the history of the redevelopment is marked by accusations that proper procedure has not been followed in the awarding of contracts and the public release of information regarding the successful tender. With the failure of the original bid in which Paramount Studios was a partner (through its parent company Viacom), the Melbourne studio does not have the luxury enjoyed by its Sydney counterpart of a major industry backer.

Plans for a state-of-the-art studio in Toronto are similarly part of a much larger program to revitalize the city's waterfront. In 2001, C$61 million was allocated to create a District for Innovation and Creativity and prepare the Port Lands for cultural, recreational, residential, and commercial uses. Within a year, two competing studio proposals had been announced for separate sites in the Port Lands. One involved a consortium that included Pinewood-Shepperton Studios and was backed by the mayor of Toronto, with the studio to be built on land owned by the City of Toronto's business corporation, the Toronto Economic Development Corporation (TEDCO). The second proposal was for a studio to be built on the site of a decommissioned power station on land owned by a Crown corporation, Ontario Power Generation. This consortium also had film industry representation, with one partner being the large Canadian film services company Comweb Group. Ground clearing began at the latter site in October 2002. In April 2003, the studio planned for the TEDCO site was shelved when the consortium failed to attract commercial backing and tenants for the development. The proposal had been strongly condemned by existing facilities providers in Toronto, who argued that they had been shut out of the process. Three months later, a deal was struck whereby expressions of interest were called for the TEDCO development, known as the Toronto Film/Media Complex, and the Comweb Group announced that it would not build a full-scale purpose-built studio but rather convert the power station into several large "effects stages" to complement the proposed studio. In July 2004, it was announced that Toronto Film Studios, one of the existing studio facilities in the city whose owners had been stern critics of the original TEDCO deal, had won the right to develop the Port Lands studio.

The most recent New York studio development, Steiner Studios, is also part of a major waterfront redevelopment, in this case the Brooklyn Navy Yard. The navy yard is a much older and more established development than either of those in Melbourne and Toronto, having been converted into an industrial park after the closure of the military site in 1966. Like the Toronto development, the studio was initiated by local government interests rather than by private-sector representatives. The then-mayor of New York, Rudolph Giuliani, had invited a group led by Miramax Films and Robert DeNiro's Tribeca Productions to "explore" construction of a studio at the navy yard, leading to the group's expressing an intention in May 1999 to commit $35 million to the project, supplemented by a $25 million low-interest loan from the City of New York and an $8 million grant from the Brooklyn Navy Yard Development Corporation. But, to the group's great surprise, the Miramax-Tribeca proposal, which might have led to Martin Scorsese's *Gangs of New York* being filmed in the city, was passed over in favor of a competing proposal from a group led by the real estate developer Steiner Equities. In October 1999, it was announced that the Steiner Equities group, which included a company that had previously been using the site for music video and commercial production, had signed a seventy-year lease to develop a studio at the navy yard.[11] Despite Mayor Giuliani's explanation at the time that "[t]he Brooklyn Navy Yard board believes that the deal with . . . the Steiner group would bring about $60 million more in revenue, and it was a more realistic deal that they could start faster—meaning within the next three or four months—and they did not require a $25 million loan," construction did not begin on the studio until mid-2003.[12]

These waterfront studios were pitched in terms of their ability to attract international production, most particularly high-budget feature films, but they were also directly related to the image of the city—in terms of either their capacity to promote it or their ability to trade upon it. For example, in its "Backgrounder" on the Toronto Film/Media Complex, TEDCO argued that in addition to the employment and economic benefits and the clustering and synergies with the arts community that might flow from the project, the studio was also important because "the glamour and publicity which naturally follows feature films such as My Big Fat Greek Wedding, Chicago, and Bollywood Hollywood, enhances the city's image and provides additional promotion for the tourist industry."[13] The Melbourne studio was one among a number of initiatives to transform the city's image and boost its global profile. The development fitted neatly with the entrepreneurial approach of the administration in power when the idea was first floated in the late 1990s, which involved a large-scale program of civic infrastructure construction, limits on public participation in planning processes, and the privatization of many governmental functions, all of which were oriented toward positioning Melbourne "as the 'events' capital of Australia" and winning for the city "a place in the second . . . order" of global cities.[14] And News Corporation's decision to build Fox Studios Australia was informed by Sydney's emerging position as a "global media city" and the company's desire to pick up on the innovations, capabilities, and expertise that go along with that moniker.[15] Fox Entertainment Group's executive vice president of feature production, Jon Landau, acknowledged as much when he said in 1994 that the recent success of Australian films had been one of the deciding factors in the decision to invest in Australia.[16]

Studios are then vehicles to propel cities "toward a competitive realm of the virtual in which image-city competes against image-city."[17] But the images presented by cinematic cities, or by places that flaunt their capacity to represent somewhere other than they are, are not the same as the kind of image promotion or "brand identity of a city" that is commonly evoked in tourism marketing or that adheres around the success of sporting teams.[18] This is evident in the case of the promotion of the Berlin-Brandenburg region of Germany (which includes Studio Babelsberg) on an English-language DVD produced by the Berlin-Brandenburg Film Commission, entitled Location Berlin-Brandenburg. The DVD contains testimonies from producers, directors, cinematographers, and production designers from Europe and North America who have lived and worked in the region. The disc also contains a six-minute show reel of locations available in the region, interspersing shots from films made in Berlin-Brandenburg with castles, parks, historic and futuristic buildings, postindustrial moonscapes, and rural idylls designed to fire the visual imagination of the international filmmaker. The package is clearly designed to sell "Location Berlin-Brandenburg" as the totality of what is available in a region to filmmakers.

In the show reel, Berlin and its surrounding areas are depicted in the four roles available to a cinematic place: to play itself, to act as an unidentified generic urban or rural backdrop, to stand in for another real place, or to represent speculative fictional places. The films in which the location stands in for another real place (as Berlin and nearby towns do for Warsaw in *The Pianist*, or for Los Angeles in *The Cat's Meow*, or for London and Paris in *Around the World in 80 Days*), and those in which speculative fictional places are realized (as in the science fiction television series *Lexx*, or casting back to an earlier era, the classic film *Metropolis*) are perhaps the ones that best showcase a city's creativity and spread the word within the film industry about the possibilities for transformation. But these are also the films that are most problematic for the kind of city image fostered in tourism promotion—either they don't exist, or they exist somewhere else. The essence of the city's competitiveness in the realm of image cities is its ability to be remade as somewhere other than it is—including, in Berlin's case, the "quintessential postmodern city," Los Angeles.[19] In this show reel,

> Berlin is a city of sights and sites, a city for rent, a city at the service of international capital, a city of surfaces which creatively parades its capacity for authentic inauthenticity, for concealing or transforming historical and spatial specificity, representing itself as a series of locations available for multiple make-overs. Berlin is a commodity whose value lies not in what it is, but in what (or where) it can be turned in to—and this is perhaps the critical difference between the cinematic city and the touristic city.[20]

One of the characters in Wim Wenders's film *Himmel über Berlin* (*Wings of Desire*) says at one point, "It is impossible to get lost in Berlin because you can always find the Wall." As the *Location Berlin-Brandenburg* DVD shows, now that the Berlin Wall has gone, it is possible not only to get lost in Berlin but to lose Berlin itself. And this is the problem confronting studios and representatives of the location interest: The studio and the city are promoted to filmmakers on the basis of a dual image, an image of the place as somewhere else—not a false image, rather an uncanny image, an image that is familiar yet unfamiliar to residents and others who "know" a place. But because these images are not targeted at the local community and may not resonate within that community, it is difficult to evoke community affect and affinity or identity with the studio on the basis of these images of place.

As we have described in this and the previous chapters, the location interest involves and enrolls many agents, with governments and their agencies chief among them. This pursuit of the location interest at the highest levels of government sanctions the remaking of policy and urban spaces to assist international film and television production because of the tangible and intangible rewards that this production can bring. But the kinds of top-down, undemocratic, nonconsultative decision-making processes that have facilitated the development of a number of studios can spark a backlash from the local community that may not view the transformations enabled by the studio in such a positive light.

Such a backlash was most obvious in the case of Sydney, where the Fox Studios Australia development aroused considerable grassroots community protest. An action was brought in the New South Wales Land and Environ-ment Court by the Save the Showground for Sydney Action Group in 1995 against the developers that cited a number of breaches of planning laws, the sidelining of public consultation mechanisms, concern over proposed uses for what was still public land, and the impact of the development on heritage-listed buildings. The local state member of parliament, Clover Moore (who was subsequently elected mayor of Sydney in 2004), introduced legislation into the New South Wales Parliament in 1996 that sought to ban the build-ing of medium-density housing on the site and to ensure that when the Royal Agricultural Society relocated to its new site at Homebush Bay, the Show-grounds site would revert to public ownership. The court dismissed the ac-tion in September 1996, with the decision upheld by the New South Wales Court of Appeal the following June. In part as a result of the level of com-munity concern over the annexation or privatization of what had been pub-lic land, the state government inserted a clause in the contract with News Corporation banning the development of anything resembling a theme park with large rides. Permission was given to establish a "Backlot tour" and an entertainment precinct, Bent Street, including cafés, restaurants, live enter-tainment venues, shops, and cinemas, that, although now run by a company separate from Fox and News Corporation, would at least appear to meet one of the objectives of the Trust that manages the parklands within which the complex sits. This objective states that the Trust's role is "to encourage the use and enjoyment of the Trust lands by the public by promoting and in-creasing the recreational, historical, scientific, educational, cultural and en-vironmental value of those lands."[21]

Conclusion

The transformations enabled by studio developments and the regular attrac-tion of international production are many and varied. Some relate directly to the film industry and the position of a production center within a national and global hierarchy. Fox Studios Australia, Central City Studios in Mel-bourne, Steiner Studios in New York, and the Toronto Film/Media Complex were all inspired in part by a fear of decline in the city's production capacity in the absence of such a facility and by the desire to be recognized or confirmed as a leading international production center. The same sense of "loss," albeit to a much lesser degree, frames discussion of international production in Los Angeles, and similar anxieties exist about being left behind in the high-stakes competition for international production. But a whole series of other transformations enabled by studio developments are only indirectly related to film and television production. The four studio developments discussed in this chapter are located in inner-city areas, rather than in edge city areas as studio developments tended to be in the years before and after World War II. They all form part of larger urban revitalization agendas in which the studio is intended to transform the landscape and change the economic base of a place.

As part of urban regeneration strategies, these studios are enrolled in entrepreneurial city planning and contribute to the image of the city as a stage.[22] This relies in part on the renovation of urban areas through a mix of developments including entertainment, leisure, and cultural facilities and attractions that generate a sense of the constantly changing experience of the city as a means to draw in investors, residents, workers, and tourists. As part of such larger regeneration projects, studios are on a continuum with galleries, museums, libraries, performing arts centers, sports stadia, motor racing tracks, convention centers, and theme parks, as well as with new economy infrastructure such as business and technology parks. They might be considered part of broader "urban entertainment development" that is underwritten by a new cultural and urban policy emphasis on infrastructure provision designed to enhance "quality of life" (for some but by no means all) of a city's residents, attract tourists, stimulate investment, rejuvenate inner city areas, and repopulate these areas with moneyed urban professionals and other new-economy workers.[23]

Like other forms of urban entertainment development, studios can "alter the texture and trajectory of places";[24] that is, they can transform physical environment and the outlook of a place and affect its image(s) and the ways in which the place is presented or marketed to residents and visitors. But because the images produced in these places may bear no obvious relation to the "real" place, they may not produce the kind of community affect in terms of the broader urban population's sense of connection with the development that planners might have hoped for. The inclusion of physically accessible space such as the Bent Street entertainment area at Fox Studios Australia is one attempt to address this problem. The construction of this usually costly infrastructure also brings with it new vulnerabilities; as new places enter the competition to service international film production, the vulnerability of all increases.

We now turn to the riskiest and most vulnerable developments, what we call "extreme" studios, which further exemplify the risks that inevitably accompany the transformative powers of the studio and international production.

Notes

1. Ben Goldsmith and Tom O'Regan, "Locomotives and Stargates: Inner-City Studio Complexes in Sydney, Melbourne and Toronto," *International Journal of Cultural Policy* 10, no. 1 (March 2004): 29–46.

2. Siegfried Kracauer, "Calico World: The Ufa City in Neubabelsberg," originally published 1926, translated in *Film Architecture: Set Designs from Metropolis to Blade Runner*, ed. Dietrich Neumann (Munich: Prestel, 1999), 191.

3. Victorian Film and Television Industry Task Force, *The Film and Television Production Industry in Victoria*, Report to Minister for the Arts (Melbourne: Victorian Film and Television Industry Task Force, September 2000).

4. Stephen Hamnett, "The Late 1990s: Competitive versus Sustainable Cities," in *The Australian Metropolis: A Planning History*, ed. Stephen Hamnett and Robert Freestone (Crows Nest, Australia: Allen & Unwin, 2000), 169.

5. Peter Hall, *Cities of Tomorrow*, 3d ed. (Oxford: Blackwell, 2002), 379–403.

6. Hamnett, "The Late 1990s," 169.

7. David Harvey, "From Managerialism to Entrepreneurialism: The Transformation in Urban Governance in Late Capitalism," in *Spaces of Capital: Towards a Critical Geography* (Edinburgh: Edinburgh University Press, 2001), 356.

8. Goldsmith and O'Regan, "Locomotives and Stargates," 34.

9. Audit Office of New South Wales, *Performance Audit Report: Sydney Showground, Moore Park, Lease to Fox Studios Australia* (Sydney: Audit Office of New South Wales, 1997).

10. Goldsmith and O'Regan, "Locomotives and Stargates," 35.

11. Jeremy Lehrer, "Brooklyn Navy Yard Deck Is Reshuffled—Development into a Movie Studio," *Shoot* 22 (October 1999); available at www.findarticles.com/p/articles/mi_m0DUO/is_42_40/ai_57796020/print (13 September 2004).

12. Lehrer, "Brooklyn Navy Yard Deck Is Reshuffled."

13. TEDCO, "Toronto Film/Media Complex Backgrounder," *Toronto Economic Development Corporation* (2003), available at www.tedco.ca/backgrounder.html (13 September 2003).

14. Louise Johnson, William S. Logan, and Colin Long, "Jeff Kennett's Melbourne: Postmodern City, Planning and Politics," in *The Twentieth Century Planning Experience*, ed. Robert Freestone (Sydney: University of New South Wales, 1998), 440.

15. Stefan Krätke, "Global Media Cities in a Worldwide Urban Network," *Globalization and World Cities Study Group and Network Research Bulletin* 80 (March 2002), available at www.lboro.ac.uk/gawc/rb/rb80.html (6 August 2003).

16. "Movie Mecca," *Telegraph-Mirror* (Sydney), 19 October 1994, 4.

17. Janet Ward, "Berlin, the Virtual Global City," *Visual Culture* 3, no. 2 (2004): 250.

18. David Rowe and Pauline McGuirk, "Drunk for Three Weeks: Sporting Success and City Image," *International Review for the Sociology of Sport* 34, no. 2 (1999): 125–41.

19. Mark Shiel, "A Nostalgia for Modernity: New York, Los Angeles, and American Cinema in the 1970s," in *Screening the City*, ed. Mark Shiel and Tony Fitzmaurice (London: Verso, 2003), 164.

20. Ben Goldsmith, "From the Ruins of Berlin: Imagining the Postmodern City," Passionate City Symposium Proceedings (Melbourne: RMIT Publishing, 2004), available at www.rmitpublishing.com.au/products.asp?type=il.

21. Centennial Park and Moore Park Trust Act 1983, Section 8 (d).

22. Hall, Cities of Tomorrow, 386.

23. John Hannigan, "Cities as the Physical Site of the Global Entertainment Economy," in Global Media Policy in the New Millennium, ed. Marc Raboy (Luton: University of Luton Press, 2002), 181–95.

24. Hannigan, "Cities as the Physical Site," 189.

CHAPTER FIVE

Extreme Dreams in Satellite Locations

The Rise of the Greenfields Studio

One feature of the contemporary period of international production has been the establishment of studio facilities in greenfields locations—places where there is little or no existing production infrastructure. These extreme developments are located throughout the world, sometimes in countries for which English is not the first language. Many are designed to attract and service high-budget international production; others are more modestly pitched at more cost-sensitive areas of production, such as television drama and movies of the week, or high-turnover short-term advertising production. Usually they are peripheral to the main centers of (domestic) production in the country. Later in the chapter, we will profile developments in the United States, Canada, Ireland, Mexico, Australia, Romania, South Africa, and Spain that illustrate different aspects of these dynamics at work.

We can see here the same dynamics of transformation discussed in the previous chapter motivating the establishment of greenfields studios. Here as elsewhere, studios and international production work as locomotives driving employment and activity in a variety of related and peripheral industries and act as high-profile vehicles for the positive international projection of a locality. What is distinctive about the studios that are the subject of this chapter is their geographic and industrial context: They are typically distant from major population centers, and typically they were not major media production centers before the studio was established. In these locations, the studio functions to create production capacity rather than to augment it. As a consequence, a range of different motivations come into play—some relating to what the studios *enable* rather than what they actually *do*. These studios are looked to as a means to generate foreign investment, create employment in new economy industries, and provide or encourage the development of particular specializations. And they are conceived as the hub of a cluster of related industries and companies. Such places aim to be a crucial cog in the international system but often through the agency of foreign intermediaries. Unsurprisingly, in some of these iterations, the relationship with tourism is strong. This not only stems from a practical need to get people to come and work for short term but also addresses the long-term needs of the location to attract people to migrate and settle there.

Both short- and long-term strategic needs help explain the close connection of the Gold Coast and Alicante studio developments with tourism (it also helps explain how staff in the Queensland Tourism and Travel commission were involved in selling the studio as part of their business tourism brief). For the Gold Coast and Vancouver, the fostering of international production provided an opportunity to diversify the regional industrial base that was heavily skewed toward farming, mining, and tourism. In Alicante, Cuidad de la Luz is part of an industrialization and industry diversification strategy that began with the establishment of a Ford car manufacturing plant some years earlier. For Alicante, the studios are designed to attract global capital to the area through the development of a large-scale theme park infrastructure in the shape of an aquarium, five-star hotels to support the theme park and the studios, and additional tourism and leisure infrastructure in circumstances where visitors are more likely to gravitate toward Barcelona and other parts of the Spanish coast. Because of these emphases on regional development, provincial governments in Spain, Australia, and South Africa are likely to be firmly focused on jobs and multiplier effects and less focused on the national cultural patrimony in their promotion of the location interest.

The problem facing these developments is that the work could conceivably disappear in a way that would be much less likely for traditional filmmaking centers such as London or New York. Film studios are risky businesses even at the best of times, and in the best of places. They can be extraordinarily expensive to build and equip, and they rely on strong and sustained connection into national or international production circuits. The risks are multiplied when studios are located in extreme or peripheral places that may have no history of international production or sometimes of any production at all. These extreme places may lack much of the film-related and ancillary infrastructure necessary to generate and attract more than the single project that may have prompted their creation.[1] Studios rely on the collaborative creative and promotional work of a cohort of mainly (but not necessarily) locally based advocates. In most cases they will rely on long-term assistance from subnational and national governments, and their establishment will often be the result of the combined efforts of policy-makers and local or international entrepreneurs who may or may not have a background in film production. Studios in places with a preexisting production culture can connect with local filmmakers (although they may bypass the local industry altogether); for extreme ventures, this base may need to be grown, with the studio itself a vital conduit between the local and international production industries.

In this chapter, we will examine in detail the range of risks facing greenfields studio developments. We will then, through a number of case studies, outline the range of reasons why these developments proceed despite these risks. We conclude that there are different reasons for studios in different places and different risk profiles in different places. The studio developments covered here are those in Wilmington, Vancouver, Dublin, Galway, Rosarito, Gold Coast, Bucharest, Cape Town, and Alicante.

Extreme Risk, Extreme Measures

Perhaps the common characteristic of all of these developments is their risk-taking entrepreneurialism. Each share an *extreme* character that defies common sense, accepted wisdom, and routine film industry risk assessments. Even when these extreme developments proceed beyond the drawing board (which many do not), the absence of an existing local production capacity can increase filmmakers' costs considerably by requiring personnel and equipment to be flown in as needed—in the process limiting anticipated cost savings for producers. Normal rules of supply and demand would seem to suggest that these sites would be too vulnerable to the ebb and flow of international production cycles either to be established initially or to survive long-term.

Some extreme studios are greenfields developments located away from the main media cities/global media cities in the country and sometimes considerable distances from existing filmmaking infrastructure and facilities, although they may generate or create such infrastructure in their locality over time. The studios seem to be inherently risky ventures in that *supply must be in search of demand*. Often they would be judged unfeasible by even the most optimistic of studio consultants.

These studios reify *extreme dreams of production*. They are either bold or foolhardy (depending on one's viewpoint) pitches for production and regional participation in the global Hollywood production system. They strive by virtue of, variously, force of will, bottomless budgets, or compelling access to place-based resources (climate, locations) to corral and channel vectors of international production. The motivation behind these studios may be to change the destinies, the self-projections, and identities of the places and individuals with which they are associated. Such endeavors are often predicated on the *Field of Dreams* logic, "build it and they will come." They seem to represent and endorse an extreme preparedness to make a place over for film production. The comparison could not be more stark with the urban entertainment and creative city agendas driving the development of inner city studios of the previous chapter. Those inner-city studios are in cities seeking to fill out their ambition as global media cities. They look relatively safe and modest compared to the greenfields developments, which seek to create a global filmmaking presence from a very low base.

Studios in extreme or peripheral places are inherently vulnerable. Created in expansionary phases of international production, they risk being the first places affected by industry contraction. This is because they are mostly sites for the production of international film and television production and little else. Neil Coe's analysis of Vancouver and its vulnerabilities can help us identify some of the broader issues greenfields sites share. Vancouver's internal dynamics reveal a "Marshallian style industrial district, with shifting networks of small firms producing an ever-increasing volume of high-quality audio-visual product." But this industrial form is entirely dependent on the "external" relations in which the whole fifty or so Vancouver soundstages are "largely dependent on flows of capital from Hollywood." No matter how progressive and innovative Vancouver's local development dynamics might be, the region is nonetheless "worryingly predicated" on international linkages and therefore macroeconomic conditions.[2]

If Vancouver, with all its undeniable advantages, is vulnerable in this way, how much more vulnerable are the studios that are the subject of this chapter? If greenfields locations are by definition always flying by the seat of their pants, those farther away from the centers of production are even more vulnerable. This suggests that while these sites may share much in common with Vancouver, Wilmington, and Orlando, this North American experience may not provide the answers to the variety of problems they are likely to face.

Greenfields studios and the business they generate are almost entirely dependent on the reputation and amenities of the place and on the spending decisions of international producers. Local actors may have little financial or creative control over these projects or even some of this reputation. While many of these studio infrastructures and facilities are locally owned and some are state owned, the Hollywood design center is able to maintain control through subcontracting networks. In split location production dynamics, key production personnel from the center are sent to the location and remain domiciled there for periods of time overseeing or managing these projects through a subsidiary. These subsidiaries may become permanent fixtures, as happened for Coote/Hayes on the Gold Coast. There is often little scope for creative control by local actors and a diminished sphere in which their creativity can be exercised. Some of these studios have experienced difficulties in securing qualified below-the-line workers and have had to rely, particularly in their early years, on fly-in, fly-out film workers to fill not only heads of department positions but also to provide competent below-the-line crews. In the Gold Coast's case, with insufficient numbers of skilled below-the-line workers available locally, crew from Sydney and Melbourne were required. Over time, these productions' labor needs can end up being met locally through training and migration, as time in the market can build levels of international producers' trust in a location.

Greenfields studios are financially vulnerable in a number of additional ways. Exchange rates can push up costs. Throughout Hollywood's history, costs have been notoriously more difficult to manage on location than in the controlled studio environment in established production locations like Los Angeles. Local circumstances can price production out of a market, for example, if permits for location shooting become too costly or bureaucratic. The popularity of a location may drive up the cost of labor, production, and ancillary services such as hotels. The cost of stage rental is a small part of most budgets but is vulnerable to competition both locally and internationally. Hawaii, for instance, is said to be approximately 50 percent more expensive than the continental United States. This means that Hawaii labor rates have had to be much lower to compensate. Writing about the prospects of the facility under construction in Alicante, Spain, Joshua Levitt saw its critical problem in attracting production turning on its cost structure.[3] Wages in Spain are not as competitive as they were in the 1960s, and large film studios run the ever-present risk of becoming white elephants.

When producers weigh up the total costs of shooting in a location—stage hire, need to fly in technicians or hire locals, ancillary costs, currency exchange rates—they can decide it is cheaper and easier to stay in L.A. or to locate in another major center with a critical mass of skilled workers. This makes extreme and peripheral places inherently more vulnerable than more proximate and developed film locations. Any lowering of production costs in the "center" vis-à-vis peripheral spaces will count severely against filming in these spaces. When the U.S. dollar is high, production has a greater chance of flowing offshore and trickling down to these low-cost environments, but when it is low, such production will tend to stay in the United States or contract to familiar international locations such as London.

Greenfields studios may also be susceptible to voter backlash or to a change in government that may result in the loss of public and political support. Taxpayers often have to foot much of the cost of the risks associated with these initiatives, and they may grow weary of shouldering this burden and question the kind of cost–benefit assumptions promoting this international integration. This may be particularly the case where these projects are tied up with huge risky developmental projects, as in Alicante.

Peripheral and extreme studios may suffer as a result of *inflexibility* that derives from the limited depth of local production capacity or a limited range of locations. Limitations on crew depth mean that it can be difficult to sustain production levels above a certain base (the very nature of the greenfields location means that this base is arrived at much more quickly with larger-budgeted productions than it is in a London or New York). Without flexibility, a characteristic necessary for reuse of both studios and locations, these studio facilities may be limited structures—in many cases these studios are the only place in town with all the limitations this assumes.

Larger global media cities have the advantage of a larger variety of spaces being available and a wider range of locations, particularly urban settings. Studios located away from major cities may not have ready access to the requisite big-city buildings and look to sustain trading off as somewhere else. Being only able to play a limited variety of stories and scenes creates obvious problems of sustainability. While greenfields studios can go some way to insulating themselves against such risks, they are still likely to be more risky than their counterparts in major centers. Some studios are less flexible than are others. A studio, like the city or region that surrounds it, trades on its reputation and builds trust in what it can do and what can be done locally by virtue of its versatility—its capacity to be somewhere and something other than it is. The greenfields studio needs simultaneously to be generic and specific; it must be anywhere and somewhere. This can be a particularly difficult act to accomplish since such sites are not always integral to a global economy of images.

A further risk arises from what may initially be an advantage of "new" places—that is, their stock of new locations. If this stock is limited or if particular locations are overused, these locations may become overfamiliar. For example, Peter Hald, the deputy director of the Swedish Film Institute, fears that Trollhättan has become such a popular location that the audience will become bored with seeing the "same old streets" in film after film.[4]

The strength of niche greenfields studios is often also their weakness. The Mediterranean Film Studios in Malta, or Fox Studios Baja in Mexico may be advantaged by their water tank features, but this strength can be dissipated as new water tanks are built in other locations. Studios known for water features may face problems securing other kinds of production.

The very "out of the wayness" of greenfields locations can create problems possibly more routinely than for production in established centers. Stars may balk at the prospect of a lack of routinely available luxury amenities, as was reportedly the case when after almost AU$20 million had been spent on preproduction, Brad Pitt pulled out of shooting *The Fountain* in Australia at the last moment supposedly because of a dearth of quality restaurants on the Gold Coast (although the offer to star in *Troy* may also have played a part in Pitt's decision). The absence of, or low level of services, attractions, and entertainments in certain Eastern European destinations is regularly cited by European competitors as a hindrance to their future development.

Where greenfields studios rely on the skills, experience, contacts, and reputations of key individuals and firms to attract regular work, changes in local or international conditions may create problems. For example, Warner Roadshow Studios on the Gold Coast lost its anchor tenant, the production company Coote/Hayes, in 2002 when the studio reoriented its focus to large-budget feature films and away from telemovie and series television work following the addition of two new soundstages. With the departure of Coote/Hayes for Melbourne, not only did the studios lose its anchor tenant, but the local production industry lost its major employer. Industry scale means that larger production centers do not suffer so acutely from a single firm closing shop in the way that the greenfields site can.

Studios may also be at risk when they are overreliant on the skills, experience, contacts, reputation, and energy of one person (e.g., Michael Lake, the CEO of Warner Roadshow Studios); if that individual left temporarily or permanently, or if he or she were to lose credibility or the confidence of investors and producers, then there would necessarily be repercussions for the studio in question.

Studios in greenfields sites also suffer from what could be termed an *agglomeration deficit*, meaning that, at least initially, they do not have the privileged set of localized clusters of firms and workers of the scale and variety that can be found in first-tier global media cities such as Los Angeles, London, and New York or in second-tier cities such as Rome, Berlin, Prague, Sydney, and Toronto. Rather, these greenfields places have limits to the level, character, and depth of their agglomeration dynamics and are not able to develop the concentration of production expertise and depth as can global media cities.

While ownership is an important issue in any studio location, it can be critical in greenfields locations, particularly if the studio is the only game in town. If the owners are in legal or financial trouble, the studio may be shrouded in uncertainty, incapable of long-term planning and vulnerable to sell-off and redevelopment for housing and so on.

The opportunistic character of many greenfields studios makes them susceptible to politicization and conflict between filmmaking and other agendas. A change of government can compromise long-term planning and policy directions. Even where they are not state controlled or where there is no direct state interest, greenfields studios may be vulnerable to political action (or inaction)—if, for example, there is no, or not enough, incentive in the form of tax breaks for producers, a studio and its surrounds become less competitive, and consequently more vulnerable. This is particularly important in greenfields sites because these incentives are a major instrument for minimizing risk and have historically been integral to Hollywood going on location. Alternatively, community concern about opportunistic developments may enhance the risks to production in a particular place, as in Baja California, where Fox was forced to take action to counter criticism by environmental activists.

A particularly important risk in the context of some greenfields sites is that of political instability and insecurity, which may be as much perceived as real. For example, there was a drop in production following 9/11 and subsequent bombings in Morocco, while in Fiji, the parliament was due to pass tax laws that would have paved the way for the construction of Studio City at Yaqara when a coup was staged and the country was thrown into turmoil.[5]

Another important risk stems from the ever-widening disaggregation of the system as the spread of production to new places increases the vulnerability of all. The Danish film commission provides an instance of this logic advertising itself for its proximity compared to far-away Sydney. This is something of a theme because it shows a bikini-clad girl and handsome man frolicking on a beach. It costs very little to add to this mix—repackaging existing domestic capability and facilities, a population with English as a second language, sophisticated ICT infrastructure—to also be competitive in this market. Clearly there is an ever-widening geography of potential greenfields sites and locations for international productions. With each new site and each new studio, another potential satellite is added, creating anxieties for existing satellites and additional opportunities for producers shopping for the best location for production.

Greenfields places may not always be as capable of learning from and applying knowledge gleaned from international production work. They do not have the capacity and the depth to apply this knowledge to new ventures as can established film and television production locations with extensive infrastructure, human capital, and long-standing networks and depth of production. Greenfields sites can only manage innovation in limited ways. They are dependent on skills of practitioners but also the available training infrastructure. While it is possible to build in such training capacity through films schools as Alicante is doing, or as on the Gold Coast, through deals with local tertiary training providers, the problem such locations face is that they are less generators of intellectual property and ideas than takers. Innovative technical and technological solutions may require firms to colocate in the global media city in order to capitalize on benefits because of the more narrow field of application of this technology within a greenfields location. Certainly this is a dynamic discernible in the Gold Coast context where a firm that had developed technology associated with a high-budget production has now established a presence in Sydney.

From Satellite to Center:
North American Precedents for Extreme Dreams

Of particular importance to our story is the emergence of Wilmington, North Carolina, and Vancouver, British Columbia, from very low bases of occasional location-based production to become two of the top six film and television production locations in North America by the mid-1990s. In 2001, *Forbes* put production spend over the seventeen-year life of the Wilmington studio now known as Screen Gems at $2.6 billion. Notable feature film and television productions include *Blue Velvet*, *Sleeping with the Enemy*, and *Dawson's Creek*.[6] While the stories of Vancouver and Wilmington will be pursued in more detail in later chapters, here we are interested in the ways in which these studios fashioned a model for the greenfields studio and set important precedents for international developments. The evidence from both places shows that extreme production locations can be sustainable. They seem to prove that it is possible to come from nothing and become a major production center. And they seem to provide the most telling instances of the capacity of film and television production to remake place and challenge assumptions about what can and can not be done in such locations with important spin-off effects on the place and the region's national and international standing. While other studios had also been established to service international production and build on existing location production outside North America in the 1980s, such as Atlas Corporation Studios in Morocco, Vancouver's and Wilmington's extraordinary success has made them models for thinking about the development of film infrastructure and capacity in places peripheral to traditional centers of film and television activity.

What later became known as the Screen Gems studio in Wilmington was built for the film *Firestarter* and opened in 1984. Vancouver's first studio, The Bridge Studios, opened in 1987. Both were preconditions for North Carolina and British Columbia becoming major North American audiovisual production centers. The Wilmington studios were set up by Dino de Laurentiis to take advantage of North Carolina's locations, lower labor costs, and workforce "flexibility" under rules that permitted the employment of nonunionized labor. While other "right-to-work" states had a minor production presence through the 1980s, de Laurentiis took this occasional location production to its next stage through a functioning Hollywood standard studio. In establishing the Wilmington studio, de Laurentiis was drawing on personal and international precedent. He had already established a studio for international and local production in his native Italy at a time when Rome was touted as "Hollywood on the Tiber."

What is notable about both Vancouver and Wilmington is the way they have transformed themselves over twenty years from centers for location production without any substantial residual infrastructure to two of the foremost production and services centers in North America. Each transformation occurred in stages. In Vancouver's case, the initial catalyst was the development by the provincial government—at the instigation of film unions and the local industry association—of The Bridge Studios as a production precinct. Over time this studio expanded, and a range of other facilities and services were also developed. The existence of The Bridge Studios and increasing demand for controlled production environments led to the establishment of additional studios in Vancouver. It now has several "cinema cities," each with multiple soundstages and ancillary infrastructure, and the city as a whole hosts over fifty soundstages.

Both Vancouver and Wilmington have been able to capitalize on the initial development of a studio. Vancouver was aided by a range of interlocking factors including the exchange rate between the Canadian dollar and the U.S. dollar that made Canada a significantly cheaper production location. In Wilmington's case, it was lower wage rates and the right-to-work provisions that ensured levels of flexibility not possible in Hollywood. Vancouver is functionally proximate in time zone and transport to the design center for the international production industry, Los Angeles. It is also notable for the extent of entrepreneurial, collaborative activity among film unions, companies, and professional associations in pursuing international production and in developing master agreements that emphasize peaceful labor relations.[7]

Wilmington is functionally proximate to major East Coast locations and boasts the largest full-service facility in the United States east of Los Angeles. The British Columbia and North Carolina governments provided incentives and invested in infrastructure throughout the period to bolster the initial foray into film and television production. Both Vancouver and Wilmington were able to establish themselves as major international production centers because the various local players worked together to provide innovative and flexible solutions to their dependence on international production. They understood the "ever present need for collaborative, organised entrepreneurialism" and "international competitiveness," to enhance their profiles and reputations as centers for international production.[8]

Without a substantial local production industry to fall back on, both places needed to find a solution to their dependency as satellite production centers on externally generated production. Both chose to become more—and not less—dependent on international production. For David Murphy, Vancouver's dependency as a filmmaking location on "global financial, distribution and exhibition mediums" nurtured and reinforced significant levels of "intra-community interdependency" that have enabled it to withstand competition for international production from other—traditional and emerging—film production locations.[9]

While both places have been the stand-out successes of the last twenty years, they are still vulnerable. Wilmington in particular suffers from the development of other low-cost locations around the world. Unlike Vancouver, production in Wilmington does not have the advantage of exchange rate differentials. Both are as much at risk—if not more so—than are larger places such as New York, Toronto, or Miami. While each has some capacity to seed the development of local production companies to take up some of the slack in down periods, neither location is strong on developing such capacity. Both need a locally based player with long-term production plans in order to remain competitive and maintain a permanent production presence. So while these places provide precedent, they are each aware of and driven by the spectral presence of competition and the ever-present worry about the flow of production drying up. Indeed, the development of more greenfields sites puts pressures on these players to innovate and renovate in order to maintain their lead.

Ardmore, Ireland

The main Irish studios, Ardmore near Dublin in the east, and Concorde Anois Teo near Galway in the west, have much to tell us about greenfields studios, film policy, the historical and contemporary dynamics of international production, and the imperatives and (sometimes frustrated) needs of the Irish film industry. Ardmore studios in County Wicklow south of Ireland's principal city of Dublin was a greenfields development when it was built in 1958 with private and state support to encourage Hollywood and British film producers to make films in Ireland. Many major productions have made use of Ardmore's facilities particularly in recent years, although often only actually shooting there for short periods. Concorde Anois Teoranta began production in 1995 in County Galway under the direction of American mogul Roger Corman. The studio was partly financed by Údarás na Gaeltachta, the regional development agency responsible for the economic, social, and cultural development of the Gaeltacht regions, on the understanding that it would act as a training facility. More than twenty low-budget feature films in the Corman mold have been made at Concorde Anois.

A number of prominent figures, including the playwright George Bernard Shaw and politician Eamon de Valera, had lent support to the idea of creating an Irish film studio in the 1930s and 1940s. Sean Lemass, who as taoiseach (prime minister) in the 1950s is widely credited with changing the ideological underpinning of Irish trade and economic policy away from protectionism toward an open market, export-oriented economy, had promoted the idea of using public and private finance to build a studio in the 1940s when minister for industry and commerce. The establishment of Ardmore in 1958 represents perhaps the first instance of an explicit international film policy designed to enable greater local participation in international film and television production networks, and to take advantage of the fact that by the late 1950s, many Hollywood films were being produced outside the United States. Ardmore was envisaged as a means to promote the location interest at a time when Irish film production was virtually nonexistent and the local television industry was in its early stages of development, but a lack of consistent support coupled with the maintenance of Ardmore as a production venue with few additional services (especially in postproduction, which tends to flow to companies in the United Kingdom or United States) and difficulties in bridging the gap between an internationally oriented studio and domestic producers have contributed to Ardmore's roller-coaster history.

In 1958, in film as in a variety of other industries, international capital was coveted through state investment in infrastructure and the provision of a variety of financial incentives, with the idea of kick-starting indigenous production, generating employment, and providing training in film trades. However, as Lance Pettitt writes, Ardmore "became fairly quickly a hireable facility monopolised by British and US studios as a production space. The plan to base indigenous film production on successful Abbey theatrical adaptations was ill-conceived and soon gave way to commercial pressures, British distribution controls and trade union practices which excluded Irish technician grade workers."[10] A large gap emerged between local and international production aspirations as the studio was governed by a "manufacturing plant" mentality consonant with other initiatives to attract foreign manufacturers.[11] This was decidedly not the creative industries cluster development strategy of subsequent developments. As Kevin Rockett explains:

> Ireland, unlike other European countries, such as Britain, did not offer state support, either indirect through a levy on cinema tickets, or through loans and grants, to indigenous filmmakers. In the 1950s, when the government eventually took a more pro-active approach toward film production, it did so not by treating filmmaking as part of a positive cultural activity, but in the same manner as any manufacturing industry. In this context, Ardmore Studios was opened in 1958, well after film studios were closing elsewhere. The hope was to encourage foreign film producers to make films in Ireland while also generating earnings on exports.[12]

For much of its life, the studio has been integrally bound to the "corporate state"[13] either through direct state investment and ownership, or through the mix of grants, loans, and tax incentives that mainly attracts British and U.S. companies. Although a commercial operation with a number of private-sector owners, the studio relied on state assistance to survive until 1973, when effectively it was run by the national television broadcaster RTÉ for two years, before being renamed the National Film Studios of Ireland in 1975. In 1982, the studio went into liquidation again, and remained closed until a takeover in 1986 by the American production company MTM (for Mary Tyler Moore) was engineered by local producer Morgan O'Sullivan, who managed the studios from 1986 to 1990 and still has offices on-site to this day.

While it might have been assumed that international productions would assist in the development of Irish capacity, this model was always going to pose difficulties. For a brief period, Ardmore was used for Irish-set stories such as the War of Independence drama Shake Hands with the Devil (Michael Anderson, 1959), with James Cagney, and the 1940s IRA story A Terrible Beauty (Tay Garnett, 1960), starring Robert Mitchum. The studios and surrounds stood in for Tibet and China in The Face of Fu Manchu (Don Sharp, 1965) and Berlin in The Spy Who Came In from the Cold (Martin Ritt, 1965). But apart from this initial period, the studio has not been so integral to international production in Ireland, although most productions make some use of the studio's other facilities, including its office space. This history has ensured that Ardmore has not driven decisions about locating production in Ireland in the way that Screen Gems drove production location decisions in North Carolina, for example. Ireland then as now continues to function principally as a scenic backdrop, with the studio acting as an extra incentive for production. This helps explain the relatively modest scale of Ardmore in the contemporary period—its stages are small compared to many available internationally. Ardmore has also suffered from the tendency of production levels in Ireland to be high in the six months from April, and lower from October to March because of the weather, the length of daylight hours, and decisions on eligibility for tax breaks that tended to be announced at the start of a new financial year in April.

Ireland is a small country seeking to punch above its weight through international production. It has a small population base that limits the development of film and television production infrastructures beyond a certain level. It is therefore not surprising that internationalizing strategies would be looked to in order to leaven these structural conditions. This happened in Ireland a lot earlier than it did elsewhere, in part because of the way that Ireland simultaneously benefits from and is used for its symbolic importance given the place of Irish stories, music, and literature within the English language and beyond.

The desire to capitalize on interest in Irish stories and the symbolic resonances of Ireland appears to have played only a minor part in the establishment of Concorde Anois Teo in the west of Ireland in 1995. Although still strongly oriented to international English-language production, this studio operates on a different model from Ardmore. It is the first major center for film production in Ireland to be established outside Dublin, and it is owned by the American movie mogul and champion of exploitation cinema, Roger Corman. According to Corman, the motivation to establish a European studio was a direct consequence of European quotas on non-European films and television programs that "was really a move against American films. As I make medium- and low-budget films, I felt I would be frozen out of Europe. I thought in the old tradition of 'If you can't beat them, join them.'"[14] Corman worked closely with the governmental minister then responsible for film, Michael D. Higgins, to develop a plan for the studios that would be financed in part by tax relief and grants from Irish government agencies, including Údarás na Gaeltachta, the agency responsible for the economic, social, and cultural development of the Gaeltacht (or Irish-speaking) regions. Corman was attracted by the prospect of low-cost labor and the subsidized training initiatives that the studio would offer, although these subsequently became bones of contention within Ireland. Several Irish unions representing film workers expressed concern about the high turnover at Concorde Anois, and the lack of an agreement with the studios over the pay and conditions of Corman's Irish employees that were low in comparison with those of film workers in Dublin.

The veteran filmmaker's keys to success—swift, low-budget genre-based production, latching onto or boosting a youth trend, and using a catchy title—affronted some within Ireland whose idea of "film" did not extend to this kind of work. The differences came to a head when *Criminal Affairs*, the first Corman film made at Concorde Anois with an Irish director (Jeremiah Cullinane), was screened at the Galway Film Fleadh in 1997 and was accused of being "soft porn." Údaras and the Department of Arts, Heritage, the Gaeltacht, and Islands became the target of criticism for certifying Corman's productions (and thus enabling them to claim tax relief) because of their questionable cultural relevance. In its defense, the department argued:

> Our obligation is to certify productions . . . under three broad criteria—employment creation, value added to the economy, and enhancement of the national culture. We are unreservedly a Department of Culture, so we do in particular give credence to Irish stories, but that cultural element does not have to apply in all cases. Nobody asked us why we certified Steven Spielberg's [*Saving Private Ryan*].[15]

The Ardmore and Concorde Anois initiatives turn on Irish self-recognition as a small, peripheral state that struggles as a "satellite" (albeit a fiercely independent one) of its larger neighbor, Great Britain, and that seeks to build on its relationship with the United States. The creation of Ardmore can be seen as part of a longstanding Irish play evident in politics as much as business of using its satellite status—proferring a public strategy of positioning itself with respect to the United States so as to maintain an independent identity and presence with respect to Britain. Ireland has long sought to play one off against the other and to construct in the process some Irish presence and advantage and attention from both. The Ardmore initiative both sought to interest Hollywood in Ireland and Irish production locations and stories and also through this interest the United Kingdom in Ireland as a viable production location, not only for Irish stories but also for geographically nonspecific productions. The aim is to secure not only production for Irish stories but also films like *Braveheart*, *Reign of Fire*, and *King Arthur*. This ensures that Ardmore is part of a history of Irish attempts to construct an alternative position in the British Isles for itself and an integral part (and an agent for) the story of Irish integration into both Hollywood and the British Isles. Like so many greenfields initiatives, it represents an attempt to deal directly with Hollywood and to capitalize on Hollywood's and America's long-standing interest in Irish stories as a way of leapfrogging habitual networks that cast Ireland and Dublin in only marginal roles.

While a number of plausible external reasons can be advanced for the resurgence of Ireland as production location in the contemporary period, domestic policy innovations undoubtedly played their part. Much of the commentary on film and television production in Ireland sees the contemporary period as emerging almost simultaneously with the symbolic shift of policy from a near exclusive reliance on international production in an international production policy aimed at generating foreign exchange in a central state-owned, part-owned facility toward a more thoroughgoing interest in and recognition of the importance of independent film activity in domestic film and television production industry capacity with the establishment in 1982 of the Irish Film Board devoted to encourage Irish production."[16] This significantly changed the orientation toward a project-based rather than manufacturing studio model of production.

The second shift a decade later turns on the explicit intersection of strategies to facilitate Ireland as a place where original creative output from Irish artists is alive and well with strategies to encourage foreign investment and offshore production in Ireland including generous tax concessions. This time around, the Irish government would internationalize not at the expense of local production but through its own actions in supporting local production and through local filmmakers taking advantage of this and helping to revitalize the country's indigenous film industry. After 1993, support for film became part of a broader effort "to put the arts and culture at the center of Irish economic policy."[17] In this mix, film had an important role to play given its capacity to "create significant numbers of jobs in Ireland." Derry O'Brien of the Irish Trade Board claimed that the choice of Ireland for the production of *Braveheart* was in part because of the tax deal negotiated between the production and the government, and partly the result of the work of the arts minister, Michael D. Higgins, in arranging for 1,500 Irish troops to be available as extras for battle scenes and in ensuring access to all government-owned castles. In this case, the careful management of both sites and both locations also held out the possibility of a break from the past, as Garry puts it (1995): "[t]heir film ambitions suggest that the Irish are no longer resigned to the perceived fate of their country—a fate that commands the young and talented to leave, and condemns those who stay to a disappointing life."[18]

Fox Studios Baja, Mexico

In the latter stages of the production of James Cameron's *Titanic*, a smog of fear and anxiety hung over pockets of Los Angeles. Sobered by the catastrophe of *Waterworld*, skittish executives feared that *Titanic's* soaring costs would sink more than an ocean liner. Built for an estimated cost of $20 million in only one hundred days, Fox Studios Baja at Rosarito, just a short drive south of the Mexican border with California, quickly turned like the movie itself from a cost to a significant and lucrative asset. Shortly before the film was green-lit by Fox, Cameron and producer Jon Landau were told to bring the budget below $110 million, excluding the cost of the studio. By this time, after a global search the team had settled on the Rosarito site as a suitable location to build the water tanks and infrastructure necessary to re-create this legendary disaster. Initially conceived and budgeted for as a temporary facility with portable, "pop-up" stages and large cement pits to hold the millions of gallons of water in which the almost full-size exterior of the ship would be suspended and sunk, the studio was soon seen by Fox executives as a workable, permanent production space.

In later tellings of the story of this extraordinary achievement, when the knowledge of its stellar success all but drowns out memories of the anxiety that attended *Titanic's* production, the symbolism of the date that construction began can only augment the mystique. "Nicknamed the '100-day studio,' Fox Studios Baja began construction on May 31, 1996, the same day that *Titanic's* hull was launched into Belfast Harbor at Harland and Wolff's shipyard eighty-five years previously."[19] At the time, some might have seen the historical parallel as an omen rather than as serendipity.

In Paula Parisi's account of this tale, Cameron had never intended to build or use facilities in Los Angeles because construction costs were too high.[20] A number of different ways of re-creating the ship and the sinking were explored, including dressing an eight-hundred-foot-long container ship with portable sets that could be remounted on a soundstage, and using the premier niche water facility at that time, Mediterranean Film Studios in Malta, for the sinking scenes. In the end, the attraction of the completely controlled environment that they could custom-build on forty acres of oceanfront land at Rosarito was greater than the use of any other stand-ins. As Parisi tells it:

> Scouring the world for large, open spaces, they came up with blimp hangars—
> 330 feet high and 1000 feet long with open space, uninterrupted by column
> support—rock quarries and a submarine plant in South Carolina. Any huge
> structure any place in the world was considered. Nothing was quite right. . . .

It soon became clear that the most effective route, the one that would offer the most control, was building their own studio. . . . Mexico was the obvious choice. The freeway-close proximity to Los Angeles and its world-class crews and equipment were bonuses. Cheap labor and real estate were necessities. They settled on Rosarito, a "resort" community, popular among Southern Californian college students in the 1970s, that had seen better days.[21]

At a time when the costs of acquisition and construction appeared only as lines on *Titanic*'s budget, when 1,500 workers were building the facility in 100 days while 400 others built and dressed sets, it makes sense that labor and land costs would loom large in thinking about the studios. But, in retrospect, Fox Studios Baja's functional proximity to Los Angeles and the large pool of Mexican filmmaking talent and expertise have been major draws for future production work.[22] The filmmakers were certainly fortunate in their timing and choice of Mexico; for political and economic reasons, the Mexican government was keen to facilitate foreign investment in the wake of the North American Free Trade Agreement (NAFTA), and shortly before the Rosarito site was acquired, Mexican law was changed to allow 100 percent direct ownership of land by foreign businesses. The recent collapse of domestic film production in Mexico also meant that many professional filmmakers were available and in need of work.

It was clear early on that the build would be substantial and that it would have considerable impact on the environment. Local fishermen and environmental groups complained about pollution and runoff that local laws did not prevent. Fishermen from the town of Popotla claimed that the volume of the catch of some species in the area around the studios had declined by 50 percent, but after commissioning a number of reports, the studios denied responsibility, pointing to the water filtration system and sewage treatment plant on site, and the less assiduous practices of other major sites nearby, including a power station.[23]

Fox Studios Baja is a quintessential extreme location. It was indirectly created by that rare kind of tragedy that bequeaths its name to the description of subsequent events. Like the film, the studio was always going to be viewed and written about in terms of scale, and indeed the numbers are mind-boggling. Through this one film, Fox Studios Baja acquired the most advanced technology and equipment for filming on and in water anywhere in the world, with innovative gimbals and hydraulics that permitted the sinking of the massive ship set. The studio has also accommodated some clustering of production services, and has tapped into the local tourist market through the adjacent Foxploration theme park. Like many of the extreme studios discussed in this chapter, Fox Studios Baja has not been uncontroversial, but it appears now to be well established as the premier global site for movies with lengthy or complex water scenes.

Warner Roadshow Studios, Australia

Although on a much smaller scale and without the level of surrounding infrastructure that has been built up in British Columbia, the establishment and subsequent development of the Warner Roadshow Studios on Australia's Gold Coast shares many parallels with Vancouver. Like the initial Vancouver complex, the Gold Coast facility was developed in a region peripheral to the country's major production centers at the instigation of a conservative provincial government. In both cases, the involvement of government was essential. In Vancouver, the provincial government financed The Bridge Studios' redevelopment, and continues to control the complex through a Crown-owned corporation. In the case of the Gold Coast, the state government secured Dino de Laurentiis's commitment to build a studio in Queensland by providing a low-interest loan of $AU7.5 million and offering a thirty-year lease of the fifty-hectare site at Coomera to facilitate construction. Loans to finance initial construction and subsequent expansion topped up the final amount of state government assistance to $AU12.5 million.[24] In both Queensland and British Columbia, the initial interest of government was spurred by a conviction that international production would be a medium for regional industrial development and diversification, and a valuable promotional appendage to the resource and tourism industries.

Importantly, this policy thinking did not align with traditional national film policy frameworks but rather came out of the industry development and job creation thinking of regional governments. The governmental interest in developing a studio was then somewhat disconnected, at least initially, from the aspirations of Vancouver's and nearby Brisbane's small domestic industries. Involvement in servicing international production gave Queensland-based filmmakers the opportunity to establish a commercial film industry through the development of a studio. Discussing Vancouver, Mike Gasher makes the point that this was "an opportunity that had been denied [British Columbia] by the concentration of the Canadian film industry in Ontario and Quebec."[25] Similarly, in Queensland's case, this opportunity was preempted by the concentration of film industry activity in Sydney (New South Wales) and Melbourne (Victoria). International production allowed both centers to overcome their status as "remote outposts" of their national film industries. In both places, Hollywood was not seen as an impediment to the development of a local film industry but as a means to grow local film production capacity through the development of a film services industry.

The Gold Coast studio has gained an international reputation for its work initially on television series such as *Mission: Impossible* and *Time Trax*, later on movies of the week (MOWs), and more recently on high-budget international feature films—*Scooby-Doo, Peter Pan, Ghost Ship*. The early focus on international television series and MOWs was in part the result of a failure to attract regular feature film production. As a consequence, the skills to service television and MOW production were built up locally over time, but this subsequently created significant disruption to a local film milieu geared to a different production logic when the studio embarked on a concerted effort to attract high-budget Hollywood blockbuster production in 1999–2000. The succession of high-budget feature films that the studio housed from 2000 fundamentally changed its profile as a production location. However, the studio has also hosted a considerable amount of production that has stretched our thinking about what "local" production might mean, such as controversial coproductions *Beastmaster* and *Pacific Drive*. While studio management and service companies have generally been willing to negotiate favorable terms and conditions for local productions on limited budgets, in general the costs of using the studio's soundstages are too high for the low budgets characterizing domestic production.

Like so many greenfields sites, the Gold Coast studio has a "frontier" quality as filmmaking infrastructure was created from a low base. This imbued developments with an improvised and provisional quality and a no-frills approach to the studio and its environs. Like its Vancouver and Wilmington counterparts, the Gold Coast studio relied on fly-in, fly-out film-workers to fill the heads of department positions while below-the-line crews came from Sydney and Melbourne to supplement the small Brisbane pool of film workers. Over time, productions' labor needs have been able to be met by locals as international producers' levels of trust in their abilities increased and as the local pool grew through training and migration.

The Gold Coast studio has transformed over time from a production precinct to a cinema city. The studio was established with four stages and a small number of on-site tenants. Initially it had limited postproduction capacity and was only able to service production shoots. Additional facilities have been added at intervals—new soundstages were built in 1990, 1996, and 2002, and the exterior water tank was constructed in 1996—and more companies have located on-site or close to the studio, thus enabling the provision of the full range of production and postproduction services.

Like Vancouver and other greenfields studios, Warner Roadshow Studios has remained more oriented to the production shoot and less to postproduction than older studios such as Pinewood-Shepperton, Studio Babelsberg, and Cinecittà. While initially a consequence of the limited skills and services available and the need to build a film infrastructure of locally based service providers from scratch, a range of factors has contributed to continuing this production-shoot orientation.

The Gold Coast is a film services center for the international film production industry and supports very limited domestic production activity that would call on an extensive postproduction sector. This has meant that film services companies located on the Gold Coast have not for the most part been able to mix and match domestic and international production in the same way, leveraging one off against the other to expand and update facilities and services, as have companies in Toronto, Montreal, Rome, Berlin, and London.

The Gold Coast, like Vancouver, depends more on international production than do Toronto and Montreal, or Sydney and Melbourne. Unsurprisingly, given their international orientation and limited domestic production, both the Gold Coast and Vancouver are better known for playing somewhere else than playing themselves. British Columbia's promotional literature explicitly invites the filmmaker to bend and change the location to fit any setting. In his 2002 study of filmmaking in British Columbia, Mike Gasher observes that the city of Vancouver has "not sufficient signifying power—sufficient star power, in Hollywood parlance—to play itself."[26] While a number of initiatives have been developed in recent years to foster local (and locally set) filmmaking,[27] and despite the recent action movie *Ballistic: Ecks vs. Sever* being set there, this remains the case. The situation is similar on the Gold Coast, where none of the major feature films produced at the Warner Roadshow Studios have been set on the Gold Coast, although in recent years a number of lower-budgeted local films have been set and produced on the Coast (e.g., *Blurred*, *Gettin' Square*, and *Under the Radar*).

The rationale for state financial support and the international promotion of Vancouver and the Gold Coast as filmmaking locations has consistently focused on the economic and employment benefits that would accrue to British Columbia/Queensland and on the glamour of Hollywood, rather than on their contribution to local film culture. Without "talk of art or national identity to confuse things,"[28] film could more easily co-opt the images and rhetorics of the nascent tourist industry and be framed in terms of state economic development, rather than cultural development. Chasing the multimillion-dollar investments that large-budget international productions would bring made sense to a province/state reared on large investments and deals with foreign companies in the pastoral and mining industries. Both centers placed considerable emphasis on establishing liaison networks and resourcing their respective film commissions with a service rather than production funding orientation. Government has been important here not only in enabling the studios to be established in the first place but also in enabling them to continue to function as integral components of the international production ecology.

The Gold Coast studio is different from its Vancouver counterparts in that the studio is adjacent to a film-related theme park. In this respect, the Gold Coast is like Orlando, where studios are connected with Disney and Universal theme parks. The studio–theme park combination was obviously important in attracting the involvement of a Hollywood major, Warner, which was probably more interested in establishing an Australian version of its movie theme park business than developing a film studio. Just as in Orlando, Florida, where the making of major Hollywood productions like *Waterboy* could help confirm the theme park as a "movie world" (and therefore permit it to be marketed not just as a consumption site but also a production site), so, too, the production of *Scooby-Doo* and *Peter Pan* was seen as helping to secure the theme park franchise in the public imagination of Hollywood on the Gold Coast.

Being part of a theme park also had other benefits, with the theme park helping to pay for the maintenance of infrastructure, including security and sharing infrastructure such as a commissary for staff. In Orlando's case, soundstages have also doubled as venues for faux productions of variety television; while in the case of the Gold Coast, a soundstage has also been temporarily used for a theme park ride.[29] As with its Orlando counterparts, the involvement of a Hollywood major was important in giving the Gold Coast studio immediate credibility. In addition, the involvement in the development of the initial de Laurentiis–led bid of an experienced industry figure like Terry Jackman ensured that the studio had significant political, local, and international industry connections.[30]

As in Vancouver, the commercial orientation of the studio on the Gold Coast was an important factor in convincing governments, investors, the film community, and the public of its value. This commercial orientation emphasizes the importance of continuity of production, given the low operating margins of these facilities—hence the value of long-term series television production (e.g., *Stargate SG-1* in Vancouver, and *Beastmaster* on the Gold Coast) or long-term relationships with major television or film production companies (e.g., MGM for Vancouver, Coote/Hayes for the Gold

Coast). But underlying the vulnerabilities of these associations, Coote/Hayes relocated to Melbourne when first *Scooby-Doo* and then *Peter Pan* required all of the studio's stages.

Castel Film Studios, Romania

Until one of the most expensive features of 2003, *Cold Mountain*, was made on its stages and around Romania, Castel Film Studios near Bucharest had a reputation for low-budget international horror and action productions. The roll call of film titles made at Castel since it opened in 1992 indicate the provenance of much of this English language exploitation production: *Subspecies 2* and *3*; *Leapin' Leprechauns* and *Spellbreaker: Secret of the Leprechaun*; *Josh Kirby . . . Time Warrior! Chapter One, the Planet of the Dino-Knights* and *Josh Kirby . . . Time Warrior! Chapter Two, The Human Pets*; *Frankenstein Reborn*; and *Hideous* are among the titles. Frontier spaces of production tend to be favored initially by low-budget productions. Cost savings can compensate for the increased risks associated with producing in a transitional society, but there can also be a creative incentive; the low-budget productions filmed in Romania in the last decade have made much use of Transylvania's mythic identity as the home of Dracula. Where better to produce a vampire film?

Romania is currently regarded as one of the cheapest places in Europe to make movies, with costs an estimated 25 to 30 percent lower than Prague, the benchmark lower-cost Eastern European location. Comparisons with other more established centers are even more striking; a standby carpenter in Romania earns less than U.S.$1 per hour, while a British counterpart could earn 400 pounds per day. Such low wage rates make crowd scenes particularly cheap to stage in Romania—a battle scene in *Cold Mountain* required nearly a thousand extras. Supplying this kind of scene is something for which Romania is well suited. Romania has a low-waged but skilled workforce and large available crew courtesy of the film and television production infrastructure maintained under the former communist regime. In the area of set construction, it is not only the labor that is cheap but also the "raw materials for construction," particularly timber, with the result that construction costs are extremely low.[31]

Since Castel opened for business in 1992, the Bucharest region's film and television production and associated infrastructure have grown. The region's telecommunications and production facilities are reliable with "post-production services and fully integrated facilities allowing further cost control for producers."[32] Bucharest now features five-star hotels and up-market restaurants; five years previously, the absence of such facilities made major international production shoots almost impossible to contemplate in the region.

Castel's production trajectory evidences a familiar pattern of development. There is an initial pattern of opportunistic lower-budgeted productions typically pitched at the lower ends of the production market. These function to build confidence and enable the studio and filming in Romania to become viewed as a less risky enterprise. They are then followed by pitches for and the successful accommodation of higher-budgeted productions.

Cold Mountain is a significant achievement for Castel and for Romania as an international production location more generally. For a country whose participation in international production has been mostly at the cheap, generic ends of production, hosting one of the most expensive Hollywood features of the year was symbolically very important. It indicates that it is possible for Romania to service high-budget international productions for which cost is not the defining consideration. The sheer scale of *Cold Mountain* is staggering, with "nearly everything from ravens to tons of artificial snow and blood" being imported and "entire farms, planted with corn and tobacco," created.[33] These costs could be justified by the look afforded by a relatively undeveloped and unfamiliar location.

Romania's wild and natural locations have played important roles in attracting international production. In the case of *Cold Mountain*, Castel Film Studios president Vlad Paunescu claims that Transylvania had the advantage of looking "like the US 150 years ago." For Gub Neal, filming *Boudicea* outside Bucharest made sense because the filmmakers "were able to get away from the development of the UK" and from the "the National Trust feel."[34]

The Romanian studios—Castel and Media Pro in Bucharest—have firmly pitched themselves as a low-cost alternative to the Prague studios and locations. In the ecology of Eastern European production, Romania is positioned to soak up the overspill of production from Prague when its studios are booked and to pick up work progressively priced out of the Prague market while its facilities, services, and locations are in great demand. But Romania's authoritarian legacy and its record of underdevelopment continues to create problems. Allegations of profiteering by some suppliers were made during the production of *Cold Mountain* while customs and bureaucracy challenged the filmmakers[35]—similar complaints were made in Prague during the filming of *Mission: Impossible*. These difficulties derive in part from the transitional nature of these economies and the transaction costs associated with situations that are not always transparent and do not necessarily obey international norms. While the savings may be considerable, the risks associated with these productions can become equally significant as unexpected costs, lack of transparency, and difficulties associated with production can push up costs considerably and unexpectedly.

Securing *Cold Mountain* was not only a confidence-building measure but also a mechanism to reposition Romania as a location for high-budget international production. The production of *Cold Mountain* demonstrated that both local facilities and personnel could handle the norms and demands of Hollywood blockbuster production. The success of the production symbolically and practically addresses and perhaps surmounts the endemic and structural weakness of Eastern European locations—their foreignness for international producers—and the cultural differences involved.

The rapid development of the Bucharest studios as sites for international production may mean that Romania's period as an extreme location is a short one. The problem Castel and Media Pro may increasingly face is how to manage their newfound centrality in more mature circumstances. Nonetheless, the Romanian experience is a powerful example of the use of low-cost labor, facilities, and locations to broker something bigger and more extensive. Romania has become, as a consequence, normalized on film production horizons to international standards and production norms, often in advance of domestic capacity to do so in other spheres.

Dreamworld Film City, South Africa

The Dreamworld Film City studio under construction in Cape Town at the time of writing is part of larger strategies by government, private consortia, and film industry figures for South Africa to emerge as a significant global force in international film and television production. This facility is touted as the country's first Hollywood-standard studio that will allow filmmakers to undertake production and postproduction on projects ranging in size from thirty-second commercials to blockbuster features. The development promises to unlock mid-Africa and South Africa locations and stories and to provide competitive and cost-effective alternative locations for international production. It turns on the twin ambitions for two of South Africa's three major cities—Johannesburg and Cape Town—to act as international gateways for foreign investment and joint ventures into Africa using African locations and resources and, second, to emulate, match, and in some areas displace Australia and New Zealand as preferred Southern Hemisphere locations for international production. Cape Town's beaches and other natural and built environments are promoted as ideal venues for European, Japanese, and other Asian advertising production, movies of the week, and feature production during Europe's winter months. In Johannesburg's case, the focus is on the range of metropolis city environments and game park environments not matched in Cape Town. The studios in these locations provide an important example of the play for global integration by South Africa and southern and mid-Africa in global production networks in the postapartheid era. South African ambition here is to use international production networks to fulfill place-making requirements by emphasizing themselves and their uniqueness while simultaneously promoting their capacity to double as somewhere else. In this sense, the strategy of targeting advertising shoots and utilizing old Cape Town infrastructure and locations makes the city a competitive and compelling alternative not only to Sydney, Melbourne, and the Gold Coast in Australia but also to Miami.

Neighboring states have little film infrastructure and are unlikely to develop any in the short term. South African companies have acted as agents for bringing these states into the global film economy, as in the case of *Ali* (Michael Mann, 2001), which was shot in part in Mozambique. These states mostly see their future as linked with a dynamic and expansive South Africa. In this context, the film services provider Sasani Film promotes itself as "post-production co-ordinator, providing producers with a consolidated package of advice on methodology, facilities and services for any film/television project in southern Africa." It is able to offer full-service facilities in both Cape Town and Johannesburg. Sasani is interesting for the largely vertically integrated character of its operations and its handling of a diverse range of location shooting on a continental basis.

In feature film, Martin Cuff of the Cape Film Commission sees the Cape's principal competition as Australia, New Zealand, Mexico, Canada, and Argentina; in TVCs, the competition is Spain, Portugal, Argentina, and Greece; in still photography, its competition as Miami, Cuba, Argentina, and Spain.[36] The South Africans see themselves as having a number of advantages as a location for international production over their competitors. In comparison with Australia and New Zealand, South Africa is in the same time zone as much of Europe and considerably closer. It has available to it arguably a greater range of exotic locations and can play on Africa as Europe's other in a way that Australasia cannot. It also has the potential to act as a major center for film and television production destined for African markets.

Cape Town is a particularly advantaged location in this mix because of its diversity of proximate locations, and streets that can double for streets in European or North American cities. In 2003, the city of Cape Town issued over four thousand filming permits, representing a fourfold increase on 1999. Cape Town markets itself as a flexible location:

The region offers widely diverse geographical and architectural locations within a short distance of the international airport. Shoots in the Cape in the last few months have recreated everything from a Roman Colosseum, St. Helena in the time of Napoleon's exile, a Hong Kong street market, a Paris fashion show, an Australian sporting stadium, South Beach Miami, 1960's London as well as numerous other generic American cities. We have Alpine mountains and lakes, tropical-style beaches or rugged rocky coastlines, rolling wheat fields and mysterious forests. We have skyscrapers and quaint English cottages, industrial plants and areas of startling physical beauty.[37]

Cape Town initially emerged as a venue for out of season advertising production work—TVCs—sourced from Europe and North Asia. Its infrastructure of smaller scale studios was skewed toward the needs of television commercial production. The Cape Film Commission claims that over the summer period from November to April, Cape Town's (advertising) Stills Production industry is the largest in the world while in terms of TVC production, it is the fifth-largest center outside California.[38] Cape Town dominates the shooting of television commercials in South Africa, with 58 percent of foreign originated commercials facilitated by South African companies filmed in Cape Town. (By way of comparison, Cape Town has only a 27 percent share of local commercials.) Eighty-four percent of the international television commercial business comes from Europe—62 percent from mainland Europe, principally Germany, France and Italy, and 22 percent from the United Kingdom.[39]

This work illustrates the ways in which participation in global production networks can evolve incrementally. TVC production has created confidence in South African locations, particularly the premier Cape Town location. Great effort has been put into securing the international parts of the city for the safety of international tourists. The effort benefited the "working TVC tourist" and provided confidence badly dented by routine reporting of law and order and violence issues.

The initial focus on TVCs took advantage of the low costs of production in South Africa to grow Cape Town into a leading television commercial production center that has "carved a lucrative niche in shooting sunny, cheap-and-cheerful commercials for packaged goods, whether cereal sports for Japan or jam jingles for Poland."[40] However, with the rand appreciating in value against the U.S. dollar, some of Cape Town's competitiveness has been eroded.

What makes the Cape Film Commission (CFC) and the Dreamworld Film City particularly special in the agenda of greenfields studio construction is the important role—essential in all areas of economic, social, and cultural life in South Africa—of black empowerment. The CFC sees itself as "responsible for driving transformation within the Film Industry, and ensuring that it becomes ever more accessible to people from historically disadvantaged backgrounds." It sees one of its tasks as being to facilitate "training initiatives to ensure participation by people of colour, and playing an introductory role for BEE companies wishing to break into the industry."[41] All of the tenders for the new Cape Town studio were judged on their black empowerment strategies.

Martin Cuff lists a number of threats facing Cape Town in its efforts to establish itself as a viable location for film and television production. He observes that it is still a long haul destination. Cape Town has wet winters, making it not quite a year-round production location like Sydney or the Gold Coast. South African central and regional governments provide only limited production support through taxation and subsidy, and there is a lack of funding for and taxation incentives aimed at local productions with little attention paid to audience development. Although postproduction facilities are being developed, they are limited. There is a lack of research and development funds. Conditions and location fees are not uniform. Foreign exchange rates can hamper technological upgrades and drive up the cost of equipment, and there is a lack of coproduction treaties to facilitate development.[42] There is also a tendency for only split location production to be done in South Africa and Cape Town rather than the total production, so that in recent years Cape Town has functioned as a location for second-unit production, and for the production of smaller films rather than big-budget international blockbusters.

These last comments about the lack of support for domestic film and television production activity open out onto the increasingly lopsided development of South African production capacity. While the economic story of international production is a positive one, the cultural and creative story is one of declining resources and opportunities for local production. Since the heyday of the 1980s, when liberal tax concessions underwrote a production slate of up to one hundred feature films per year, there has been a huge contraction down to some three or four locally produced features per year.[43] Whereas the revival of interest in international production in Ireland was based on the combination and intersection of the cultural and creative focus on locally produced films and an international film friendliness, South African circumstance made this less possible. There is also the additional problem that the preferred destination for international productions—Cape Town—is not the hub of the local film and television production industry that is headquartered in Johannesburg, with the two largest broadcasters, the South African Broadcasting Corporation and the private broadcaster MNET, having production facilities and head offices there. This ensures that Johannesburg and the province of Gauteng benefit most from the South African Broadcasting Corporation's (SABC) commissioning processes.[44] The logical entailment of this is that Cape Town would need to develop its own regional film and television production initiatives to make up the slack, although this will require careful negotiation of the interactions and intersections of the local and international production sectors.

Ciudad de la Luz (City of Light), Spain

Southern Spain played a starring role in "runaway" production of the 1960s and early 1970s when it featured as a location for spaghetti westerns and high-budget Hollywood blockbusters such as *El Cid* and *Lawrence of Arabia*. At this time, director Luis Garcia Berlanga advocated for a new studio to service international production, but international production has been sporadic over the last four decades.[45] Until recently, Spain has not been seen to have had the necessary infrastructure of a modern large studio or the necessary ancillary service and film-friendly policy mechanisms, including regional film commissions, to support international production. In addition, Spain has made significant economic progress since the death of dictator General Franco in 1975. It is no longer the low-cost production center it was during the 1960s, but this is not the ambition of the massive studio, Ciudad de la Luz, that has been proposed for Alicante.

When completed, it is claimed that the studio will include six soundstages— two of them twenty-five thousand square feet; deep tanks, to open in 2005; and a fifty-four-acre backlot capable of handling multiple productions through flexible screens. It will also host an in-house film school and is explicitly pitched at luring big productions from the United States.[46] The development is being financed by the Valencia Regional Government, which is investing over $U.S. 300 million. This represents eight times Spain's annual film subsidy fund.[47] It is one among a number of film-related developments on the part of Spanish regional governments that now considerably outstrip the central government in support of film production and film production infrastructure. While Cuidad de la Luz has not yet cost as much as the Babelsberg refurbishment in Berlin, it is at the high-end of the scale of "studio ideas"—those studios that have been imagined and that exist in commentary but not in reality.

While the studio represents a massive investment in film and studio infrastructure, its location does raise a number of issues. In the 1960s, international production tended to take place in the province of Almeria, some distance from Alicante, and left no lasting legacy of use today. The Valencia Self-Governing Region hosts approximately one-seventh of the Spanish film, video, and television industry, involving some seven thousand workers and six hundred companies, but much of this base is concentrated in the city of Valencia. The proposed studio's distance from Spanish production centers and from Valencia, the closest large production center, may make it difficult to sustain any ongoing connection with these industries, and locally initiated film production activity may take some time to emerge. If Allen Scott is right in that places need to be more than sites for international production in order to become sustainable, then Alicante's problem is that it is outside the normal production loops and is of such a scale and lavish appointments that may be out of reach of local producers. So Alicante may not have the synergies between local and international production, and it may thus be more vulnerable to periods of underutilization until local critical mass is reached.

Alicante is clearly pitched and developed as a "satellite" production location that is to be more a satellite of London or Hollywood than of Madrid or Barcelona. A number of advantageous attributes of the location help explain the enthusiasm for the studio. There are strong, historic connections with Northern Europe through tourism and expatriation. The large expatriate British community and the infrastructure that has grown up to service international tourism on the nearby Costa Brava and Costa del Sol will reduce the strangeness of the location for English-language filmmakers and audiences. The region is able to supply English-language competences as there is a history of dealing with foreign tourists and companies on a routine basis. The Alicante studio becomes, like those on the Gold Coast and in Orlando, a logical extension of an existing regional facilities and services orientation.

The proposed facility will be oriented to large-scale blockbuster production. Split up in a way that enables a number of productions to use the site at the one time, it can have productions just coming in to use the water tank or just coming in to do the production. This makes it well-suited to split location production and also the large-scale megaproduction utilizing all the soundstages. The water-tank features promise to make Alicante competitive with facilities in Malta and Mexico. Its backlot is also designed to facilitate contemporaneous productions through the use of acoustic screens—this not only ensures the capacity to handle a number of productions simultaneously but also ensures that the backlot can service multiple sets for the same films.

The recent establishment of a film commission to promote the region as a location for international production should boost the studio's chances of securing whole and split location productions. The region provides distinctive architecture, particularly churches and housing, to represent itself as itself.

But as in the earlier era, it may be that it is the location's capacity to stand in for somewhere else that ultimately determines its fortunes.

Conclusion

So why, given the heavy burden of risk that they carry, are studios developed in greenfields locations? Typically these studios are the principal vehicles for integrating places and spaces into wider international markets principally for English-language production. They constitute satellite industrial districts. We find, therefore, in these studios perhaps the clearest expression of the logic of globally dispersed, networked production, and the importance of local intermediaries in facilitating global circuits of production, consumption, and finance. They are a response to the openness and competitiveness of global film and television production. And they constitute its limit case. They represent an identifiably new form that has been fed by the globalization and dispersal of economic activity under the project-based system of international production. They have become that much more feasible by the development of telecommunications capability.

As satellite production locations, these studios are at the service of the center. They seek to normalize their offering as much as possible and may aim to become an *extension* of what is available at the center. Typically, they propose themselves as *the center displaced*. As Frank Capra Jr. of Wilmington's Screen Gems studio puts it, "When people get here they realize that it really operates very much like an LA studio, with support facilities like on an LA lot. They feel at home."[48] As satellites, these precincts do not, at least initially, seek or aspire to the alternative center status of a London, Berlin, or Sydney. Rather they seek to become "at a distance" *appendages* imitating, simulating, and complementing the resources at the center. They work within their limits and explore these to secure areas of local advantage and benefit. In this sense, these greenfields sites are the purest expression of internationally networked and integrated production, but they are also the most vulnerable parts of that system.

Notes

1. An example of a single project creating studio infrastructure is *Titanic* and Fox Baja in Mexico; the Gold Coast studios in Australia were initiated with a view to hosting *Total Recall* and were built despite the film being produced elsewhere.

2. Neil M. Coe, "A Hybrid Agglomeration? The Development of a Satellite-Marshallian Industrial District in Vancouver's Film Industry," *Urban Studies* 38, no. 10 (Sept 2001): 1770.

3. Joshua Levitt, "Cameras, Sound, Money, Action . . . : Critics Are Asking If Investments in Film Studios May Not Be Enough to Bring in the Scale of Film-making the City Needs," *Financial Times*, 31 October 2002, 3.

4. Tom de Castella, "Way Out West," *Sight and Sound* 14, no. 1 (January 2004): 9.

5. Passage of the laws was delayed until June 2003, and the Studio City development is now reported to be proceeding.

6. Tim W. Ferguson and William Heuslein, "Cape Dear," *Forbes*, 28 May 2001, 132.

7. David G. Murphy, "The Entrepreneurial Role of Organized Labour in the British Columbia Motion Picture Industry," *Relations Industrielles/Industrial Relations* 52, no. 3 (1997): 531–53.

8. Murphy, "The Entrepreneurial Role of Organized Labour," 549.

9. Murphy, "The Entrepreneurial Role of Organized Labour," 549.

10. Lance Pettitt, *Screening Ireland: Film and Television Representation* (Manchester: Manchester University Press, 2000), 38.

11. Kevin Rockett, "Phases of the Moon: A Short History of Cinema in Ireland," *Film Comment* 30, no. 3 (1994): 25–28.

12. Kevin Rockett, "Irish Cinema: The National in the International," *Cineaste* 24, nos. 2–3 (1999): 23.

13. Desmond Bell, "Communications, Corporatism, and Dependent Development in Ireland," *Journal of Communication* 45, no. 4 (1995): 70–88.

14. Steve Brennan, "Galway Getaway," *Hollywood Reporter*, 5 September 2000, I-8.

15. Hugh Linehan, "Corman Uncovered," *Irish Times*, 22 August 1997, 13.

16. Rockett, "Phases of the Moon," 25.

17. Patrick Garry, "A Different Voice: An Industry Is Born," *Commonweal* 122, no. 6 (1995): 17.

18. Garry, "A Different Voice," 17.

19. Ed W. Marsh, *James Cameron's* Titanic (New York: HarperCollins, 1997), 14.

20. Paula Parisi, Titanic *and the Making of James Cameron: The Inside Story of the Three-Year Adventure That Rewrote Motion Picture History* (London: Orion, 1998), 90.

21. Parisi, Titanic, 90–91.

22. They have also stimulated the dreams of other prospective studio operators such as Francesca Fisher, who announced plans in 2004 to build the first of a number of regional Mexican studios. Fisher's plan involves six soundstages, production support services, a technical film school, an outdoor mall, and a backlot. See Ken Bensinger and Pat Saperstein, "Filmmaker Plans Lavish Studio," *Variety*, 5–11 April 2004, 13.

23. See "Fishermen Try to Hook Titanic," *Variety*, 3 March 1997, 67; "Fish Story," *Hollywood Reporter*, 3 February 1998, 12; Talli Nauman, "Titanic Prompts Pollution Study," United Press International, 6 April 1998.

24. Sue Pavasaris, "Lights, Camera, Ahern! Queensland Film Gets a New Start," *Filmnews* 18, no. 9 (1988): 3; Warner Roadshow Studios, *The Economic Effect of Warner Roadshow Movie World Studios on the Film and Television Industry in Queensland* (Gold Coast, Australia: Warner Roadshow Studios, May 1992), 7.

25. Mike Gasher, *Hollywood North: The Feature Film Industry in British Columbia* (Vancouver: University of British Columbia Press, 2002), 46.

26. Gasher, *Hollywood North*, 118.

27. See Neil M. Coe, "The View from Out West: Embeddedness, Inter-personal Relations and the Development of an Indigenous Film Industry in Vancouver," *Geoforum* 31 (2000): 391–407.

28. Sandra Hall, "Queensland Takes the Plunge," *Bulletin*, 18 December 1979, 65.

29. Another Gold Coast theme park, Dreamworld, houses a different kind of studio; each series of the Australian version of the television show *Big Brother* has been filmed in a specially built house within the Dreamworld complex.

30. Jackman had been general manager of two of Australia's largest exhibition chains—Hoyts and Birch, Carroll and Coyle—had overseen Hoyts's involvement in high-profile Australian productions, and had sold *Crocodile Dundee* in international markets, helping to make it the most successful feature in its year of release and still the most commercially successful Australian feature film of all time.

31. Phelim McAleer, "Where Stars Stroll in the Streets: The Film Industry: Producers Are Flocking In, Attracted by Cheap, Skilled Labour," *Financial Times*, 14 October 2003, 2.

32. Phelim McAleer, "Hollywood's Finest Flock to Romania: Cost Savings and Varied Scenery Make the Former Communist State a Hot Destination for Filmmakers," *Financial Times*, 25 June 2003, 10.

33. Ian Fisher, "On Dracula's Terrain, an Infusion of New Blood," *New York Times*, 22 July 2003, A4.

34. McAleer, "Where Stars Stroll in the Streets," 2.

35. Fisher, "On Dracula's Terrain," A4.

36. Martin Cuff, *Business Plan 2003/04 Including Industry Growth Strategy, Marketing Strategy, Film Development Strategy* (Cape Town: Cape Film Commission, June 2003), 17.

37. Cuff, *Business Plan 2003/04*, 38.

38. Cuff, *Business Plan 2003/04*, 3.

39. Cuff, *Business Plan 2003/04*, 4.

40. Emiko Terezono, Peter Hudson, Amy Kazmin, Ian Bickerton, and John Reed, "Creative Minnows Hunt Big Fish: Rich Imaginations and Inspirational Settings are Helping Advertising Backwaters Emerge in to the Mainstream," *Financial Times*, 18 November 2003, 10.

41. Cuff, *Business Plan 2003/04*, 2.

42. Cuff, *Business Plan 2003/04*, 10.

43. Cuff, *Business Plan 2003/04*, 6.

44. Cuff, *Business Plan 2003/04*, 5.

45. In the early 1990s, the BBC built an extensive "studio" near Malaga for a soap opera based on the lives of British expatriates in Spain, *El Dorado*, but the show was canceled after a year.

46. John Hopewell and Emiliano de Pablos, "Gov't Backs Top Studio Complex," *Variety*, 19–25 January 2004, 10.

47. Hopewell and de Pablos, 10.

48. Ferguson and Heuslein, "Cape Dear."

CHAPTER SIX

From National to
International Film Studios

This chapter charts the contrasting experiences, fortunes, and strategies of three studio complexes—Barrandov in the Czech Republic, Cinecittà in Italy, and Studio Babelsberg in Germany. Each of these studios was built before World War II and designed to be a national production epicenter, although each has hosted international production at various times. All were transformed in the 1990s with a view to servicing principally English-language film production, but each remains important to domestic film production in their respective countries, is home to at least one television network, and hosts a considerable amount of local and international television production.

As "national film studios," these facilities typically employed large numbers of film workers across a variety of functions and services and commanded considerable governmental and public investment and attention. The size of these facilities, and the symbolic and political investment in them, played major roles in determining the scope, scale, and style of domestic film production before the 1990s as well as the type and amount of international production they could serve in both the past and the present. As each was partially or fully privatized in the 1990s, their workforce and commitment to local production diminished, but each remains the subject of broad public debate, a legacy perhaps of the local filmmaking community and the wider public's sense of "ownership" deriving from their prior status as national film studios. Each studio now operates in radically different circumstances from those of earlier periods, and each now competes for production with a host of new or revitalized facilities in their own country and internationally.

The three studios have adopted different strategies in recent years to deal with changing circumstances, and each has embraced a different mix of local and international film, television, and new media production work. A particular focus in this chapter will be on the way these studio complexes have evolved in response to changing domestic and Europe-wide political and economic circumstances over the last two decades, including the fall of communism and with it the privileged and protected position enjoyed by national film studios; the division of Czechoslovakia and the reunification of Germany; and the policy priorities, funding strategies, and expansion of the European Union.

Barrandov

Named after the French geologist and paleontologist Joachim Barrande, who had worked on the site in the nineteenth century, the Barrandov Studios were built on a hill to the southwest of Prague between 1931 and 1933. The studios were owned by the brothers Milos and Vaclav Havel, the uncle and father of the first president of the Czech Republic, as a means to supplement their film distribution business, which had been affected by restrictions on film imports by producing sound films in Czech for a hungry national market. National production sustained the studios for much of the 1930s and particularly in the period of communist rule from the late 1940s until the late 1980s, but international production—which dominates Barrandov's contemporary history—was a feature of the studios' output from the early days. As Czech film historian Jaroslav Brož writes, "For reasons of prestige and in order to demonstrate the advantage the new studios offered to prospective international producers, the A-B company [Barrandov's parent company] undertook to produce itself foreign language versions of three costly historical superfilms designed principally for distribution in France" in the 1930s— Julien Duvivier's French-language version of *Le Golem/The Golem* (1936) and multilanguage versions of Viktor Tourjansky's *Volga en flammes/Volha v plamenech/Volga in Flames* (1933) and Nicolas Farkas's *Port Arthur* (1936).[1]

Shortly after the occupation of Czechoslovakia by the Nazis in 1939, the complex was expropriated and overhauled as part of the "'Germanizing' and 'Aryanizing' of the entire film industry." Three huge new interconnecting stages were built at Barrandov between 1941 and 1945 as it "became the most important bridgehead of German production outside the borders of the Reich," and these stages remain the complex's main draw to this day.[2] Barrandov's technology and equipment base was supplemented by materials brought from Berlin and confiscated from occupied France and from the Cinecittà studios in Rome. In the last two years of the war, Barrandov became increasingly important for German cinema production as facilities in Berlin and Munich were damaged by Allied bombing.

During World War II, an underground film committee made plans for the postwar resurrection and reconstruction of the Czech film industry, and as a consequence, the film industry was among the first industries to be nationalized by presidential decree late in 1945.[3] Antonín J. Liehm argues that the "rise in the prestige of [Czech] film . . . during the Nazi occupation" due to the limitations on Czech production at this time, which actually encouraged a culture of experimentation among filmmakers, coupled with a pent-up demand for "serious artistic" films and heightened interest in national cultural expression worked to create support and acceptance for the nationalization of the film industry.[4] The expertise and equipment available in the Barrandov and Hostivar Studios were essential to the success of this project.

From the 1960s, the Barrandov complex was periodically hired to international filmmakers as a means to earn valuable foreign currency. In 1964, West German producers made the first full-length non-Czechoslovak feature there. German production constituted a substantial part of the complex's foreign film production in succeeding decades, and it remains important to this day as Germany's importance in film and television finance and consumption grows. Hollywood producers also made use of the facilities before the fall of the communist regime, with *Yentl* and *Amadeus* filmed there in the early 1980s. In 1987, Canada and Czechoslovakia signed a coproduction treaty that led to a variety of projects being made at Barrandov in the 1990s and assisted in developing links between Canadian and Czech companies.

The contemporary turn to international production as the mainstay of Barrandov's work began with the Velvet Revolution of 1989, in which the communist regime was replaced by democratic and market-oriented systems. Under the new government, Barrandov's annual state subsidy of 170 million crowns (then approximately U.S.$6.3 million)[5] was slashed. Although the regional Czech government was convinced to inject 120 million crowns (ca. U.S.$4 million) into local filmmaking in 1991,[6] 1,700 of Barrandov's employees were made redundant as the facility came to terms with newly straitened circumstances.[7] The domestic production sector was hit hard by the political upheaval and the subsequent decision to privatize the Barrandov complex.

Plans to privatize the studios in the early 1990s were bitterly resisted by many Czech filmmakers, who formed the Association for the Foundation of

Czech Cinematography to lobby against the plans. The group warned that a fully commercial studio would be devastating for local production.[8] In response, the Ministry of Culture kept a "golden share" in the complex, a move designed to guarantee that the complex was used for filmmaking and that Czech filmmakers continued to have access to the facilities. But in 2000, the golden share was declared legally invalid by a commercial court, and the state's influence over the operation and future of the complex was diminished. In its place, it has been proposed that future owners sign a contract with the state that would ensure continuity of production and guarantee some amount of local production.

In June 1992, the complex was sold to Cinepont (later renamed AB Barrandov), a company entailing twenty-five film managers and workers headed by Barrandov's executive officer Vaclav Marhoul, for 500 million crowns (then ca. U.S.$20 million), although the final payment of 250 million crowns was not made until 2000.[9] In the first years of the country's political transition, the studio's management team sought to exploit cost advantages over other facilities to service international production and attract coproductions to keep the complex going. In 1992, the complex initiated the first Eastern European location market at the Karlovy Vary film festival to promote international production in the region. Four years later, the steel company Moravia Steel became the majority shareholder in AB Barrandov.

Under Marhoul's management, Barrandov pursued a dual strategy of attracting international film and television production and becoming a major domestic communications corporation. It expanded its media holdings to include a radio station, a movie magazine, and an advertising company, and planned to develop a theme park. The studio was also involved in the production of twenty-five of the sixty Czech-language films made between 1992 and 1996, with Marhoul claiming that the studio had suffered substantial losses on its local production.[10] In 1997, Marhoul left Barrandov after a loss of 170 million crowns (ca. U.S.$5 million) in the previous year. With Marhoul's departure, the studio returned to a focus on coproduction and facilities rental for largely international clients. Barrandov's current primary owner, Moravia Steel, has been open to offers for the complex since 1997, and all likely buyers mention the need to invest in studio infrastructure. In May 2002, Moravia Steel's 80 percent share in Barrandov's holding company was put out to public tender, although according to studio sources, the company is no longer seeking to sell the facility.

Since the privatization of the studios, various attempts have been made to connect productively with the local film industry. In 1992, a foundation and a script development fund were established by the complex's owners to contribute to the funding of Czech films. In addition, the State Fund for the Support and Development of Czech Cinematography was established to distribute profits from sales of films in Barrandov's film library to the production and distribution of local films. However, this remains a sore point between the studio and the government. The culture minister lodged a suit against AB Barrandov in 1998 to recover 117 million crowns in copyright royalties owed to the fund.[11] The fund had been seriously depleted in recent years as a result of falling revenue from cinema attendance, its other source of funds.

As a state-controlled entity, Barrandov produced between thirty and forty feature films annually, and the vast majority were Czechoslovak productions. Pre-1989 funding was awarded through semiautonomous film units closely connected with the Barrandov complex. After 1989, the local film industry entered a period of sustained crisis, with the number of domestic features dropping dramatically as state subsidies were slashed. Financing for Czech film production is now competitively awarded to individual projects by the State Fund of the Czech Republic for the Support and Development of Czech Cinematography. This can be supplemented by grants and loans awarded by the European Union's production support schemes and by individual European coproduction partners, with France playing the most prominent role. The Czech Republic was barred from membership of the European Union's (EU) MEDIA Plus program for some time because Czech audiovisual legislation did not conform to EU standards.[12]

Czech television companies have increasingly become important financiers of Czech film production in the last few years.[13] In 1994, Eastern Europe's first nationwide commercial television channel, TV Nova, began a production relationship with Barrandov by commissioning a children's program, a game show, and a soap opera. In 1999, TV Nova relocated to the Barrandov complex following a dispute with the broadcaster's primary service provider, CNTS. The dispute is currently before the courts.

In the context of a transitional society, the partial collapse of the local production industry made Barrandov very interested in presenting itself almost exclusively as a facility offering skilled crews and specialized skills to the international film production industry. For Barrandov, international production became a means of keeping the facility going. In a sense, this was the only strategy available to them. In a postcommunist society the government was neither able nor committed to sustain funding for a state-run facility, which became perceived to be a liability. The international production industry allowed the complex to be kept going—and upgraded where possible.

Although the reputation of the complex and of Prague as a location was damaged by the price inflation and red tape experienced by the production of *Mission: Impossible* in 1995, since 1999 a significant number of major international productions have been lured to the city. The boom in production after 1999 has encouraged the establishment of a large number of production and production services firms, with about three thousand listed in the city's 2001 film directory.[14] Smaller firms tend to work with larger firms on a film-by-film basis, in sharp contrast to the pre-1989 system, in which film units "usually led by a well established director, comprised several directors, as well as screenwriters, cameramen, set and costume designers, and sometimes even actors, all salaried employees who only received bonuses upon the completion and release of a new film."[15] Another studio complex, Prague Studios, was established on the site of a former aircraft factory to service the growing volume of international production. The site on the outskirts of Prague contains three soundstages that are claimed to be the largest in Central Europe.

Barrandov has its limitations, particularly its lack of extensive, modern, on-site postproduction facilities (although the availability of a range of postproduction services in Prague offsets this absence), and the reluctance of its parent company to invest in new infrastructure. A U.S.$10 million digital visual effects facility was mooted in 1996 but did not eventuate, largely as a result of management upheavals and the reluctance of the complex's owners to make the necessary investments. The dearth until recently of ancillary facilities such as five-star hotels in and around Prague has also been cited as a hindrance to future growth. The film-processing laboratories in the complex recently upgraded their equipment, increasing capacity from 1,000 to 2,800 meters of film per hour, at a cost of 25 million crowns. The laboratories are reported to generate around 35 percent of the studio's revenues.[16] In November 2001, it was announced that an additional 4,000 square meters of soundstages would be built.

Despite the need for investment in facilities, international production at Barrandov, as in Prague more widely, is booming, with the studio complex competing with a growing number of facilities for a share of footloose international production. At one level, the contemporary concentration of international production activity in Prague is surprising. The Czech Republic is a small country, and until recently there was no film commission infrastructure supporting, facilitating, and encouraging international production. Nor was there a system of governmental incentives and tax breaks encouraging location production. Furthermore, the country's domestic film production collapsed in the transition to a market economy and a differently organized production base.

Yet Prague has not only been able to maintain a significant studio complex, Barrandov, but also to generate the establishment of new one, Prague

Studios, a refurbished former aircraft factory built to American production specifications a few years ago—all without the benefit of a healthy domestic film production sector, governmental agency assistance, or incentives.

There are several reasons behind Prague's current position as a major production venue. First, the city's built environment has advantages as a prize location for film production and television commercials alike. As producer Anne Pivcevic, puts it:

> There's a huge range of unspoilt architectural styles and landscape to be found here, the like of which I've seen nowhere else in Europe. One huge plus point is that it escaped bombing in the World War II—you can walk into any Prague street, any village or café, and find what appears to be a ready-made set.[17]

The city's architecture makes it a favorite for period productions, and it has seen recent re-creations of Europe in medieval times (*A Knight's Tale*), the eighteenth century (*The Scarlet Pimpernel, Plunkett & Macleane*), the nineteenth century (*From Hell, Shanghai Knights, Oliver Twist*), and the twentieth century (*Anne Frank*). In an attempt to cash in on this feature, the Prague City Council increased location permits and rental fees in 2002 by around 500 percent, but, following pressure from local and international producers based in the city, these increases were reversed late in 2002.

Second, Prague is advantaged by the existence of both skilled crew and substantial studio complexes. Skilled crew can supply production services to international production with labor costs around 40 percent cheaper than in the United Kingdom or United States. Indeed, a ready pool of skilled, underemployed film workers was available, as a large proportion of Barrandov's several thousand–strong workforce was laid off in the early 1990s with the industry moving to private contractors on a film-by-film basis.

This shift in employment led to a lack of unionization among film workers and an absence of strict work rules, making for a compliant labor force. To this day, wages continue to remain low in comparison to other international production centers. However, there is growing concern in the Czech Republic that the country's imminent accession to the European Union will result in rising prices and wage inflation, thereby wiping out what to date has been the Czech film industry's primary competitive advantage.

Prague film workers' considerable skills in set construction and art direction are also significant factors in attracting production, particularly when coupled with the facilities of the city's studio complexes. This combination of skills and facilities means that more of the production can be done in Prague, with sets built in soundstages and backlots to complement the city locations. The combination is also proving useful in attracting science fiction productions, particularly to the new Prague Studios (both *Dune* and *Children of Dune* were filmed at the Prague Studios).

A third factor that helps to explain Prague's seemingly disproportionate share of current international production is the particular importance of foreign, particularly American, capital and companies as investors. Unlike other continental "media cities," Prague's infrastructure is substantially maintained by money from outside Europe. A number of non-Czech, usually but not always American, production companies have been established in the city over the 1990s as English-language international production developed. One of the most active and successful small firms located at Barrandov is Stillking Productions Ltd, now Stillking Films, a company founded by Briton Matthew Stillman in 1992. The company has grown from a tiny advertising and music video production house to a major Czech media player. It made the film XXX, starring Samuel L. Jackson, in Prague, and it is regularly reported to be a potential buyer of the Barrandov complex. In April 2002, Barrandov hosted a delegation of independent American producers in an effort to win more midrange international production.

Finally, both Barrandov and Prague have a long-standing history of engagement with the international production industry, stretching back to Barrandov's initial construction in the 1930s. Barrandov is best known today for its international production services, but while few Czech films make use of the complex's stages and set construction expertise, the studio does provide a range of services to domestic film production, including costume, prop, and camera hire, and film processing. Barrandov's current situation as one of the major European venues for high-budget, English-language, studio-based feature film production is of course a far cry from its previous status as an epicenter of local production. Given the size of the Czech market, local production is unlikely ever again to sustain the facility on its own, but while Barrandov Studios and the city of Prague continue in 2004 to attract high volumes of international production, there can be no guarantees that these volumes will be maintained in the long term. Competitors in London and Berlin also argue that Prague has been "shot out," meaning that what was once the city's principal attraction—the diversity of its architecture and locations—is now a disadvantage as so many films have filmed there. This may not affect Barrandov, however, as many of the feature films shooting there now have substantial studio-based components and extensive built sets rather than relying on found locations.

It remains unclear how the Czech Republic's accession to the European Union will affect film production in the country, with claims that wages and costs will rise disputed by local industry figures. Access to EU funding, co-production, and media programs may provide some compensation should prices rise. The recent move to establish a Czech Film Commission should also be of benefit to international as well as local production.

Cinecittà

The 400,000-square-meter or 99-hectare plot of Cinecittà, formerly on the rural edge of Rome but now surrounded by urban sprawl, contains 22 production stages ranging in size from 400 to 3,200 square meters, a 10-hectare outdoor shooting area, 280 permanent dressing rooms and offices, 21 makeup areas, 82 prop stores, workshops and warehouses, a sizeable water tank, 40 editing rooms, and 7 sound mixing and dubbing rooms equipped with the latest digital sound equipment. Cinecittà also owns a further 2,000 acres of backlot on an estate near Lake Bracciano. Cinecittà Studios employs the entire workforce, which can be hired in whole or in part by producers using the facility. It is without doubt one of the most important studio facilities in Europe, not only for its capacity to service film and television production but also for its symbolic value as an icon of Italian production and a conduit between the Italian industry and the world. For example, it was no accident that the launch of Italian pay-TV network Sky Italia, majority owned by Rupert Murdoch's News Corporation, was held at Cinecittà in May 2003.

Federico Fellini once said

> all meetings, relationships, experiences, trips, begin and end for me in the studios at Cinecittà. All that exists outside the gates of Cinecittà is an enormous storehouse to visit, to plunder, to transport avidly and tirelessly inside Cinecittà. Maybe it is a privilege, maybe a servitude—but it is my way of being.[18]

The love affair between Fellini and Rome's Cinecittà Studios continues long after the great director's death. Number one on the studio website's list of ten reasons to shoot there is "Following in Fellini's steps—shooting at his 'temple of dreams' and enjoying *La Dolce Vita*." The opportunity to work on the same stages as this Italian master has inspired filmmakers like Martin Scorsese to shoot in Rome, but while Fellini's spirit permeates almost every aspect of the studio's self-promotion, there is much more to its story.

Cinecittà literally means "cinema city," an apt moniker for this huge complex that remains the largest in continental Europe almost seventy years after it was built. The studio was constructed at the direction of industrialist and film entrepreneur Carlo Roncoroni and the Fascist government's general director of cinematography, Luigi Freddi, to a design by the architect Gino

Peressutti on the site of another studio that had been mysteriously destroyed by fire. Although the studio was not technically owned or operated by the government until 1938, the dictator Mussolini associated himself closely with the project, laying the foundation stone in 1936 and presiding over the opening ceremony in 1937. The complex was bombed by the Allies and looted by the Germans during World War II, and it was used first as a prisoner of war camp and later a center for displaced persons immediately after the war. Indeed, the prohibition placed by the American military immediately after the war on filming at Cinecittà was one of the main impetuses behind the distinctive shot-on-the-streets style of Italian neorealist filmmakers such as Vittorio de Sica and Roberto Rossellini.

When filmmaking was again permitted there, Cinecittà became for many years the only substantial rival European location for high-budget international film production to the United Kingdom's Pinewood and Shepperton. Cinecittà's reputation as "Hollywood on the Tiber" was established in the 1950s and 1960s when it hosted epic productions such as *Quo Vadis?* (1951), *Ben Hur* (1959) and *Cleopatra* (1963), spaghetti westerns, including *A Fistful of Dollars* (1964),[19] and dramas such as *Roman Holiday* (1953). But at the same time, it was also the epicenter of Italian feature film production, with as much as half of the total Italian film output in some decades produced at Cinecittà since its opening in 1937. Historian of Italian cinema Peter Bondanella describes the two decades between the late 1950s and the late 1970s as "the golden age of Cinecittà."[20] Fellini made nearly all his films there—including *La Dolce Vita* (1960), *8 1/2* (1963), and *Fred and Ginger* (1986). The studio also featured prominently in Fellini's semiautobiographical feature *Intervista* (1987).

Spiraling debts in the late 1960s and 1970s, in part as a result of the Hollywood studios' withdrawal from European production and retreat to Los Angeles, at this time led to a decline in Cinecittà's output and profile. Changes in the rules governing the employment of foreigners in films made in Italy in the early 1970s also had a significant impact upon production activity. Dino de Laurentiis claims he left Italy in 1970 because "a law came in saying you must use mostly Italian people in making films"—before this law, he claimed "that it had been 50:50, spread any way, so that in *War and Peace* (1956) I could use stars like Audrey Hepburn and Henry Fonda and an American director King Vidor alongside an Italian cameraman, designer and so forth."[21] The security situation in Italy further discouraged offshore film activity and investment—particularly after a series of high-profile terrorist actions in the mid-1970s.

International production at Cinecittà consisted not only of production generated elsewhere but also of production generated by Italian companies and creative producers, such as Carlo Ponti, Dino de Laurentiis, and Alberto Grimaldi. Ponti's retirement and the departure of de Laurentiis and Grimaldi to the United States in the 1970s robbed the complex of its impresarios and severely reduced the volume of work coming into the studios.[22] In addition, the golden generation of directors—Fellini, Visconti, de Sica, Antonioni—who had helped create Cinecittà's reputation were entering their twilight years. These directors had used the studios extensively and were capable of commanding the attention of local and international investors. Their departure from the filmmaking scene was then a further blow to Cinecittà's fortunes.

In the 1980s, some of the land owned by Cinecittà was sold for housing and retail development in order to reduce the studios' debts—the Roman forum built for *Cleopatra* became a shopping mall known as Cinecittà 2. High-budget international productions such as *Once Upon a Time in America* (1984), *The Name of the Rose* (1986), *The Last Emperor* (1987), and *The Adventures of Baron Munchausen* (1988) returned to the studios and marked a partial recovery, but Cinecittà faced continuing structural and systemic difficulties.[23]

Italy's increasingly complex tax bureaucracy contributed to making Cinecittà a less film-friendly environment than its U.K. competitors, Pinewood and Shepperton.[24] Cecchi Gori, Italy's largest film distributor, claimed in a 1996 *Financial Times* article that "the Americans have stayed away because we need their money so badly that we give them an unfair deal," citing disincentives such as value-added-tax (VAT) and "tax surprises." Apparently, nontransparent tax laws could create surprises, uncertainties, and delays for producers. As Cinecittà's administrative director Degli Esposti recalled in 1996, "I had an American producer who wanted to make a film at Cinecittà but who was still waiting for the return of VAT on his last production eight years ago. I went to the government and got them to hand it over. It is absurd that Hollywood companies must keep an office open for years after making their film just to reclaim taxes."[25]

At the same time, the fortunes of Italian cinema were changing. Domestic box office revenues declined dramatically after 1976, which, in combination with falls in the core European markets for Italian cinema—France and Germany—reduced the returns to Italian filmmakers and meant in consequence that the new generation of filmmakers would not have access to the capital or infrastructures of the earlier generation. These difficulties were offset to an extent by the explosive growth of television production in the wake of the advent of commercial television stations and later networks, after a 1976 ruling that the public broadcaster RAI's monopoly was unconstitutional. The needs of domestic television rather than cinema began to drive patterns of investment in Italian audiovisual production, and Italian film-makers became oriented toward television rather than cinema.[26] Indeed, the Italian broadcasters—public and private—became over the 1980s and 1990s the major investors in Italian feature film production released in cinemas.

This situation left Cinecittà increasingly isolated. Its orientation had been toward high-budget international productions and local feature productions with big budgets and international partners. Neither characterized the new situation. As a result, Cinecittà lost some of its central role in defining audiovisual production in Italy and was increasingly bypassed. With budgets for features and TV drama production typically lower, and lower expectations in terms of image and sound standards, the Cinecittà soundstages were too expensive for many productions. Designed to accommodate many films at once, its extensive facilities were soon underutilized as producers shot on location or used smaller, cheaper, and less well-equipped studios. In addition, the policy of decentralizing RAI's television production further eroded Cinecittà and Rome's central position. When RAI formalized its arrangements for drama production in 1995, Cinecittà was to be the venue for coproducing its feature film slate and investing in features, while Milan was to specialize in TV movies, Turin sitcoms, and Naples soap operas.[27]

Domestic television work became an increasingly important component of Cinecittà's operations. In the process the studios became, almost by default rather than plan, a media city in which television and advertising production would contribute around 40 per cent of its annual revenue by the mid-1990s.[28] But consistent production levels could not be guaranteed. In May 1993, as thousands of props and items of furniture were auctioned off to meet some of the studios' debts, Cinecittà was "host to a single Italian television production."[29]

Toward the end of the 1990s, Cinecittà again became a significant destination for high-budget international feature production as well as a major center for local television and feature production. In recent years, *The English Patient* (1996), *Daylight* (1996), *Titus* (1999), *The Talented Mr. Ripley* (1999), *U-571* (2000), *Gangs of New York* (2002) and *The Passion of the Christ* (2004) have been shot at Cinecittà. At the same time, the complex has become a center for Italian television production, with television companies occupying some if its biggest stages with "live shows and quiz games . . . beamed to millions of households" and teenagers queuing up "at its gates in the hope of making a career in television."[30]

As was the case for Barrandov in the Czech Republic and Babelsberg in Germany, the renovation of Cinecittà in the 1990s was tied to a strategy of (partial) privatization that was not only seen as necessary to attract international production but considered "critically important in helping restore Italian cinema."[31] Cinecittà Studios SpA was privatized in 1997, and in 1998, its parent entity was launched as a joint-stock company known as Cinecittà Holding SpA, with the Italian government retaining a controlling interest through the Department for Arts and Cultural Activity. Cinecittà Holding is currently the largest shareholder in Cinecittà Studios (17.5 percent). The Istituto Luce SpA, a government-owned structure that operates in the production, distribution, and exhibition sectors and is the main national film archive, owns 7.5 percent of shares in Cinecittà Studios, with other major shareholders being the Aurelio de Laurentiis film production company Filmauro Srl, which owns 15 percent; the electrical appliance mogul Vittorio Merloni (15 percent); clothing manufacturer Diego Della Valle (15 percent); Vittorio Cecchi Gori, owner of the largest Italian film distribution and production company (11.25 percent); film producer and distributor Robert Haggiag (7.5 percent); and the Italian bank Efibanca (7.5 percent).

In recent years, a variety of strategies have been pursued to make Cinecittà a viable media city studio complex, some highly innovative, and some modeled on the success of other complexes elsewhere. After the construction of the shopping mall Cinecittà 2 in the 1980s, a number of schemes have been hatched to make Cinecittà "more than a studio." A proposal to build a communications center to support Cinecittà's "cinematographic vocation," featuring cinemas, teaching facilities, and a museum was partially implemented in 1994.[32] Cinecittà Studios' sister company Cinecittà Entertainment manages the studio's logo and brand, produces the studio's two theme television channels, Cinemovie and RAI Sat Cinema, and produces the annual David di Donatello–RAI Uno film awards. Various attempts have been made to establish a movie theme park on the Cinecittà site, the most recent resulting in the establishment of Cinecittà World Inc. in April 2003, but to date the theme park has not progressed beyond the drawing board. A studio tour opened in 1994 to exploit domestic and international tourist interest in "the principal site of Italy's golden age of filmmaking."[33] In March 2004, Cinecittà launched Cinecittà Campus, a training institution for theater, dance, television, cinema, and fashion inspired by the Actor's Studio in New York.

A variety of strategies have been adopted to redevelop Cinecittà as a "working film and TV studio,"[34] with an emphasis on planning the integration of film and television production, rather than accommodating conflicting demands on the ad hoc basis that had previously been the norm. From 1994, Cinecittà's management team sought agreements with public and private audiovisual companies, particularly the major private broadcaster (then

Fininvest) and the public broadcaster RAI. The agreement with RAI involved a commitment to coproduce "eight Italian films and invest in 17 other projects."[35] These initiatives acknowledged the reality of Cinecittà's already significant dependence on both state and commercial television.[36] The 1995 program to "relaunch" Cinecittà centered on a "digital village" with a view to creating "an integrated audiovisual services company" and moving away from the complex's image as principally a "space for rent."[37] The digital village proposal formed part of the plan for Cinecittà to explore synergies between television and cinema, and to play a role in the development of interactive multimedia products through partnerships with telecommunications companies.[38] In short, Cinecittà was being positioned as a leader in new media innovation and an incubator for film, television, and new media partnerships, but it was not until 2001 that Cinecittà Digital opened for business.[39]

Alongside these plans to make Cinecittà more than a film studio, considerable efforts have been made to make the complex "more than Italian" by enabling Cinecittà to compete with studio complexes around the world for international production work. In this regard, emphasis has been placed on

- its position near a variety of locations in and around Rome and its extensive backlot,
- the prices it charges (a favorable exchange rate),
- its traditional skills in set decoration, costume design, and set construction,
- its upgraded postproduction facilities, and
- its capacity to offer "full service."

To assist the studio's competitiveness, much energy has been expended to build up its liaison network, improve its profile with international producers, and generate business. Cinecittà maintains offices in London, Rome, and New York, and in July 2003, it created Cinecittà Financial Consulting to facilitate the financing of international projects, broker partnerships with Italian investors, and assist producers to negotiate a path through the Italian tax system.

Cinecittà's management actively pursued international partnerships in the 1990s and early 2000s with varying degrees of success. Major international production companies were courted and encouraged to set up shop in Rome in an effort to echo the situation in the 1950s and 1960s when Hollywood majors based themselves in Rome and bankrolled Italian-language production for European and American audiences while simultaneously producing high-budget English-language feature films. Miramax established a subsidiary, Miramax Italia, in 2000 to finance and distribute Italian films and to coordinate the company's international production in Italy. The renewed American interest in filming in Italy and financing Italian projects was termed "Miramaxizzazione" in honor of the leading role played by the company,[40] but Miramax Italia was radically restructured in 2003 and ceased to exist by the middle of 2004.

Links were also forged between Cinecittà and other studio complexes to share work and infrastructure. In 1994, Babelsberg and Cinecittà signed a cooperation agreement covering the sharing of costumes, sets, and possible cofinancing of productions.[41] Cinecittà was also used for high-budget features in conjunction with the water tank facilities in Malta for Dino de Laurentiis's production *U-571*, the veteran producer's first film in Italy for many years.

One of Cinecittà's claimed advantages over its international competitors is the studio's practice of retaining sets constructed for particular films rather than dismantling them at the end of the shoot, in accordance with normal industry practice. Recycling and renovating existing sets enables producers to "build sophisticated physical sets at a fraction of the normal cost."[42] Both Martin Scorsese's *Gangs of New York* and Mel Gibson's *The Passion of the Christ* made use of recycled sets when filming in Rome. This practice requires considerable space to store prebuilt sets with a view to their later reuse and so is unsuitable for many studio complexes where there are limits on the possibility of expansion and where space is at a premium.

The turnaround in Cinecittà's fortunes in recent years and its success in attracting international and domestic film and television production prompted the purchase in 2003 of the rival Roma Studios facility, formerly owned by Dino de Laurentiis and previously known as Dinocittà. Cinecittà and Roma Studios were hosting rival U.S. television series on the Roman empire in 2004 when the latter was virtually destroyed by fire in an echo of the conflagration that presaged the construction of Cinecittà in the 1930s. Despite fierce competition from old rivals such as Pinewood-Shepperton, Babelsberg, and Barrandov, as well as from new domestic players such as the Lumiq Studios in Turin[43] and facilities in Eastern Europe, Cinecittà remains an important player in international film and television production.

However, despite ongoing discussions between film industry representatives and the Italian government, there is no tax shelter legislation in Italy similar to that on offer in many other countries that are competing for international production work. In combination with the relatively high costs of production in Italy compared to some other European locations—particularly the emerging Eastern European centers—and the strength of film unions, which has protected wages and conditions but acts as a disincentive for some international producers—Cinecittà finds itself at a disadvantage in relation to its competitors. As a consequence, the studio management have had to continually innovate and try new strategies in core business areas and beyond to maintain Cinecittà's position among the elite studio facilities. Cinecittà's history and the prestige that attaches to it have been important factors in attracting high-profile international clients, but the variety of different plans and ideas that have been put forward in recent years to keep the facility in business perhaps illustrate the limits to which it is possible to trade on these intangibles in the contemporary production environment.

Studio Babelsberg

In the twelve years after it was privatized in 1992 and sold to a subsidiary of the French corporation Compagnie Generale des Eaux (now the international media conglomerate Vivendi) and a British property development company for about DM140 million, around €1 billion were invested to transform the historic studio complex at Babelsberg near Berlin into the prototypical media city development, complete with theme park, film school, museum, the latest digital facilities, and an extensive area for the offices of media companies. In mid-2004, Studio Babelsberg was sold to a group of German investors led by Carl Woebcken, managing director of Berlin Animation Film, and Christoph Fisser, managing director of the Munich studio facility Studio Atelierbetriebe Schwabing (SAS) for €1.[44] The sale of Studio Babelsberg had been the subject of much speculation ever since the expiry of the agreement between Vivendi and the agency responsible for privatizing the assets of the former East Germany that the facility would not be sold on for ten years after privatization. The choice of new owners did not meet with unanimous approval; the studio workforce sent an open letter to German chancellor Gerhard Schroeder criticizing the choice and raising fears about the future of Studio Babelsberg.[45] At a press conference shortly after the takeover was made public, the new owners announced that Vivendi had provided €18 million as "start-up financing" and that "the main strategy is and remains the orientation of the studios to large, international cinema."[46] But, according to Woebcken, the deal was more than just a commercial transaction:

> Studio Babelsberg is not just a business venture for us. . . . It's overwhelmingly an affair of the heart. Babelsberg is a legend, but it's also a business. If the legend is to survive, it has to stand on solid legs. . . . That's our mission: We want

to make Babelsberg fit for the future so that in 10, 20 or 50 years there will still be a living legend and not just a dead myth.[47]

Like Cinecittà, the modern Babelsberg relies to a great extent on (parts of) its history in the marketing and promotion of the contemporary facility. This is a somewhat ironic strategy, given the heterotopic character of a film studio and the play with history and the real that characterized production at Babelsberg in its heyday in the 1920s and 1930s. On a visit to what was then the Ufa Studios in Neubabelsberg, the German critic Siegfried Kracauer wrote of the "world made of papier-mâché" in which everything is "guaranteed unnatural and everything exactly like nature."

> The masters of this world display a gratifying lack of any sense of history; their want of piety knows no restraint—they intervene every-where. They build cultures and then destroy them as they see fit. They sit in judgement over entire cities and let fire and brimstone rain down upon them if the film calls for it. For them, nothing is meant to last; the most grandiose creation is built with an eye to its demolition.[48]

The Babelsberg complex has a long and checkered production history, with the first (glass-walled) film production studio built on the site in 1912 by the Berlin film company Bioscop. The facility was expanded several times after World War I, and following the merger of the leading German film companies Universum Film AG (Ufa) and Decla-Bioscop in the 1920s, the facility became "the legendary 'Ufa film city,' the company's major fortress in its competitive war against Hollywood," a state-of-the-art facility and the largest film studio in Europe at that time.[49]

> The new filming hall with its steel framework and massive walls measures 123.5 meters long by 56 wide and 14 high at the catwalks. With all auxiliary space included, the total floor area is about 8,000 square meters and the total enclosed space 20,000 cubic meters. The facility has all necessary technical equipment and options. The large hall can be divided by movable masonry walls so that several major films and a number of smaller films can be shot at the same time.[50]

The combination of technical developments, high capital investment, the organizational expertise of producers like Erich Pommer, and the imagination and inventiveness of filmmakers and crafts workers enabled the creation of what Klaus Kreimeier describes as "a new type of film studio."[51] The vast majority of Ufa's output in the 1920s was produced on the stages at Babelsberg, including such classic films as *The Blue Angel* (1930) and *Metropolis* (1926). The catastrophic failure of the latter film upon release was one of the major factors in the financial disaster that befell Ufa in the late 1920s and precipitated the company's transformation into a vehicle for the promotion of initially conservative and ultimately Fascist political causes.[52] In 1929, the facility was equipped for the production of sound films with the construction of the "Tonkreuz," or "sound cross," composed of four studios laid out in the shape of a cross, which survives to this day. Kreimeier argues that with the addition of the Tonkreuz and surrounding workshops, editing and viewing rooms, a special-effects studio, and a laboratory, "the old film city had been transformed into a modern media center"[53]—the precursor of the media city that would emerge on the Babelsberg site in the 1990s.

Adolf Hitler and his Minister of Propaganda and Public Enlightenment, Joseph Goebbels, well understood the propaganda value of film, and Babelsberg remained an important production center after the Nazis took power in 1933. Later in the decade, Ufa became a state-owned company, with Babelsberg a principal production venue into the World War II years until Allied bombing forced much production to shift to the Barrandov studios in Prague. In late April 1945, advancing Soviet troops reached the complex, with fighting continuing there into May. Curt Reiss describes the scene: "Soviet tanks are making their way over torn-up pavement and along streets dotted with dead horses and made almost impassable by toppled lighting towers. This street had been constructed for the film *Refugees*. Back then, this was all props; now it is a horrible reality."[54] Much of the technical equipment and facilities at Babelsberg were dismantled by the Red Army and taken to Moscow at the end of the war, but the studios were not completely destroyed. In the division of Berlin and Germany after the war, the studios were located in the Soviet zone, and Babelsberg became the home of the state film corporation DEFA (Deutsche-Film-Aktiengesellschaft), which monopolized film production in the East for over forty years. Approximately seven hundred films were made at Babelsberg in this time. Following the unification of Germany in 1990, the federal government committed DM3 million to support the production of a number of feature films at the studio and enable it to continue to function in the transition from state control to privatization.[55] In 1992, the studio was sold by the Treuhand, the agency responsible for privatizing the holdings of the former East German government, to a subsidiary of the company that later became Vivendi.

Since the fall of the Berlin Wall and the unification of East and West Germany, local, regional, national, and European governments and agencies have poured a huge volume of public monies into the complex, first to enable it to continue to function in the immediate aftermath of the fall of the East German state that had sustained it for over forty years, and subsequently to assist its renovation and transformation. In March 2001, a Babelsberg spokesman estimated that half of the investment in the complex over the previous decade had come from European Union sources and from national subsidies.[56] The studio has been assisted by the fact that the Brandenburg region is a priority development area with low (by European standards) socioeconomic indicators. But some of the funds have flowed because of the symbolic importance of renovating the complex as part of the larger efforts to restore Berlin as a media, cultural, and political center in both the reunified Germany and a rebuilt Europe. Announcing a contribution of DM2.75 million toward the renovation of the studio's postproduction facilities in 1993, the European Commission declared that it "considered the aid could be authorized because of the importance of the project for the European film industry in economic and particularly in cultural terms."[57]

German unification "resulted in the erosion of aspects of the GDR's [German Democratic Republic] cultural heritage and ensured its subordination" both to the film culture of the former West Germany, and to the demands of the international production market.[58] The East German state film-distributing monopoly, Progress Film-Verleih, had guaranteed the exhibition of DEFA product, but this disappeared along with the studio's annual production subsidy when the communist government was overthrown.[59] About 1,600 of the studio's 2,400 employees were made redundant, although some were reemployed as tour guides for the theme park, which opened on the studio lot in 1991. Helen Hughes and Martin Brady have argued, "The story of the transformation of what was potentially one of the most lucrative assets of the GDR into the privatized concern of Babelsberg Studios GmbH was at the heart of a debate over not only the future of film in eastern Germany but also the industry as a whole."[60]

Studio Babelsberg is situated in the German Land (or state) of Brandenburg. As a former East German territory, Brandenburg receives considerable structural funding from the federal German government and from the European Union for regional economic development. The information and communication technology (ICT) and media industries have been singled out for support in Brandenburg as key economic drivers, recognition in part of the achievements and prospects of the studio and the media city.

In June 1994, Brandenburg, as one of the new German Länder, received a share of DM26 billion in structural assistance from the European Commission toward regional economic development. This assistance, which was provided under the EC's Community Support Framework (CSF) 1994–1999, prioritized seven areas. The Babelsberg developments fit five and possibly six of these areas.[61] In 1999, when structural funds were allocated for the 2000–2006 period, Brandenburg was listed as an "Objective 1" region, making it eligible for a share of the €19 billion allocation to Germany. This funding goes to partnerships between public authorities and the private sector.

A key component of the refurbishment of the complex after privatization was its transformation into a media city. The site was divided into three different areas of use:

- film, television, and media production;
- residential; and
- recreation/entertainment and retail, which includes the theme park Filmpark Babelsberg and the studio tour.

Between 1993 and 1997, more than sixty buildings on-site were demolished, and the remaining buildings renovated. In the ten years after privatization, about DM1 billion was invested in the site to upgrade basic infrastructure, including roads, sanitation, electricity, and high-speed fiber optic cable as well as production infrastructure.

In the film, television, and media production area of the site, what we call the studio complex, new and renovated facilities include

- the Television Center, containing four large television studios;
- the Center for Film and Television Producers, containing office space for tenant media companies;
- a new broadcasting center for the television broadcaster Ostdeutsche Rundfunk Brandenburg (ORB);
- the Babelsberg FX Center, containing fourteen thousand square meters of studio space for digital film production, a preview theater, office space, and a virtual studio for show production and real-time 3D rendering; and
- a new building to house the Konrad Wolf College for Film and Television, and another to house the Museum of Broadcasting.

This suite of media production facilities and services has been established in the years since Babelsberg ceased to be the East German national film studio, and they are prominent, tangible indicators of the physical transformation of the facility. The studio complex includes all the elements we can expect to find in such a facility: 16 stages, the full range of production and postproduction facilities including more than 250,000 costumes and more than 1 million props, production offices and workshops, a digital telephone network, and high-speed fiber-optic cabling throughout the complex.

The complex is also home to over 130 tenant companies working in a variety of areas of media production and services, some resident in the digital postproduction FX Center. Babelsberg houses the television networks ORB and ZDF, a film school, a technical school, the offices of the independent professional association Film Association Brandenburg, and the regional film commission, Filmboard Berlin-Brandenburg. The studio's art department provides set construction and decoration services not only to film and television production but also to leisure and entertainment events and facilities including theme parks.

The range of public/governmental and private functions and networks that Babelsberg helps to organize and interweave are a further notable aspect of the contemporary facility. As noted earlier, the complex is home to a public broadcaster, a private broadcaster, a training institution, and the regional film commission. In 1996, Studio Babelsberg established the Media Initiative Babelsberg, a mechanism to assist in networking media companies both in the complex and in Brandenburg more widely, and to promote and market the media city and its tenants. In 1998, in partnership with the German regional investment bank Investitions Bank des Landes Brandenburg (ILB), the studio established a film production finance and management company, Studio Babelsberg Independents (SBI), specifically to invest DM50 million annually in production by small and medium-sized production companies in the Berlin-Brandenburg region.[62] This partnership appears to have now been wound up.

More recently, at the Babelsberg Media Conference held at the complex in August 2001, a new joint marketing venture known as "production.net berlin babelsberg" involving the four main studio complexes in the Berlin-Babelsberg region—Studio Berlin, Park Studios, Studio Babelsberg, and Berliner Union Film—was formed to facilitate cooperation among service providers and win both national and international production for the region. The production.net is part of the larger "media.net berlinbrandenburg," an alliance of about ninety media, IT, and communications companies based in the region.

Since the late 1990s, and particularly since the death of co–chief executive Rainer Schaper in March 2001, Studio Babelsberg appears to have changed the focus of its business model from the simple provision of production services and facilities to all comers toward a greater interest in coproduction. Studio Babelsberg Independents was established in 1998, and later in the same year, Babelsberg International Film Produktion, a media investment fund managed by Dutch bank ABN Amro, was also set up to attract international production and to build on the partnership between Studio Babelsberg and Hallmark Entertainment.

Ample evidence suggests that Studio Babelsberg should be a major player in the international production market. It is centrally located in Europe, apparently well placed to profit from European Union initiatives to encourage audiovisual coproduction, to develop skills and training, and to build on a culture and tradition of film production and innovation to become a key European center for ICT industries.

Yet over the last decade since privatization, the studio has not been as successful in attracting medium- to high-budget international production as might have been anticipated by its owners and managers. It faces considerable domestic competition from other facilities in Berlin as well as from established production entities in Munich, Düsseldorf, Cologne, and Hamburg. There has been some suggestion that since the filming at Babelsberg of Jean-Jacques Annaud's *Enemy at the Gates* in 2000, Roman Polanski's Camera d'Or and Academy Award winner *The Pianist* in 2002, and *The Bourne Supremacy* in 2003, this situation will change and the studio will become an increasingly favored venue for international production. But despite the high quality of German crews—*The Bourne Supremacy* hired over 80 percent of its crew locally—the malleability of Berlin's locations, and a range of initiatives offered by the regional film agency Medienboard Berlin-Brandenburg and the state of Brandenburg itself, relatively high production costs in Germany may continue to discourage some international producers. In addition, German facilities such as Babelsberg have also been at a disadvantage until recently in that, unlike similar systems in the United Kingdom, Canada, and Australia, the German system of tax shelters, which has provided hundreds of millions of dollars for high-budget English-language feature film productions such as the *Lord of the Rings* series, *Mission: Impossible 2*, *Shallow Hal*, *The League of Extraordinary Gentlemen*, and *Battlefield Earth*, did not contain conditions requiring the use of German actors or the filming of some or all of the film in Germany itself. None of these films was shot in Germany.

Considerable television production is done in Germany, but Studio Babelsberg had limited success in attracting projects despite the presence of the local public broadcaster and UFA Film and Television, a subsidiary of Bertelsmann, which also owns the television network RTL. The development of the Babelsberg FX Center digital production space was jeopardized when the developer went bankrupt in 1999, and although it was completed, some of the space remains vacant.

On a more positive note, the site does boast a leading film school, and the studio is at the heart of the Medienstadt, a development designed to function as a crucible of innovation in digital media production. The future appears bright, then, for the studio as a center for training, research, and development. Production at the studio increased by 20 percent in 2003, and Studio Babelsberg Motion Pictures has recently entered a number of international projects as coproducer, including *The Bourne Supremacy*, *Around the World in 80 Days*, and *Alien vs. Predator*, which—should the features prove successful—could help offset some of the studio's losses and will also act as an incentive to draw production to the facility.

A recently launched film financing scheme backed by the state of Brandenburg has enabled Studio Babelsberg to cofinance projects shot at the studio, including Kevin Spacey's *Beyond the Sea*, and Studio Babelsberg Motion Pictures, under Head of Production Henning Molfenter, has acted as a coproducer on a number of projects financed under the British sale-and-leaseback schemes that require at least three European partners.[63] Studio Babelsberg distinguishes itself from its local competitors and from many of its international competitors by virtue of the extent of production services offered to incoming producers. It cannot compete on labor prices with the Czech Republic or Romania, but many of the ancillary services—hotels, car rental, and so on—are on a par with or cheaper than its competitors.

Like Cinecittà, Studio Babelsberg competes on the basis of the quality of its infrastructure and the expertise of its workforce. It also has the added advantage that despite its history (or, rather, in the former East Germany to some extent *because* of its history), the built and natural environment of Berlin is relatively unfamiliar to global cinema audiences; that is, Berlin has not featured as prominently either as itself or playing somewhere else in recent English-language films as have other European cities from London to Prague. Although the volume of international production in Prague shows little sign of slowing, competitors argue that the city is "shot out"—meaning that its variety of locations have been filmed so many times that they have become overfamiliar to the international filmgoing audience. Berlin, by contrast, is claimed to be the up-and-coming destination for international productions.

In his article "Hollywood in Germany/Germany in Hollywood," Peter Krämer describes German audiences' embrace of Hollywood films over the last thirty years and Hollywood's long love affair with German filmmakers, but he has nothing to say about international production shot in Germany, perhaps because until relatively recently, Germany has served principally as a source of finance, talent, and revenue for international films shot elsewhere, rather than as a location in its own right. The recent growth in high-budget international production at Studio Babelsberg may go some way to changing this view, but much more international production will need to come to Berlin if the new owners' desire for the facility to remain a living legend for another fifty years is to be realized.

Notes

1. Jaroslav Brož, *The Path of Fame of the Czechoslovak Film: A Short Outline of Its History from the Early Beginning to the Stream of Recent International Successes* (Prague: Československý Filmexport Press Department, 1967), 24.

2. Klaus Kreimeier, *The UFA Story: A History of Germany's Greatest Film Company, 1918–1945* (Berkeley: University of California Press, 1999), 338.

3. Brož, *The Path of Fame*, 32–35.

4. Antonín J. Liehm, *Closely Watched Films: The Czechoslovak Experience* (White Plains, N.Y.: International Arts and Sciences Press, 1974), 22–23.

5. Craig Unger, "Prague's Velvet Hangover after Their Revolution," *Los Angeles Times*, 12 May 1991, 20.

6. "Czech Films to Receive State Subsidies Again," *Reuters News*, 3 April 1991, available at http://global.factiva.com (28 May 2002).

7. Audrey Choi, "Filmmakers Adjusting Focus for the Future," *Wall Street Journal Europe*, 31 January 1994, 38.

8. Ian Katz, "The Tread of a Velvet Tightrope," *The Guardian*, 4 June 1992, 24.

9. "Czech Barrandov Studios Sold," *Hollywood Reporter*, 26 June 1992, 4; Lenka Studnickova, "Barrandov Deal Off Due to a Lack of Capital," *Prague Business Journal*, 27 November 2000, available at http://global.factiva.com (28 May 2002).

10. "Prague Film Studio Incurs Losses on Czech-Language Films," *Pravo*, 15 January 1996, 1, 4.

11. "Culture Minister Sues AB Barrandov," *CTK Business News*, 23 April 1998, available at http://global.factiva.com (28 May 2002); "Czech Studio Landed with Copyright Bill," *Screen Digest*, 1 June 1998, 126.

12. Ministry of Culture of the Czech Republic, *Report on the State of Czech Cinematography in 2000* (Prague: Ministry of Culture of the Czech Republic, 2001), 6.

13. Ministry of Culture, *Report*, 15.

14. "Czech Republic: Take One: Prague," *Newsweek International*, 19 March 2001, 84–85.

15. Dina Iordanova, "East Europe's Cinema Industries Since 1989," *Media Development* 3 (1999): 14.

16. "Barrandov Laboratories Have World-Parameters Equipment," *CTK Business News*, 16 November 2001, available at http://global.factiva.com (21 September 2004); "Barrandov Film Studio Expects CZK 100 mln Drop in Revenues in 2001," *Interfax Czech Republic Business News Service*, 24 November 2001, available at http://global.factiva.com (21 Sept 2004).

17. Kate Connolly, "Bridge for Hire—$7,000 a Morning," *The Guardian*, 12 April 2002, 8.

18. Quoted in Daniel J. Wakin, "Even in Death, Fellini Assumes Epic Proportions: All-Night Wake Held at Rome Studio," *New Orleans Times-Picayune*, 2 November 1993, A11.

19. Peter Bondanella notes that twenty-five westerns were made at Cinecittà prior to *A Fistful of Dollars*. Peter Bondanella, *Italian Cinema: From Neorealism to the Present*, 3d ed. (New York: Continuum, 2001), 253.

20. Peter Bondanella, "From Italian Neorealism to the Golden Age of Cinecittà," in *European Cinema*, ed. Elizabeth Ezra (Oxford: Oxford University Press, 2004), 253.

21. "Epic Fade-Out in Rome," *Financial Times*, 12 October 1996, 1.

22. John Phillips, "Italy Sells off Dream Factory on the Tiber—Cinecittà Film Studios," *The Times*, 27 August 1994, 12.

23. "Cinecittà," *Unesco Courier* (July 1995): 68.

24. Deborah Ball, "Film: Privatization May Spur Lethargic Cinecittà—Storied Studio Refocuses on International Filmmakers," *Wall Street Journal Europe*, 9 December 1997, 4.

25. Carlo Degli Esposti quoted in "Epic Fade-Out in Rome," 1.

26. Ball, "Film: Privatization May Spur Lethargic Cinecittà," 4.

27. Mark Dezzani, "RAI Gets More Domesticated," *Broadcast*, 17 February 1995, available at http://global.factiva.com (21 September 2004).

28. Ball, "Film: Privatization May Spur Lethargic Cinecittà," 4.

29. David Willey, "The End as Lights Fade Forever at Italy's Hollywood," *The Observer* 23 May 1993.

30. "Cinecittà," 68.

31. Giovanni Grassi, "Italy to Privatize Cinecittà," *Hollywood Reporter*, 6 September 1994, 1.

32. "Ente Cinema's Three-Year Plan Proposes Creation of Communications Centre in Rome," *Il Sole 24 Ore*, 7 December 1994, 9.

33. "Italian Film Studio Going into Tour Business," *Variety*, 5 July 1994, B7.

34. Grassi, "Italy to Privatize Cinecittà," I1.

35. Dezzani, "RAI Gets More Domesticated."

36. Victor L. Simpson, "Liz's Queenly Bed Snapped Up for $4,500: Huge Italian Film Studio, Cinecittà, Auctions Off Thousands of Props," *The Globe and Mail*, 2 June 1993, C3.

37. "Cinecittà Prepares for Relaunch with New Agreements," *Il Sole 24 Ore*, 4 July 1995, 9.

38. For references to "multimedia products" see "Board of Ente Cinema Approves Three-Year Relaunch Plan," *Il Sole 24 Ore*, 6 July 1994, 16; and for references to telecommunications companies and TV/cinema synergies, see "Ente Cinema Reports Losses in 1993, Draws up Relaunch Plan," *Corriere della Sera*, 6 March 1994, 19.

39. Cristina Clapp, "Digital Cinecittà—How Two Innovators Using Quantel and Other Leading-Edge Technologies Are Advancing the Science of Digital Intermediates," *Digital Cinema*, 1 December 2002, 20.

40. Elisabetta Anna Coletti, "'Made in Italy' Label Gains Celluloid Cachet," *Christian Science Monitor* 92, no. 220 (4 October 2000), available at http://csmonitor.com/cgi-bin/durable Redirect.pl?/durable/2000/10/04/p1s4.htm (3 September 2004).

41. "Europe: Cooperation between Studios," *Media Monitor*, 18 March 1994, 4.

42. Michael Goldman, "Set Incentives," *Millimeter* 29, no. 11 (1 November 2001): 9.

43. Carole Horst, "Winter Games, Lumiq Studios Bring Northern Region an Edge," *Variety*, 27 October 2003, B2.

44. Martin Blaney, "Vivendi Universal Sells Babelsberg Studios," *Screen Daily*, 14 July 2004, available at www.screendaily.com/story.asp?storyid=18410 (6 September 2004).

45. Martin Blaney, "Babelsberg Workforce Protest at Takeover," *Screen Daily*, 16 July 2004, available at www.screendaily.com/story.asp?storyid=18426 (6 September 2004).

46. Martin Blaney, "New Babelsberg Chiefs Outline Studio Strategy," *Screen Daily*, 22 July 2004, www.screendaily.com/story.asp?storyid=18494 (6 September 2004).

47. Ed Meza, "Studio Exex Allay Worries," *Variety*, 26 July 2004, 15.

48. Siegfried Kracauer, "Calico World: The Ufa City in Neubabelsberg," in *Film Architecture: Set Designs from Metropolis to Blade Runner*, ed. and trans. Dietrich Neumann (Munich: Prestel, 1999), 191.

49. Kreimeier, *The UFA Story*, 72.

50. *Reichsfilmblatt*, 22 December 1926, quoted in Kreimeier, *The UFA Story*, 99.

51. Kreimeier, *The UFA Story*, 100.

52. See Kreimeier, *The UFA Story*, 158–72.

53. Kreimeier, *The UFA Story*, 181.

54. Quoted in Kreimeier, *The UFA Story*, 362.

55. "Government Stresses Desire to Maintain DEFA," *Sueddeutsche Zeitung*, 21 February 1991, 31.

56. Mark R. Johnson and Vanessa Liertz, "German Studio Transforms Itself into a Coproducer," *Asian Wall Street Journal*, 21 March 2001, N5.

57. "EC Approves $1.6 mil in Babelsberg Studios Aid," *Hollywood Reporter*, 2 November 1993, I2; "Germany: Extra Cash for Babelsberg," *Media Monitor*, 12 November 1993, 4; "Babelsburg [sic] Opens 'Biggest' Euro Film Studio," *Pro Sound News Europe*, January 1994, 1.

58. Leonie Naughton, "That Was the Wild East: Filmpolitik and the 'New' Germany," paper presented at History and Film Conference, Brisbane, November 1998.

59. Mark Heinrich, "East German State Film Studio Feels Cold Wind of Capitalism," *Reuters News*, 25 April 1990, available at http://global.factiva.com (21 September 2004).

60. Helen Hughes and Martin Brady, "German Film after the *Wende*," in *The New Germany: Social, Political and Cultural Challenges of Unification*, ed. Derek Lewis and John R. P. McKenzie (Exeter: University of Exeter Press, 1995), 276.

61. "Structural Funds: The Commission Approves the Community Support Framework for Germany 1994–99," IP/94/564, 21 June 1994; *European Union*, available at http://europa.eu.int/ (26 February 2003).

62. "German Studio Launches Production Outfit," *Screen Digest* (October 1998): 218.

63. Ed Meza, "Film-rich Region Targets more Prod'n," *Variety*, 2 February 2004, B8.

CHAPTER SEVEN

Still Exceptional?

London's Film Studios

London's film studios deservedly hold prominent places in both historical and contemporary accounts of English-language film and television production. In the twentieth century, the United Kingdom was the principal location for American production outside the United States, although in recent years this position has been challenged by Canada. Approximately 80 percent of film production in the United Kingdom and 70 percent of digital and media production companies are based in and around London. Virtually all studio-based feature film production in the United Kingdom has been, and continues to be, concentrated in the "western wedge" around London, in the massive purpose-built complexes at Pinewood, Shepperton, Denham, and Borehamwood;[1] at the smaller facilities at Ealing and Elstree; or, more recently, at facilities converted from other uses, such as the former aircraft manufacturing plant at Leavesden and, to a lesser extent, the former distillery at Three Mills in London's Docklands.

Unlike many studios in continental Europe, the initial development of studios around London was not motivated by governmental interest in rationalizing or centralizing domestic production through a single, dominant studio complex. Then as now, London's studios were typically founded on a mix of British and American entrepreneurialism, and a combination of the desire of some—but by no means all—within the British film industry to attract and work on large-scale, high-budget production, and the ambition of major Hollywood players to establish and enhance a permanent production presence in a key international market. Such a presence would provide a means to take advantage of the large stock of British stories, locations, and personnel and to tap in to London's creativity.

American-initiated and -financed projects have long been important to film production in the United Kingdom, not only in terms of technological development, training, and employment of British skills and creative expertise, but also in terms of the creation and maintenance (and sometimes the demise) of infrastructure such as studio facilities. Various Hollywood majors have owned and built studios in the United Kingdom since the 1920s, and occasionally individual feature film projects have created lasting physical infrastructure. The highest-profile and most successful example of this phenomenon is the former aircraft manufacturing plant at Leavesden, which was first used for the production of the James Bond film *GoldenEye* and has subsequently been home to the first four *Harry Potter* films, but there are a number of other examples, including the 007 Stage at Pinewood, once the largest in the world, which was first built for the James Bond film *The Spy Who Loved Me* in 1976, and the aerodrome at Hatfield near London, which was used for the filming of Steven Spielberg's *Saving Private Ryan* and later the television miniseries *Band of Brothers*.

Here as everywhere, cost has always been a factor for international producers in deciding where to base major projects, but the cost of using these facilities alone is rarely the sole or most important concern. The competitive advantage of these studios stems in part from the quality of United Kingdom crews and facilities, in part from the familiarity and confidence in their capacity, which derives from the long history of successful and cost-effective production in the United Kingdom (in contrast with extreme locations, which must build confidence and familiarity over time), and in part from the privileged position London occupies in global cultural production and creative networks.

The boom in American production in the late 1990s and early 2000s, coupled with the concurrent discovery of the economic power and potential of the "creative industries," has again inflated the "studio idea"—the often intense commitment to building infrastructure to service international production that is an integral part of the location interest—in various parts of the United Kingdom. The studio idea is also integral to the view from the top of the future of film production in the United Kingdom. Production infrastructure—"state-of-the-art studios and post production companies, complemented by outstanding companies operating at every level of the international film business"[2]—is one of the three key ingredients in Sir Alan Parker's, former chair of the United Kingdom Film Council, recipe for "making the United Kingdom a film hub for the twenty-first century."[3] This vision is by no means uncontested within the industry; responding to Parker's speech in the British film magazine *Sight and Sound*, director Alex Cox criticized the Film Council's (and the industry's) London-centrism, described the studios as "underused . . . branch office[s] of Los Angeles," and questioned the wisdom of "giving up on distinctly British films and making co-productions with the Americans" since "[i]t has been tried by British producers on many occasions. It has always failed."[4]

It has recently been argued that the historical and contemporary stability of Britain's production base has been dependent on "the availability of American production finance provided by the large, internationally dominant US distributors."[5] Independent British producers have always been to some extent dependent on and subordinate to the U.S. majors, as evidenced by the fragility of small firms faced with the booms and busts in British filmmaking, and the historical reliance on American capital. Small production firms and independent producers are cast in one of two roles in their engagement with international production:

- *dependent*: complementing and serving the interests of large firms; [or]
- *innovative*: operating in (often founding/developing) specialised new products or markets but remaining vulnerable to the potentially fatal attentions of large organisations.[6]

This structural assessment of the British production sector has three constants: the recurrent emergence of a cohort of independent producers, the short life many production companies will enjoy, and the enduring power of the majors. But to this list should be added a fourth constant: the consistent ability of the large British studio complexes, most particularly Pinewood and Shepperton, to attract very high-budget, blockbuster productions. All of the major studio complexes in the United Kingdom provide services to—usually international, sometimes British—film producers, and while most have diversified into television production and the rental of office space, the survival of each has to some extent been dependent on their ability to attract and service feature film production. Like the smaller independent producers, the studio complexes also need to be innovative in their strategies and business practices. The specter of the early 1970s, when the long boom in American production in the United Kingdom burst so spectacularly, continues to hang over the British industry. But it may be that the experience and memory of such a large-scale withdrawal of finance—which distinguishes the United Kingdom from many of its current competitors for American film business—gives the British film industry and in particular its major studios a contemporary advantage in that most are developing innovative business models and expansion plans to weather the inevitable, coming cyclical downturn. Each of the major United Kingdom studios has adopted a different strategy. We will now look at each in detail.

Pinewood-Shepperton: Merger and Expansion

Faced with what Sir Alan Parker described as the "colossal transformation" in international film and television production at the beginning of the twenty-first century as more places and facilities around the world compete for the same business and erode some of their traditional advantages, the United Kingdom's two largest studio complexes, Pinewood and Shepperton, have adopted a dual strategy to maintain their position in the international production pecking order. In 2001, Pinewood's new management team bought out their counterparts at Shepperton and merged the two facilities in order to increase their flexibility and enhance their capacity to service every size and type of film and television production. Such a strategy was in keeping with the experience of other key United Kingdom film institutions in the late 1990s and 2000s, including the creation of the United Kingdom Film Council from the variety of disparate support agencies, the amalgamation of a number of industry guilds, and the merging of several regional Independent Television (ITV) broadcasters. The merger of Pinewood and Shepperton heralded a new era of collaboration rather than competition between these historic rivals. In June 2004, the Pinewood-Shepperton was floated on the London stock exchange, raising about £46 million and valuing the company at about £100 million. The joint facility has a number of unique assets that give Pinewood-Shepperton a considerable advantage in competing for large-scale international film production, including inside and outside water tanks and the 007 Stage, one of the largest in the world.

The merger was followed by an ambitious plan to internationalize the operations of the two studios and capitalize on one of their great strengths—their reputation—to create a global studio brand. In partnership with local firms and with the initial backing of the municipal government, Pinewood-Shepperton became prime movers behind plans to develop a new state-of-the-art facility in Toronto. Although the initial bid failed in 2003 and a revised bid lost out to a local consortium in 2004, Pinewood-Shepperton has continued to seek partnerships with other facilities internationally. This strategy is consistent with the emphasis of the United Kingdom Film Council under Sir Alan Parker—who directed a number of films at Shepperton—that international collaboration is the way forward for the British film industry:

We need to encourage greater British involvement in international film production, by creating strategic alliances with new territories outside Europe who are already playing host to big-budget productions and are hungry for more, at the same time ensuring that British talent—technicians and craftspeople—work on these films. . . . Over time, . . . non-traditional filmmaking countries will build their own film industries as they further develop their own skills. But if we form partnerships with them now, we will have a much better chance of supplying services to them—particularly our high-end skills—as their industries mature.[7]

Before their merger in 2001, Pinewood and Shepperton were already the largest studio complexes in the United Kingdom and epicenters of substantial agglomerations of media businesses with intensive transactional networks.[8] This clustering is the basis of their leading position in the industry both in Britain and internationally. The merger of these two existing media cities, situated about twenty-four kilometers apart but linked by an intranet, created a mega–media city that is able to pitch for and accommodate more high-budget production work because this work can be more efficiently spread and sequenced across both facilities than if they were to remain operating as independent entities. The merger also coincided with the British government's focus on creative industries as a sector to be fostered, partly by the active solicitation of foreign production through the British Film Commission (now part of the United Kingdom Film Council), which obviously laid great emphasis on the major studio complexes. It was also consistent with the 1998 extensive review of the British film industry, "A Bigger Picture," which argued for the creation of a stable production base as a means to produce the necessary "good quality" jobs in the core information and knowledge-based industries. After the merger, the combined facilities host more than two hundred service companies and together contain thirty-seven soundstages of varying size. Productions using the complexes are also able to call on the substantial number and variety of media-related firms and facilities that have built up immediately adjacent to the facilities and in the greater London area.

With the rise of British competitors such as Leavesden and the increasing technical and infrastructural capacity of studios around the world, Pinewood-Shepperton has needed to rethink its competitive strategy. Its response has been to build on its relationships with film, television, and commercial production companies and exploit the flexible character of its facilities in order potentially to service every size of production. Efforts to "rationalize" the use of facilities stem from the space problems created by international films taking up studio space for extended periods of time. With a history of competing against each other for the same production work, the merger arguably permitted the two studios to bid from a consolidated and united rather than separate and fragmented position. The merger also needs to be seen in light of the loss to their major emerging rival, Leavesden, of *Harry Potter and the Philosopher's Stone* when reportedly, "individually, they did not have enough sound stages to accommodate the U.S.$130 million adaptation."[9] A combined Pinewood-Shepperton not only would have a competitive edge over its domestic and international rivals in its core high-budget feature film market but also would be in a position to move into areas it had previously not actively competed in.

Another way in which the combined Pinewood-Shepperton operation has sought to retain its leading edge is through the expansion of its capacity to service television production. At Shepperton, television and commercial production became increasingly important in the 1980s, but it is at Pinewood where most of the television business is currently concentrated. The turn to television had first been taken at Pinewood in the late 1960s in response to the withdrawal of U.S. production when two new stages were built specifically for television. These stages were subsequently converted for film production, before being reconverted in 2000–2001 into state-of-the-art digital television studios capable of hosting productions with live audiences up to around two hundred people. The decision to develop digital television production facilities was made shortly after the complex was taken over by a consortium led by Michael Grade, former chief executive of Channel 4, and the fact that two television stages already existed—with the all-important flat concrete floors underneath the timber floors which had been put in during the conversion to film sometime in the 1970s—meant a considerable cost saving over building from scratch. The availability of these stages enabled Pinewood-Shepperton to win production from existing studios in Britain and decisively to enter the market for United Kingdom television production. The quiz show *The Weakest Link* was lured to Pinewood from Magic Eye Studios in Wandsworth, while Pinewood also hosts a number of BBC sitcoms. Television production currently accounts for approximately 10 percent of Pinewood-Shepperton's turnover, a figure that is expected to grow over time. Digital television is at an advanced stage in Britain compared to the rest of the world, and the move to develop digital television production facilities is designed to cement the complex's position as Britain's leading production facility. In the short term, the move is focused on the domestic British television production market, but the addition of these facilities also serves to place Pinewood-Shepperton in a strong position to compete for international digital production work.

Ealing Studios: Innovation in Space, Technology, and Production

Ealing Studios has been a working studio since 1902. From its heyday producing films that spawned a new genre—the Ealing comedy—to acting as a satellite production venue for the British Broadcasting Corporation (BBC), and for a short period in the 1990s operating under the auspices of the National Film and Television School, Ealing Studios has been a landmark in the British film and television production environment. Its current owners, a consortium of three companies—film producer Fragile Films (which made *Spiceworld, The Movie* at Ealing), San Francisco new media company The Idea Factory, and U.S. property developer The Manhattan Loft Company— bought the site for £10 million in 2000, and it quickly announced plans to reinvigorate the studios' brand. As one of its current owners, Barnaby Thompson, told *The Guardian* in 2002, "There were certain qualities the word Ealing conjured up [during its heyday]—good films, good directors, acting talent and a certain kind of innate Britishness. We want to make it a home for British talent."[10]

Ealing also has a long history of innovation in production practice. Under its current owners, the operations of the studios have diversified, and a variety of pioneering strategies have been adopted. According to co-owner John Kao, "Ealing Studios seeks to be an innovator—in the quality of the space we create, in the content we make, in the technologies we use." The redevelopment of this famous studio complex foregrounds, perhaps even more explicitly than other larger media city developments, the importance of its rental property development strategy and a related emphasis on creating a digital precinct of companies, some of which may not have a media focus.

The day-to-day running of the facility, its marketing, and efforts to attract external production are the responsibility of Ealing Studios Operations, while a separate entity, Ealing Studios Enterprises, is responsible for content production and creative partnerships. Ealing has adopted a business model for renting out space that is significantly different from that of most studios. Most studios expect to earn around 70 percent of their revenue from the short-term rental of production space, with the remainder coming from longer-term rentals to service companies. Ealing Studios, by contrast, anticipates earning between 60 and 70 percent of its income from the rental of office space to visual-effects and other digital service companies like those currently clustered in the Soho area of central London, and only 30 percent from the rental of its conventional studio spaces. The studios also host a variety of live public events including comedy nights and the Ealing Film Festival. Ealing is prohibited from expanding beyond its current footprint as the site is surrounded by residential, commercial, and educational sites, but the buildings and grounds are in the process of being comprehensively transformed. Ealing is now home to Europe's first full-scale digital animation facility, part of the effort to turn the studios into a state-of-the-art "media village."[11] The redevelopment is pitched beyond the studios' traditional focus, with the aim of bringing together tenants and skills from film, television, and new digital media. Ealing's cluster strategy is specialized, with its digital production aspect foregrounded through its first redeveloped area, a digital animation studio.

Ealing Studios is also centrally involved in the creative industries strategy of the local council. In partnership with Ealing Studios and Thames Valley University, Ealing Council was awarded £40,000 in January 2003 from the London Development Agency to commission a study into creative industries in the borough. Building on the several clusters of creative industries located in and around Ealing, key local players, including the studios, committed to working collaboratively to achieve a number of strategic objectives:

- create a role for Ealing as the United Kingdom competitor to San Francisco, L.A., and Paris for screen-based media;
- create within Ealing a United Kingdom center of excellence for creative industries lifelong learning through physical and virtual links;
- create a learning, enterprise, and knowledge exchange, specifically as a focus for multicultural talent; and
- re-create Ealing as an exemplar of urban renaissance.[12]

Ealing Studios is at the core of the Ealing "brand" that the local council's media strategy, Creative Links, is seeking to establish and promote. As well as being designed to develop local businesses and create jobs, Creative Links may also provide an opportunity for Ealing Studios to take advantage of the area's growing concentration of Asian, and particularly Indian, film production and distribution enterprises and become a principal production resource—or center of excellence—not only for the Bollywood industry but for content destined for the growing number of United Kingdom television channels aimed at Asian diasporic communities.[13]

Besides being a rental facility available for hire by domestic or international productions, a hub for new media development, and a major player in local creative industries strategies, Ealing is returning to its former status as a studio in the Hollywood sense of the term. That is, it makes its own films and commissions its own dramas under its own name. As one of Ealing's owners told a recent Parliamentary inquiry, "What we are primarily interested in doing is finding a way of building a new kind of content producing and distribution studio that is a mirror to some extent of our Hollywood counterparts, but obviously completely different, because the environment here is completely different."[14]

In addition to producing films and television programs under its own banner, Ealing has negotiated a coproduction alliance with the producer of *Shrek*, John Williams, and his company Vanguard Films to produce a slate of high-budget feature animations for Disney. Vanguard Films is the principal tenant in Ealing's new digital animation studio.

Paralleling Pinewood-Shepperton's internationalization strategy, Ealing Studios is also leading a consortium with Spanish and German companies that is bidding to take over the Bulgarian national film studios. The intention to privatize 95 percent of Boyana Film Studios in Sofia in a two-stage public tender was announced by the Bulgarian government in June 2004, with the future owner expected to commit to maintaining the site as a production venue for at least ten years, to produce at least two Bulgarian films a year during the first three years of the deal, and to invest approximately €6 million in the first four years after the sale.[15] Boyana, which was established in 1962, has three soundstages and currently entails three main units—a film production unit, a film laboratory, and an animation unit—on a huge hundred-hectare site approximately five miles from the center of Sofia. Ealing's plan offers producers the prospect of basing themselves in the United Kingdom and accessing the cheaper facilities and ancillary services in Bulgaria for part of the shoot. Ealing's proposal for the privatized Boyana facility includes investment in new production equipment, construction of a music recording studio, and possibly coproduction of live-action and animated features. The American companies Kodak and New Image have also been involved in discussions with the Bulgarian government about the future of the facility.[16] At time of writing, a final decision had not been made on the bid for Boyana, but the effort to internationalize illustrates the innovative approach of Ealing's owners to studio management and film production services.

Leavesden Studios: From Blank Canvas to Media Park

Despite the recent success of the *Lord of the Rings* trilogy, the *Harry Potter* cycle, and the *Star Wars* movies, the most successful, long-running film series has been those featuring the British secret agent James Bond. From the early 1960s to the early 1990s, the Bond films were integral to the survival and success of Pinewood Studios. More recently, the needs of Bond have created two new studios, one of which—Leavesden—became the United Kingdom's newest regular venue for blockbuster production.

After choosing to film *Licence to Kill* in Mexico, Eon Productions was unable to rent space at Pinewood due to the production there of *First Knight* when it returned to the United Kingdom to film *GoldenEye* in 1994. During their search for a suitable United Kingdom base within easy reach of London, the team came across a site owned by the Ministry of Defence in Hertfordshire that had originally been developed as an airfield and aircraft manufacturing plant during World War II. The site contained two large factory complexes and a thousand-yard-long runway. At its peak, more than three thousand people were employed at the plant, manufacturing and testing aircraft, plane engines, and parts, but construction ceased and the plant closed in 1993. According to veteran production designer Peter Lamont, "Not only could you get more than three Pinewood lots on this site . . . you could put the whole of Pinewood under cover" in the massive hangars.[17]

The production team converted some of the undercover space into five huge soundproofed stages and an adjacent model stage. Much of the site is protected greenbelt land, which means that development is strictly controlled, but as a result, it has the advantage of a clear horizon, so that large outdoor sets can be built and filmed from multiple angles without the need to disguise or later edit out anachronous buildings. In part as a result of the size and flexibility of the site, a larger proportion of the shoot than is usual for Bond films was studio based. Despite the costs of constructing soundstages, office accommodation, and workshops, installing power and lighting grids, and upgrading roads and related infrastructure on-site, it is likely that Leavesden was a less expensive proposition for Eon Productions than renting space at Pinewood or another existing facility elsewhere in the world.

Although the site was originally conceived as a one-off production venue, it soon became clear that with the extent of investment and renovation on-site for *GoldenEye*, its accessibility from London, and the local availability of skilled film workers given the site's proximity to other existing studios at Elstree and location within the western wedge in which much of the U.K. crew and infrastructure are situated, coupled with the continuing demand for large studio spaces in Britain, Leavesden had a future as a regular production venue. As the Bond team's one-year lease on the site was drawing to a close, a number of other producers, including the *Star Wars* team, were attracted by the prospect of having sole occupancy of such an environment and expressed interest in making use of the facility. Investors with an eye on the development potential of the site were also becoming interested. In November 1995, outline planning permission was granted by the local council to use one of the factory buildings as a film studio and to redevelop the remainder of the site for a variety of uses including housing, offices, a studio tour, a family leisure center, and sports and playing fields. In the same month, the site was bought by George Town Holdings, a Malaysian-based operator of pharmacies, supermarkets, and department stores, who "pledged to spend £150–200 million on developing it into a studio and entertainment complex" with adjacent residential and business park areas.[18] Both Eon Productions, the force behind the Bond films, and the U.S. major studio Warner Bros. were rumored to be planning to build a theme park on site, but they were put off by the complexity of the planning process given the site's greenbelt location.[19]

In 1999, George Town Holdings sold the majority of the Leavesden site to a United Kingdom property developer, MEPC, which believed that the area northwest of London would be "the natural successor to the Thames Valley" for expansionist and start-up technology and dot-com companies.[20] In March 2000, MEPC applied for planning permission to develop almost forty thousand square meters of high-tech office accommodation on the site, and it flagged its ambitions to develop up to one hundred thousand square meters (or nearly one million square feet).[21] But a massive fall in the proportion of office space taken up by high-tech companies in the area between 2001 and 2002 and the success of the production of the first *Harry Potter* film at Leavesden refocused MEPC's attention on the media sector.[22] Part of the site was subsequently sold off for housing development as MEPC changed its business strategy for the Leavesden site to a residential and media-focused industrial park that, like the Ealing Studios redevelopment, has been aimed at drawing media businesses out of Soho in central London. A substantial new studio facility was also planned but has yet to be built. The residential and business park areas of the site are completely separate from the area currently used for filming.

This is Leavesden's great advantage and one of the features that distinguishes it from the other major United Kingdom studios: It is a "blank canvas." There are no permanent commercial tenants on-site and consequently no hope, expectation, or requirement that incoming productions use the services of companies that have a preexisting relationship with the facility—in contrast with some other United Kingdom studios. Each production that uses the site must bring in its own crew and support services. The entire site is available for rent on a film-by-film basis to individual productions, meaning that there are none of the conflicting demands on the studio space that can occur where a facility hosts multiple clients simultaneously. The flip side of this, however, is that the facility is poorly placed if there were to be a drop-off in the demand for studio space from large-scale blockbuster feature films. It is not set up to service ongoing television or other kinds of production. Most recently, the site has hosted the production of the first four films in the *Harry Potter* series.

In the decade since it was first used for film production, many grand plans have been proposed for the site, but the studio continues to function as a four-wall facility available for rent on a film-by-film basis. While its long-term future as a film production venue remains in doubt, as long as the United Kingdom continues to enjoy a boom in international production, it is likely to remain a vital piece of the U.K. film infrastructure, at least in the short to medium term.

Elstree and Three Mills: Television and Government

Elstree Studios, one of Britain's oldest functioning production venues, and Three Mills Studios, one of the newest, are very different facilities in terms of their locations and histories, but they share several common features, including a recent orientation to television production work and the ownership interest of local government. Elstree Studios is a good example of Peter Hall's argument that large-scale audiovisual production tends to be "displaced to peripheral but accessible locations" away from the center of cities.[23] It is close to Leavesden Studios, just north of the western wedge in which much of London's filmmaking infrastructure and labor force is concentrated. Three Mills, by contrast, is located in London's Docklands, to the east of the City of London in a converted distillery. In terms of the total space available, Three Mills is one of the United Kingdom's largest facilities, but while it is eminently capable of managing the demands of small and medium-sized feature film productions, its sixteen soundstages are best suited to television production, music video, and commercial work. Like Ealing, but unlike Elstree and the other large facilities in outer London, Three Mills is accessible via the London Underground (subway). Both Elstree and Three Mills can and do host feature film production, but in recent years television production has been a core business for each.

After a decade of disuse and neglect, and six years after almost half of the site was sold off for a supermarket development, Elstree Studios was purchased by the Hertsmere Borough Council for almost £2 million in 1996. The council oversaw extensive renovation of the site and underwrote the construction of two new soundstages at a total cost of about £10 million.[24] Repair work is ongoing and expensive, costing over £500,000 in

2001–2002. The studios were leased to a specially formed company, Elstree Film and Television Studios Ltd., for seven years in 2000, with local planning conditions ensuring that the site cannot be used for any purpose other than film and television production until 2013. In the years after 2000, the council spent hundreds of thousands of pounds on external consultants to advise on ways in which millions of pounds of investment could be raised to enable the studios to remain commercially competitive. Under competition rules, the council must put the subsequent lease out to tender, and a public meeting in May 2004 was told that in order to raise the millions claimed to be necessary to enhance the attraction of the facility to film and television producers, the council would have to offer a lease of more than one hundred years.[25] Elstree is currently home to the British version of the global hit television quiz show *Who Wants to Be a Millionaire?*, the British version of the reality television game show *Big Brother*, and the Disney/Spyglass feature film version of *Hitchhiker's Guide to the Galaxy*.

The former bottling plant and distillery on twenty acres at Three Mills Island in London's Docklands was bought in 1995 by the Workspace Group, a company that was established in 1987 as the vehicle for the privatization of part of the Greater London Council's industrial property portfolio. The company quickly gained a reputation for transforming urban properties into flexible business accommodation for small to medium-sized enterprises. With approximately £10 million investment, the semiderelict Three Mills site was transformed into a media complex comprising production stages, rehearsal spaces, offices, a preview theater, prop stores, and an apartment development. It has hosted the production of feature films, including *Lock, Stock and Two Smoking Barrels*, *Code 46*, and *28 Days Later*, the animated feature *The Corpse Bride*, and television programs including *Big Brother*, *London's Burning*, and *Footballers' Wives*. While the studios' location to the east of London makes it less accessible and less attractive for the established feature film industry concentrated in the western wedge, it has proven popular with television and music producers and low- to mid-budgeted feature film producers seeking a location closer to the center of London. In mid-2004, the site was bought for £22.5 million by the London Development Agency (LDA), an agency of the London mayor's office intended to grow business and jobs in the city. Three Mills features prominently in the mayor's vision for creative industries in the capital as one of a number of planned "Creative Hubs" that will provide workspace and support facilities for creative industries workers and businesses.

Conclusion

This chapter has outlined the variety of strategies adopted by different London studios to maintain and enhance their profile in the competition for film and television production work. Acutely conscious of the cyclical nature of the studio business, these studios have diversified their businesses in efforts to develop alternative revenue sources in preparation for leaner times ahead. International production remains one of the keys to viability, but the range of different approaches adopted by the studios to "future-proof" their operations—merger, expansion, internationalization, property development, office space rental, and a turn to television and new media production—means that they are generally better prepared than their predecessors to survive the cycles in production.

London's studios are indeed still exceptional in that some of their core advantages remain—their reputations and those of United Kingdom crews and technicians, and the residual importance of the United Kingdom as creative inspiration, production venue, and market for Hollywood productions. The recent governmental attention to creative industries as future economic and employment drivers and ongoing reassessment of the orientation of the British film industry have reinforced the position of these studios in the global feature film production ecology.

Notes

1. Denham closed in 1952, Borehamwood closed in 1970.

2. Sir Alan Parker, "Building a Sustainable UK Film Industry: A Presentation to the United Kingdom Film Industry," UK Film Council, 5 November 2003, available at www.ukfilmcouncil .org.uk/usr/downloads/BaSFI.pdf (20 February 2004).

3. Parker, "Building a Sustainable UK Film Industry." The other ingredients are distribution and skills.

4. Alex Cox, "Britain Is Big Enough," *Sight and Sound* 13, no. 1 (January 2003): 6–7.

5. Helen Blair and Al Rainnie, "Flexible Films?" *Media, Culture & Society* 22, no. 2 (March 2000): 187.

6. Blair and Rainnie, "Flexible Films?" 193.

7. Parker, "Building a Sustainable UK Film Industry."

8. Nicholas cited in Allen J. Scott, *The Cultural Economy of Cities: Essays on the Geography of Image-Producing Industries* (London: Sage, 2000), 103. Scott contrasts the "sizeable agglomerations around the Pinewood and especially the Shepperton studios" with their French counterparts. This might help explain why the French studios have not been as able to capitalize on international production dynamics as other studios have.

9. Adam Minns, "Pinewood-Shepperton Eyes European Expansion," *Screen Daily*, 12 February 2001, available at www.screendaily.com/story.asp?storyid=3994 (28 February 2003). A

certain amount of production of the film was based at Shepperton, with some postproduction at Pinewood.

10. Angelique Chrisafis, "Ealing on a Roll as Deal Revives Studios," *The Guardian*, 24 May 2002, 9.

11. Adam Minns, "UK's Ealing Studios Set for $100m Revamp," *Screen Daily*, 14 June 2001, available at www.screendaily.com/story.asp?storyid=4966 (28 February 2003).

12. Ealing Council, *Report on a Strategy for Creative and Media Industries in Ealing*, 2003.

13. "Ealing Creative Links: Outline Strategy for the Creative Industries in Ealing," (London: Era Ltd, 2003), available at www.era-ltd.com/strategic_work/EalingCreativeLinks.pdf (15 September 2004).

14. Barnaby Thompson, oral evidence before House of Commons Culture, Media and Sport Committee 29 April, quoted in House of Commons Culture, Media and Sport Committee, *The British Film Industry*, Sixth Report of Session 2002–2003, vol. 1: 28.

15. "Bulgaria Offers Boyana Film Studios for Sale," *SeeNews*, 15 June 2004, available at www.see-news.com (21 September 2004); "British Ealing Eyes Bulgaria's Boyana Film Studios," *SeeNews*, 25 June 2004, available at www.see-news.com (21 September 2004).

16. "Kodak, New Image Join Efforts for Boyana Film," *Pari Daily*, 13 July 2004, available at www.news.pari.bg/cgi-bin/pari-eng.home.cgi (15 July 2004).

17. "The Business," *Sight and Sound* 5, no. 11 (November 1995): 5.

18. Louise Bateman, "*Star Wars* Casting Its Lot with Leavesden," *Hollywood Reporter*, 9 September 1996.

19. Despite its involvement in finding and establishing the facility in the first place, Eon Productions was unable to secure the studio for the filming of the next in the Bond series, *Tomorrow Never Dies*, because an agreement had been reached with the producers of *Star Wars* to film the fourth film in that series at Leavesden. With the assistance of a new organization, Herts Film Link, an alternative site was found for Bond at another nearby disused airfield, which became known as Park Street Studios. This facility is no longer operational as a film studio.

20. Stuart Watson, "The Dream Crashes," *Estates Gazette*, 12 October 2002, 106.

21. Helen Osborne, "Studio in the Frame," *Estates Gazette*, 18 March 2000, 84.

22. Watson, "The Dream Crashes," 106.

23. Peter Hall, "The Future of Cities," *Computers, Environment and Urban Systems* 23 (1999): 177.

24. "When Film-makers Seek Workspace," *The Times* [London], 14 May 1999, 33.

25. "Elstree in Need of £20m," *The Stage*, 13 May 2004, 3; "Search on for Film Studios Big Spender," *This Is Local London*, 15 May 2004, available at www.thisislocallondon.co.uk/search/display.var.490200.0.search_on_for_film_studios_big_spender.php (21 September 2004); "'Disgraceful' Waste," *This Is Local London*, 19 May 2004, available at www.thisislocallondon.co.uk/search/display.var.491044.0.disgraceful_waste.php (21 September 2004); "UK Studios: Watch This Space," *Televisual*, 2 June 2004, 30.

CHAPTER EIGHT

"The Same but Different!"

Canadian Studios and
International Production

People all over the world rave about the great outdoors and stunning film locations in British Columbia. We offer the great indoors, where you can create a location that's out of this world. Welcome to The Bridge Studios.[1]

The website of Vancouver's Bridge Studios emphasizes the capability of this studio to create extraordinary locations in a place surrounded by spectacular built and natural environments. While every place in the pursuit of its location interest seeks to stitch together its purpose-built studio spaces and its urban and natural environments as potential film sets, none has had the need to do so quite as much as has Canada—the Great White North. While Vancouver has the significant advantage over its counterparts in Toronto and Montreal in that it is possible to shoot the great outdoors on a year-round basis (its Canadian competitors are limited by extreme Canadian winters), it is still handicapped compared to its L.A. counterparts by forty inches of rain per year. The great outdoors needs to be securely tied to the "great indoors"— the soundstages and interior sets. From the late 1980s, studios have been developed to simulate exterior settings on stages and purpose-built backlots. These studios range from the purpose-built gated facilities of Vancouver and Montreal to the extensive network of small to medium-sized studios, converted warehouses, and permanent sets in Toronto.

The location interests of Canada's major film locations—Vancouver, Toronto, and Montreal—over the 1990s and 2000s have centered on effectively combining purpose-built, enhanced, and found natural and built environments. Canada provides perhaps the clearest indication of the extent to which location has become the totality of what is available in a place, from stages and backlots to existing natural and built environments, from the range, skill, and depth of film service providers and crews to the liaison services available to producers. The location interest turns on the ensemble of elements including the centerpiece of the studio. Canadian location interests have been brilliantly successful not only in developing and marketing facilities but also in securing financial incentives from various levels of government to further encourage this production. Canada has, as a consequence, become the international benchmark against which other countries measure themselves and find themselves wanting.[2]

Canada is the preferred destination for international production outside the United States. Canada's share of so-called economic runaways increased over the 1990s from 63 percent in 1990 to 81 percent in 1998.[3] In 2002–2003, Canadian sources estimated "foreign location production" to be worth C$1.9 billion.[4] Vancouver and Toronto are third and fourth, respectively, behind Los Angeles and New York as major film production centers in North America by direct expenditures in 1999 and 2000.[5] While the combined production expenditure in both Canadian cities is just one-fifteenth L.A.'s share of production, this combined amount is approaching that of New York and is considerably higher than the shares achieved by Orlando, North Carolina, Chicago, and Miami (fifth, sixth, seventh, and eighth, respectively).[6] If we then add Montreal—Canada's second city—which has emerged strongly in the late 1990s and early 2000s as an international production destination—then three Canadian cities are among the top ten motion picture production locations in North America.

From the standpoint of the design interest, Canada is a particular and special place—both the same and different. Canada and Canadian studios are simultaneously *part of* an increasingly integrated production, exhibition, and distribution market for film and television production firmly headquartered in Los Angeles; and they are *apart from* the United States in that Canada not only produces its own film and television but does so in significant volumes in the French as well as the English language. So while it is possible to say that Canada is probably as close as one can get to "producing in" and "being in" the United States without actually being there, it is nonetheless the case that, as in other foreign jurisdictions, Hollywood filmmakers need to negotiate exchange rates and foreign currency, particular tax laws, establish companies, and redress locations to remove specifically Canadian visual and iconic references as they would in other countries. It is just that Canada is more accessible, so there are likely to be fewer things needing to be redressed, fewer currency problems, no accent problems, less visible differences, smaller operational risks, and crews who are "intimately acquainted with the nuances of American television."[7] There is also the added bonus of stars happy not to have to leave North America while working on location. Canada and the United States share a border, time zones, urban landscapes, and intimate understandings of each other's ways as befits two countries that are each other's largest trading and investment partners. Canada is then like everywhere else (other than the United States) in functioning as an international location for globally dispersed production. And it is like the United States in that it shares a partially integrated *domestic* audiovisual market and North American culture with the United States.

Canadian Studios and International Production

Given that Canadian audiences have been factored into the *domestic* business models of U.S.-based film producers and television operations from film and then television's inception, American-initiated and -financed projects have long been a component of film production in Canada. Typically, Hollywood producers took *intermittent* advantage of the concentration of production expertise, facilities, and personnel available in Toronto and Montreal and went on location elsewhere in Canada. What has changed with the dispersal of production in the contemporary period is the emergence of Vancouver, Toronto, and Montreal as satellite production centers undertaking *continuous* production. At the same time, Canadian connections with Hollywood design interests have never been so close, with Canadian banks financing many major Hollywood film projects in the 1980s and 1990s.[8] And this is not confined to Hollywood; to give but one example, the Canadian investment bank CIBC World Markets provided the finance for the Australian company Village Roadshow's U.S.$1.2 billion production fund, much of which has been spent on, or is intended for, Village Roadshow's multipicture joint production venture with Warner Bros. Additionally, the development of cable television has further dispersed production, with *Variety* reporting that in 1992 Canadian fare accounted for about 30 percent of the original programming on American cable networks, making Canada the largest supplier of original programming on U.S. cable.[9] Paul Attallah argues that these developments stem from a change of policy as the concern shifted from a national cultural mind-set concerned with cultural protection to a concern for cultural export.[10]

Policy changes in the late 1980s underwrote studio and other infrastructural development, training, and employment of Canadian skills and creative expertise to work on international and local production. Vancouver—the most proximate of Canadian locations to Los Angeles—emerged as the foremost site for foreign location production, with three major studios now developed (Bridge Studios in 1986–1987, Vancouver Film Studios in 1989, and the 1999 renovation of North Shore Studios—now Lions Gate) and numerous converted warehouse spaces being used for filmmaking from the mid-1980s. International production was the "main game" in Vancouver, with the city being defined by international production and its new studio infrastructure. Here the previous absence of infrastructure to service international production mandated the development of purpose-built studios to create and then secure Vancouver's competitive advantage.

Vancouver's experience spurred Montreal and Toronto to change their approach to securing international production and developing studio infrastructure. In Toronto and Montreal, local productions already defined film and television production and made up substantial local, domestically oriented production industries serving Canada's English- and French-speaking populations. For these cities, international production would act as a "supplement" to the dominant portion of production work—the domestic local industry. Consequently, the Toronto and Montreal approach to international production focused on enhancing and extending existing production capacity and infrastructure that had originally been created for domestic production. This helps explain why the development of large-scale studios came later to both cities. In Toronto's case, existing domestic production capabilities were well suited to low-budget international production and split location production particularly between New York and Toronto. This ensured that international production needs could be met through the extensive conversion and refurbishment of warehouses alongside the development of smaller purpose-built studios geared to television production. Studio businesses like Toronto Film Studios and Cinespace grew out of the consolidation of these spaces into networks of soundstages. These stages were then used for high-budget productions such as *Chicago* and go some way toward explaining why Toronto was still aspiring to build a mega state-of-the art studio in 2004.

Montreal's record in securing international production lagged behind Vancouver and Toronto over the 1990s—with no international production being made there at all in 1992.[11] This helps explain, perhaps, the earlier turn to studio development in that city. While there was evidence of warehouse conversion as in Toronto, Montreal's problems in securing international production undoubtedly focused entrepreneurial and governmental attention on the development of purpose-built studios as a key competitive measure. The phenomenal growth of Mel's Cité du Cinéma Studios from the mid-1990s was aimed at securing high-budget blockbuster production for the city while serving the needs of the local Francophone industry. Expansion in 1999 and 2002 increased the size of stages available and the complexity of the work able to be undertaken at the network of studios. Mel's example encouraged the development in 1999 of a second purpose-built space, Ciné Cité Montreal, in a former air force base by a consortium that included North Shore Studios (Lions Gate) cofounder Paul Bronfman.

The Canadian push for location production is an extension of the original push by U.S. cities and states to develop film commissions and other agencies to attract location production to their territories. Indeed, Alberta's film commission was one of the first in North America when it was established in 1972.[12] Like their American counterparts, Canadian city and provincial governments realized the value in pursuing a location interest from an early stage and saw it as their business to facilitate environments conducive to the hosting of film and television production. As with the U.S. pattern evident in successful U.S. locations such as Wilmington, Orlando, and Miami, Canada's boom in international production over the 1990s was integrally connected with the pursuit of the location interest by provincial and city governments in British Columbia, Ontario, and Quebec.

As noted in chapters 2 and 3, public-private partnerships in which governments take an important facilitating role have been critical to the development of Canadian studios. While studios in Vancouver and Montreal had significant state support and encouragement by way of investment and loans from their respective provincial governments, there were considerable differences of emphasis on the part of their respective governments. Conservative British Columbian governments were concerned with regional industry development and services industry "rationales" for investment and support.[13] In Quebec, leftist and cultural (separatist) agendas supporting facilities were integral to the Parti Quebecois's state-interventionist[14] and separatist logic of establishing the conditions for Quebec autonomy. (Here a studio was just one more piece of necessary cultural and social infrastructure for the nation in waiting, with assistance to both Cité du Cinéma and Ciné Cité Montreal being a natural extension of this orientation.) Although state involvement in the Toronto Film/Media Complex raised many difficulties for the city's existing facilities providers, public-private partnerships still played a significant role in facilitating the development and ensuring that it was established under transparent circumstances and marketplace rents.

As in London, various Hollywood majors have intersected with Canadian studios and contributed to their development, but there are important differences. London studios benefited from London's privileged status as part of the design core of international film and television production in ways Canadian locations were never able to. Large-scale productions and valuable franchises like the Bond and Harry Potter films initiated the development and redevelopment of studios. By contrast, Hollywood majors might build or refurbish an additional soundstage, as happened in Vancouver for *Stargate SG-1*, or develop a specialized set such as the White House set and interiors Warner Bros. maintains in Toronto's Kleinburg Studios. This lower-level Hollywood interest has been a consequence of the type of work Canada—and Toronto in particular—has been best known for over the past twenty years.

Much of the discussion of runaway production to Canada revolves around movies of the week and television series that have significantly smaller budgets than blockbuster feature films. On lower-budget movies-of-the-week and television series production, overheads can be as much as 30 percent lower in Canada, in addition to other savings resulting from buying out residuals and reduced health and pension costs.[15] The tenor of this discussion means that Canada, unlike the United Kingdom, is often perceived as only operating at the lower end of the production spectrum. Susan Christopherson sees Canada as a particular beneficiary of the trend by producer/distributors to "develop low cost production centers for that portion of their programming that does not require specialized inputs or high production values."[16] Something of this low-cost production center dynamic is well captured by Katrina Onstad in 1997:

> Canada has become the Pawtucket of TV, attracting shows that are marketed for an international audience, such as Vancouver-filmed *The X-Files* or *The Outer Limits*, and B-list series featuring stars who don't mind relocating. Why? Quite simply, we're cheaper, and so we've become a kind of fraternal twin to LA, the twin who doesn't quite have the style of its sibling but makes up for lack of panache in plain old industriousness.[17]

This suggests a particular role for Canada in the ecology of audiovisual production as a low-cost backlot for Los Angeles. Some confirmation of this is provided by 1999–2000 estimates by the Entertainment Industry Development Corporation that put the Canadian global share of movie-of-the-week production at 45 percent.[18] Cost has always been an important factor for international producers in deciding to base major projects in Canada with exchange rate differentials between the Canadian and U.S. dollars making production in Canada often significantly cheaper than in the United States. But the cost of using Canadian facilities and crews alone is rarely the sole concern. Other issues can be equally important, as the sheer number of higher-budgeted television series and feature productions in Canada indicate. Canadian competitive advantage has turned on the capacity to deliver quality crews and facilities and appropriate locations, coupled with producers' confidence in Canadian ability deriving from recent successful and cost-effective production.

Canadian stories and locations are only intermittently the reason for producing in Vancouver, Toronto, or Montreal. Contrast this with the circumstances of London and New York, where the actual location is part of the very reason for producing there. London has global recognition as both a setting and generator of global stories that no Canadian city can emulate but all desire.[19] What Canada has had to offer Hollywood has been the benefits of its continental physical contiguity—the capacity to appropriate Canadian natural and built environments within what Mike Gasher has called a shared "continental cinemascape."[20] Thus, Hollywood filmmakers have been able to appropriate British Columbia, "emphasizing its physical geography, the topographical, climatic, and natural historical features that adjoin the province to Washington, Idaho, Montana and Alaska."[21] In a similar fashion, Toronto and Montreal have been able to take advantage of their "continental similarities" and the interchangeability of their respective built environments. This continental geography also facilitates split location production such as The Pledge, which was made in Vancouver and Reno, Nevada, or The Whole Nine Yards, which was shot in Montreal and Chicago, which has benefited Canadian studios.

Unlike many of its international counterparts that centralize production around a single location like London or Paris, Canada has three main international production locations. This means that no Canadian city has the kind of local ascendancy as does London or Los Angeles. In 2001–2002, 94 percent of the "foreign production" in Canada passed through these three centers, with Vancouver accounting for 51 percent, Toronto 33 percent, and Montreal 10 percent of foreign, mostly U.S.-sourced film and television production.[22] These continental dynamics have created three different kinds of media cities. Whereas domestic production has been a defining element for Toronto and Montreal, international production has played that role in Vancouver. This is clearly evident in the production industry statistics for the 2002–2003 financial year. While British Columbia (B.C.) (Vancouver) is the leading Canadian location for "foreign location production," Ontario (Toronto) and Quebec (Montreal) clearly eclipse B.C. in terms of levels of overall production, with B.C. (at C$1,041 million) coming a distant third behind Ontario (C$1,968 million) and Quebec (C$1,450 million).[23] Put another way, international production dominates British Columbian film and television production with an 80 percent share of production in the province against Ontario's 20 percent and Quebec's 25 percent.

If the historical competition between Toronto and Montreal is a continuing and defining cultural and economic contest over more than a century, the emergence of Vancouver as Canada's clear third film production center has introduced a new dynamic. Each city is in competition for the label Hollywood North. But each "Hollywood North" represents very different Hollywoods and filmmaking futures—Toronto claims this status "because it often doubles as New York in US television series and big Hollywood stars are routinely spotted in the city" and because it is—when local film and television production are taken into account—the largest film and television production center in Canada.[24] Vancouver claims this status because it secures the largest proportion of Hollywood location and medium- to higher-budgeted features. Finally, Montreal claims the title because it has been able to secure important major blockbuster productions and has enough star power to represent itself providing a diversity of international and period locations with its "one-of-a-kind architecture."[25]

Unlike London studios, which often host a combination of local and international production, the major studios in Vancouver mostly provide services to international film producers. Its domestic-oriented industry has grown up in part because of the services and skills established for international production. By contrast, the situation in Montreal and Toronto is similar to London in that neither city depends on this international production. The many stages and converted warehouses in Toronto and the purpose-built Montreal studios service both local and international production. The business models of the Montreal studios are based in part on the synergies available between lower-budgeted local production and higher-budgeted international feature production. While Canadian domestic production in English and French provides the dominant proportion of film and television production expenditure in both cities, the international and local components are in direct, synergistic relation. In all three cities, the needs of domestic and international production must be balanced, but in each city the production mix is quite different. In any downturn of local production, Montreal and Toronto would be more affected than Vancouver; but by the same token, in any downturn in international production Vancouver would be more affected than both Toronto and Montreal. The 2000s would provide telling examples of each possibility.

Megastudios, Crisis, and Stagnation

If Canada was the success story of international production in the 1990s, the 2000s have not been as kind to Canadian location interests. On closer inspection, this should not be so surprising. The continental geography, proximity, and integration with U.S. markets means that Canadian film and television production is in lockstep with U.S. economic developments. Just as the prospect of actors' and writers' strikes drove studio shoots in 2000–2001, the noneventuation of the strikes meant production slowed in both Canada and the United States over summer 2001. International production business declined in the wake of the 9/11 tragedy, leaving Canadian studios empty in the fall.[26] And Toronto had its own problems with an outbreak of the contagious virus SARS affecting rates of incoming production. In late 2002, industry unemployment in Vancouver hit nearly 50 percent in the wake of "a plunge in telepic orders, overuse of locations, the soft economy, concerns about crew depth and—ironically—even lower costs and sweeter incentives elsewhere."[27]

Some of the value proposition of Canada as a production location had been wiped out by the substantial appreciation of the Canadian dollar against the greenback, which made Eastern European studios more attractive propositions. This mostly affected "small-budget, marginal shoots like telefilms and independent features that might look to remain in Hollywood or go elsewhere internationally to shoot their projects."[28] Canadian production centers and studios faced the prospect in the 2000s of unstable levels of international production in the wake of structural change, exchange rate movements, intense competition from other locations, and economic slowdown.

Problems with international production coincided with problems in the domestic industry. The advent of and enthusiastic uptake of reality television squeezed drama production globally with consequences for domestic and international production in Canada. Further compounding the problem was the loosening of governmental regulations with funding cutbacks of Canadian production by government and television networks. This ensured that Montreal and Toronto were hit particularly hard in 2002–2003. A downturn in local production in 2003 pushed Ciné Cité Montreal toward receivership.

In these circumstances, large purpose-built studios became more, not less, important as securing higher-budgeted productions became the goal of Canadian location interests. Denis Seguin reported industry consensus when he claimed that "one element, more than any other, will dictate supremacy in film production in Canada: the motion picture studio." Seguin was here noting the importance of the "big build on the $100 million budget productions" where "a huge and complicated set" would be required to allow the camera to be "so far away from the action that the entire surrounding space must be dressed for its role." In these circumstances, the production has to "spend more money, and it needs a really big soundstage."[29]

Vancouver and Montreal seemed well equipped to manage this transition. Each city had added new stages and facilities in the late 1990s and early 2000s to accommodate this rise in imaging standards and support the digital production of blockbuster and special effects driven features. Vancouver location interests have consistently been able to adapt to market changes in international production. Just as over the 1990s Vancouver was the most important location for the production of movies of the week and for both high-profile and lower-budgeted television series, in the 2000s it has become known for its steady stream of medium-budget and blockbuster features and international TV series. As a consequence, the city has experienced a coordinated response to make its locations and its infrastructure more competitive for the servicing of international production. Montreal had sufficient studio space of the requisite scale to host a large-scale blockbuster production such as Martin Scorsese's U.S.$130 million *The Aviator* in 2003.[30]

Toronto, by contrast, has continued to rely on its large stock of warehouses and converted or smaller purpose-built spaces. Where Montreal and Vancouver use their megastudios to secure international production, Toronto is by contrast more like New York—a set of smaller spaces for production and a postproduction powerhouse. As in New York, there has been debate in Toronto about the need for a megastudio. Such a facility is seen as remedying the loss of big-budget Hollywood blockbusters to Vancouver, Montreal, and other locations—but it is also seen as something of a furphy given the focus in Toronto on split location production, the central importance of commercial production (over C$200 million in 2002), and local production requiring soundstages but not so much the "big build" stages required for *Aviator*, *Catwoman*, or *Gothika*, for example. But by the early 2000s, production infrastructure in the guise of mega state-of-the-art studios had become an ambition of all three major production centers.

Vancouver

Much is made of the savings associated with producing in Vancouver and its role as a niche site for low-cost, cost-conscious productions. Much is also made of its capacity to stand in for the Pacific Northwest. But Vancouver's story is also one of continuing involvement in higher-cost television series and blockbuster feature production and of Vancouver locations, including studios, standing in for an immense variety of locations. Integral to this story has not only been the sheer amount of "great indoors" provided by Vancouver's fifty stages and associated infrastructure capable of hosting forty productions simultaneously in the city, but also the fact that of this 875,000 square feet of studio space, 40 percent is provided in eighteen purpose-built stages in five studio complexes, with all soundstages measuring more than twelve thousand square feet.[31]

Vancouver's indoor spaces are skewed toward servicing high-end productions while proximate locations enable the re-creation of a huge variety of U.S. and international settings. *The X-Files* (1993–1998) is a case in point of this Vancouver studio-location and high-budget story. This enormously successful television series produced out of North Shore Studios (now Lions Gate) had from inception a large budget for a television series. It was to be a freaky, off-beat science-fiction show from a creator who had never directed a television episode. In 1995, the series directly injected C$33 million into the local Vancouver economy.[32] The choice of Vancouver for this series, and the availability of purpose-built studio space constructed and run by a Hollywood insider—Stephen J. Cannell—was very much based on the convenient functionality of Vancouver and surrounds. The city was ideally placed to play the "continental" reach and style required by the series. The fact that one could "ski on a nearby glacier in the morning—even in summer—and sail the Pacific in the afternoon" enabled the *X-Files* to "place every show in a different setting—an Air Force base, an Indian reservation, a small town in Iowa," without venturing far from the studio.[33] This is precisely the kind of proximity to natural and built locations that has attracted producers to Los Angeles for many years.

Perhaps because *The X-Files* showed just how versatile Vancouver could be, the city has continued to play a surprising range of locations and historical time periods—Mendocino, California, in *Jennifer Eight*; Concrete, Washington, in *This Boy's Life*; Brooklyn in *The Commish*. It has been the location for period films such as the remake of *Little Women* and for *The Highlander* TV series in which Vancouver and environs doubled as "Elizabethan England, Mongolia in 1060, or Vietnam in 1969."[34] B.C. Film Commissioner Susan Croome saw this mix of the natural and built environment, when coupled with the capabilities of its soundstages, skilled crews, tax incentives, and attractive exchange rate, as making for a comparative advantage over other production locations:

> We have a huge number of location looks and can even replicate 13 out of the 15 bio-climatic zones of the world. We have desert with cactus, the Rocky Moun-

tains and glaciers, the crashing waves on the west coast of Vancouver Island, and vineyards that look like Provences. And there's Vancouver's great urban look.[35]

Vancouver's functional proximity—a two-and-a-half-hour flight from Los Angeles—has been especially important to it. It is closer to Los Angeles than either Miami or Wilmington, and it is in the same time zone as Los Angeles. This has allowed its functional integration as Canada's west coast extension of Hollywood and enabled the city to become a premier location production center for Hollywood production.

Bridge Studios

Bridge Studios is situated on a fifteen-acre site and currently has 120,000 square feet of soundstages, 40,000 square feet of production offices, and 35,000 square feet of workshop facilities. Among its stages is a large 40,000-square-foot special effects stage that is one of the largest effects stages in North America,[36] attracting big builds such as *Jumanji*. The addition of a special effects stage significantly enhanced the attractiveness of both the studio and Vancouver as a destination for international production. Typically the studio hosts several projects concurrently. In July 2003, it was hosting two television series productions (*Dead Like Me* and *Stargate SG-1*), commercials, and a blockbuster feature, *Scary Movie 3*. According to the studio's website, it has hosted over a hundred productions over its life.

The facility started life as a steel-manufacturing plant for bridges (the steel girders for San Francisco's Golden Gate Bridge were built there). It was bought by the public water and transport utility BC Hydro and Transit in the mid-1970s and used as a bus repair depot and occasional film production venue. The first movie shot there was the 1982 feature *Mother Lode*, starring Charlton Heston. The set for that film was sold to the producers of the first Rambo film, *First Blood*, which was partly shot there. Later *Iceman* and *The Clan of the Cave Bear* used the facility. This history of the intermittent production of movies in the space undoubtedly encouraged government investment to build soundstages, develop property offices, and convert a warehouse into an effects stage. The British Columbian government transformed it into a permanent production venue in 1986–1987 after lobbying from the film industry. The complex is a "four-wall facility," meaning that producers rent only the soundstages from the operators and must access services and labor from other sources.

The studio is now part of the Bridge Business Park, a mixed-use site that also includes offices, light industrial, retail, restaurants, and a hotel. Since 1989, the studios have been run by the British Columbia Pavilion Corporation, a Crown corporation that is also responsible for BC Place Stadium and the Vancouver

Convention and Exhibition Centre as part of its brief to provide the "right places for any range of event experiences."

In mid-2002, the provincial government issued a request for proposals to privatize the studio. The logic behind this disinvestment—which was still to take place at the time of writing—was that the B.C. government had bought and refurbished the site in 1988 to nurture the then-nascent film industry. As John Harding of the BC Pavilion Corporation put it, "the government's outlook is that now that the industry is successful, it doesn't need that nurturing. . . . We don't need to be in the business of operating film studios."[37]

Lions Gate Studio

This purpose-built thirteen-acre production facility opened in 1989. It was created by U.S. producer Stephen J. Cannell and Paul Bronfman's Comweb Group. The studio is best known for hosting the X-Files from 1993 to 1998. At the time of its opening in 1989, it was Canada's largest film and television production facility, with six stages and nine tenant service companies. Initial construction was aided by a C$4.3 million loan from the provincial government. Lions Gate, which purchased the studio in 1998 for U.S.$24.5 million (C$36 million), also has a long-term lease on another five-acre, two-soundstage facility in Vancouver, Eagle Creek Studios, which has hosted the films Cats and Dogs and Insomnia (2002).

Lions Gate contains a backlot of facades of commercial districts, residential neighborhoods, retail space, office buildings, courthouse, and a small-town main street. This variety of architectural styles is seen as assisting producers to use studio space to double for a variety of North American cities. It is also one way of getting around Vancouver's "newness" as a city.

Lions Gate borders on the Pacific Ocean and is situated at the base of the Coastal Mountain range. Like its counterpart Vancouver Film Studios, Lions Gate has built two new stages in the past two years, both of which are 20,500 square feet with 40-foot clear ceilings.[38] It sees itself as catering to "large US-based productions."[39] In July 2003, for instance, it was hosting Catwoman, Scooby-Doo 2: Monsters Unleashed, and Scary Movie 3 (this last movie was also using the effects stage in the Bridge Studios). While the studio became famous for its hosting of a television series, it has been as much oriented to supplying high budget feature production as television series production.

Vancouver Film Studios

The Vancouver Film Studios began life as Northstar International Studios in 1985 when an existing commercial structure was renovated to become shooting and production space. Its present owner, the McLean Group of Companies, acquired the business and buildings in 1987 as part of its consolidation of ownership of commercial real estate in the precinct containing the original studio. The McLean Group's principal focus when it acquired the studio was commercial warehousing and residential development, and initially the owners viewed film and television tenants as filling a short-term need until a long-term tenant could be located. However this viewpoint changed with the growth of film and television production in Vancouver.

Growth rates of 35 percent in the Vancouver production services industry in 1996 and 1997 prompted the McLean Group to relaunch Northstar International Studios as Vancouver Film Studios in 1998. A further six purpose-built soundstages and associated support spaces were constructed between 1999 and 2003 with the aid of a loan from the British Columbia government in 1999 for C$20 million to go toward the C$70 million redevelopment of the site. This allowed existing warehouses previously used for filmmaking to be renovated and permitted new soundstages to be built. The site also incorporates a helipad and has a one-gigabyte fiber optic backbone—this extensive IT infrastructure, which included "about 1,200 computers and 1,200 IP phones," was integral to the production of X-Men 2 (2003) and Santa Clause 2 (2002).[40] The Vancouver Film Studios now occupies forty acres with thirty of these devoted to film and television production. It has ten purpose-built soundstages and a variety of production support buildings. In late 2002, it had 250,000 square feet of studio space.

The Studios prides itself on the quality of its spaces, claiming that it "compare[s] favourably with the best facilities in the world" and that it incorporates innovations in "construction materials and dimensions, power, and sound-proofing." It claims to have built in important fiber and network backbone infrastructure "at the construction phase" as a means of anticipating the increasingly complex "technological demands of our tenants." The Vancouver Film Studios typically hosts about eight features at a time.[41] It produces a regular stream of A-features—most recently I, Robot and Paycheck. It also caters to midbudget features such as a production based on a video game, Alone in the Dark.[42] Over the period there has been a trend away from the production of series and toward (higher-budgeted) features. In 2003, it produced seven features, two pilots for TV series, and one TV series; in 2000, it produced six features, one movie of the week, six TV series, and one TV pilot.

Toronto

There are approximately 1.3 million square feet of soundstage space in Toronto—this amounts to some ninety stages distributed across twenty-seven sites. In total space, Toronto has almost half as much again as that available in Vancouver. Only approximately 8 percent of Toronto's studio space is purpose built, while 92 percent is supplied by converted warehouses and other assorted industrial facilities. Most purpose-built stages have an average size of about nine thousand square feet and are not consequently pitched at high-budget production.[43]

There are two different kinds of conclusions that location interests and design interests have drawn about Toronto from these facts and figures. The first is that it is a location that has organically built a network of small to medium-sized soundstages and backlots to service local and international production. With Toronto responsible for about 40 percent of total film and television production in Canada, this has affected how Toronto actors have pitched for and accommodated international production. The main game for location interests has been Toronto's role as the "design center" for English Canadian film and television production—both in dollar value and absolute numbers of productions. So in 2003, of Toronto's 214 major TV and film productions, 174 were Canadian and 38 were U.S. productions, and a further 2 were from other overseas destinations.[44]

The subsidiary game of servicing international production has grown in a way that builds on and takes advantage of this local production and postproduction capacity. The city's popularity with international producers turns on a number of factors. First, they can take advantage of the facilities, services, and cost structures built up for Canadian domestic film and television production—this is the image of Toronto as a "telepic Queen." Second, there is its capacity to provide cheap, alternative location and studio shooting spaces in which Canadian locations can render a generic, urban U.S. look and double for New York locations in particular. Third, an incredible array of backlots and studio sets have been built in Toronto studios to service international production that are available for production, ranging from White House sets to interiors of shopping malls. Fourth, Toronto is attractive for its "state-of-the-art range of recording, dubbing, editing, printing and other postproduction services" that promoters claim—and New York alone could dispute—is unequaled in North America outside Los Angeles.[45] Finally, Toronto also has the added advantage of a live theater market that is legitimately claimed to be the third largest in the English-speaking world after New York and London.

From these factors a very particular and distinct story emerges of a set of design and location interests centered on the lower to middle budgets of film and television production, on the one hand, and split location production needs, on the other. The average expenditure on foreign projects in Ontario was only C$13.1 (U.S.$9 million)—well below the average Hollywood film budget of U.S.$58 million.[46] Toronto has a niche in this area, and this niche is the story of the transformation of Toronto from "a cheap place to shoot cheap films" and commercials into the third-largest film and television production center in the world.[47]

The second conclusion to be drawn from this story is the absence of a large purpose-built megastudio in the city that prevents the city from pitching for and securing the very high-budget international productions. This is a story of Toronto falling behind other competitor locations not only in Canada but in "Los Angeles, London, Sydney, Prague and other secondary production centres scattered throughout North America and Western Europe."[48] The Toronto advantage in low- to medium-budgeted domestic and international production and commercials is now insufficient: It should have more upmarket aspirations to pitch for projects around the average Hollywood film budget of U.S.$58 million and above. To do so, it would need a megastudio that would permit the city to become a "market maker" rather than a "market taker."[49] Location interests are here seeking to introduce, through the Port Lands megastudio development, another strata to the city's ensemble of facilities and services and accommodate particular design interests.

> It's been a truism in Toronto film circles for the last decade that while the city has sufficiently talented crews to host "runaway productions," it's been bypassed by *Titanic*-sized Hollywood films—movies with budgets in excess of $150-million involving support staff of as many as 2,000 persons—because it has lacked an appropriately huge, purpose-built, state-of-the-art facility. Now, with the port lands project nearing reality, the theory is that runaway business that once went to Montreal or Vancouver will be rerouted to Toronto, thus restoring the Ontario capital's lustre as the real Hollywood North.[50]

The strategy is both a response to the downturn in production in lower- and midbudget productions and a response to the opportunities available in blockbuster film production. In these circumstances, the existing facilities such as Toronto Film Studios are disparagingly referred to "as a rabbit warren of reclaimed warehouse space on Toronto's Eastern Avenue known rather grandly as Toronto Film Studios" (TFS).[51]

The two conclusions are not as mutually exclusive as they initially appear. The irresistible logic for a megastudio is overblown. Toronto already has large, purpose-built, clear-span stages. Wallace Studios—the only Toronto studio facility owned and operated by women—is a private waterfront studio complex featuring two clear-span studios with a third under construction. Its Studio 1 is claimed to be one of the largest single clear-span studios in the world—at eighty-five feet high and fifty-four thousand square feet; while its second studio, at forty-two thousand square feet, is sixty-five feet high. With its existing mix of facilities, Toronto has handled Hollywood productions of considerable scale whether it be *Chicago* in 2001 or *Resident Evil: Apocalypse* in 2003.

At the same time, Toronto does have a considerable advantage over competitor locations in North America given its variety of standing sets. Toronto Film Studios has a wide-bodied economy class airplane cabin and cockpit, a period private plane, and a Gulf Stream–style jet cabin. It also has a New York–style apartment, brownstone townhouse, and police precinct and associated holding cells. Downsview Park studios feature a penitentiary set with visiting area and segregation room, and Fraser Avenue studios has ten jail cells. Epitome Pictures specializes in this kind of facility: It has a mall interior, a school, and a prewar/present-day city neighborhood exterior backlot with matching interiors. Bars/restaurant sets can be found in Studio Works, Downsview Park, and CorkTownWorks Inc.

With changing standards of imaging and production and the availability of alternative purpose-built spaces, producers may be less inclined to put up with rough conditions on Toronto soundstages. When Canadian producer Don Carmody shot *Chicago* in Toronto in the winter of 2001, he needed a huge space that was then bigger than any purpose-built soundstage in the city—he found it in an uninsulated warehouse. He recalled that his "dancers were freezing their asses off."[52] But the response to this need does not have to be a megastudio—it could equally be the network of studios spaces including now very large clear-span studio space. Similarly, the pitch for the US$100 million production is not the only response to the growing need for "specialized, higher-per-capita projects." Just as the US$100 million budget Hollywood production has become the norm, so, too, has the higher-budgeted feature production destined for DVD release and television series that are transforming elements of what was once the movie of the week into US$20 to $50 million productions and the higher-budgeted television drama series. Toronto's existing facilities, which have undergone continuous upgrades, would seem to be particularly well placed to take advantage of these shifts.

Toronto markets itself as a location destination in a variety of ways. It is one hour by air from New York and shares a similar climate. It offers a generic "Urban USA" feel. It also provides in some of its neighborhoods—like the east-end Beaches area—wood frame residential architecture that closely resembles that in U.S. cities. It has an ethnically diverse population and a variety of neighborhoods. It can double effectively for New York at a fraction of the price. Its mix of streetscapes and people ensures that it can also stand in for Washington, Chicago, Florida, Vienna, Warsaw, Tokyo, and Teheran. Toronto's lower crime rates than U.S. cities and public and cultural amenities can also make it an attractive production location.

Design interests have focused on Toronto as a place for split location production. Of these split locations, standing in for New York has been a constant. Here producers typically do a week or two of filming in New York (or another U.S. city) and then come to Toronto for interiors and in some cases exteriors that can double for New York (and elsewhere). In this split location shooting with U.S. locales, Toronto secures the lion's share of production.[53] The mechanics and functionality of the continental geography for split location production and the importance to it of Canadian financial involvement can be seen in the case of *Good Will Hunting*. With Don Starr's consortium of investors coming into this production at a late stage, the rest of the film was shot in Canada at Toronto Film Studios and locations to attract Canadian tax concessions. So when filming wrapped up on Friday in New York, the entire operation was loaded into a fleet of trucks and hauled across the border to Toronto. By Monday morning, the actors were back at it, on a Toronto-cum-Boston set, near the University of Toronto.[54]

Cinespace Film Studios

Cinespace Studio Management owns/operates about four hundred thousand square feet of studio space, production office space, and set storage and lockup space at its four separate Toronto facilities. Its Marine Terminal 28 studio is an inner-city waterfront facility with four stages, five production office suites, and a secure five-hundred-car parking lot. Its Booth Avenue facility has four stages totalling 105,000 square feet. Kleinburg Studios has two soundstages and two floors of production offices and support space. Stage 2 includes permanent sets of the White House's Oval Office, while Stage 1 has the Great Hall and "Halls of Justice." Kleinburg is situated on fifteen acres adjacent to a river and conservation lands affording outdoor filmmaking possibilities. The Cinespace website[55] claims that since the late 1980s, the company has "constructed more production space than anyone else in Toronto" and that "well over C$1 billion" worth of Hollywood and Canadian production has been carried out in its studios.

Toronto Film Studios

Toronto Film Studios (TFS) is the other large provider of film and television studio complexes in Toronto, operating 17 stages with over 360,000 square feet of space on around 30 acres close to downtown Toronto. The Rose Corporation established TFS in January 1998 when it acquired a studio facility that had gone into bankruptcy. In 2001, a ten-acre property immediately east of their main lot was purchased for expansion purposes; in 2002, it acquired under lease from the Toronto Economic Development Corporation a 40,000-square-foot clear-span building to secure bigger studio builds, and in 2003, it acquired from Alliance Atlantis the 86,000-square-foot, 7-acre broadcast facility called Cinevillage. Cinevillage boasts as its anchor tenant the major Canadian broadcaster, creator, and distributor of filmed entertainment, Alliance Atlantis, and is geared to specialty cable channel programming. In 2004, TFS won the reopened tender to develop the megastudio complex on the Port Lands waterfront site. TFS also operates a production services arm that supplies the range of camera, lighting, grip, and electrical generating equipment to the motion picture and television producers using the facility and beyond. And, as noted earlier, it has a number of standing sets that have been used by many productions—thereby encouraging split location production with other studios.

The reasoning behind the acquisition of Cinevillage is indicative of the contemporary logic of alliances between studio operators and domestic producers. For TFS president, Ken Ferguson, the purchase was a component of the company's plan to create a "much-needed film and television campus in Toronto." For Alliance Atlantis, selling to TFS locked in long-term access to high-quality production, broadcast, and related facilities at Cinevillage while allowing for the fluctuating demands for studio facilities. This move made sense for them as the studio space was a "non–core asset," and divesting it gave the management time and corporate resources to focus on core operations.[56]

The Rose Corporation is a Toronto-based real estate investor/operator and merchant bank providing debt and equity financing. The company regularly enters into joint ventures with commercial and residential builders and developers in southern Ontario, and it has long-term holdings in hotels and seniors' residences, in addition to its film studios.[57] Toronto Film Studios is part of the company's rental properties division, which includes, besides the film studios, self-storage miniwarehouses and commercial properties. The Rose Corporation became involved in studio facilities on the basis of the steady growth of the film and television industry in Toronto since the early 1980s and its assessment that cable channels had contributed to an increased demand for new film and television product. With the winning of the bid to construct a megastudio complex aimed at attracting the US$100 million–plus productions to Toronto, TFS competitors—the existing large players like Cinespace and small to medium-sized studio facilities—worry about TFS crowding out the competition and that the city "will end up subsidising the megastudio."[58] Perhaps it might come to dominate Toronto soundstages in the way that Mel's Cité du Cinéma has in Montreal.

Montreal

In 2003, Montreal hosted three features—*Gothika*, *The Aviator*, and *The Terminal*—all US$60 million–plus productions with one, *The Aviator*, coming in at $130 million. International location production in English has been growing steadily from the nadir point of 1992, when no international productions were shot in Montreal. Purpose-built studios with large stages have played an important part in the emergence of Montreal as a significant location production destination. The large inner-city stages "just five minutes from downtown" and purpose-built facilities near the municipal airport combine with Montreal's diverse built environment to provide the two key components of the city's location interest pitch. The city is often used as the ideal North American location to play Paris and other European locales. As a contemporary North American city, it is also able to play the contemporary American city—indeed, the city has played New York in over thirty productions.

The city's diversity of architecture is seen as a core asset enabling the city to double as New Delhi in *The Day after Tomorrow*[59] and nineteenth-century Europe with Old Montreal itself looking "very 18th century." Montreal competes with the cheaper production facilities in Eastern Europe by emphasizing the possibilities of using the city's diverse architecture for exteriors instead of building sets.[60] The Montreal production mix is changing. Writing in *Variety* in 2003, Norma Reveler notes that of the thirty-three productions shot in Montreal that year, twenty-five were smaller domestic budget productions while eight were "foreign with significant budgets." The international, principally high-budget English-language productions were becoming an important feature of Montreal's mix alongside "numerous lower-budget, domestic French-language productions" that have defined its industry.[61]

At the same time, the Montreal studio sector has become consolidated into one large company—Mel's Cité du Cinéma—covering the existing Cité du Cinémas and Ciné Cité Montreal, which was acquired by Mel's after it went into receivership. This move to consolidate holdings into a megastudio has precedent in the Pinewood-Shepperton partnership but makes the new combined entity "the only [big] game in town." The Montreal Film and TV Commission head, Daniel Bissonnette, was reported to be concerned that this amalgamation into "one megacity" would limit the possibility of "any new injections of funding" into the Film and TV Commission.[62] At the same time, Montreal is as vulnerable as anywhere else to elected provincial governments passing budgets aimed at cost reductions that include a decrease in tax credits for film and TV production.

Mel's Cité du Cinéma

Mel Hoppenheim began what became Cité du Cinéma in 1988 with the acquisition and conversion of the historic Theatre Expo de la Cité du Havre. Five stages were added in 1994. Hoppenheim's partner, Locations Michel Trudel, is a film service provider specializing in cameras and lighting equipment. This first Cité du Cinéma was claimed to have "quickly pumped an estimated C$250 million into the local economy and created more than 500 new jobs." The second La Cité du Cinéma, entailing three stages, was added in 1999 at a cost of C$14 million. These stages were later used for *The Sum of All Fears*, *The Score*, *The Human Stain*, and *The Day after Tomorrow*. Construction on the third Cité du Cinéma began in 2002 with an investment of C$15 million. It consisted of four stages that were seen to be capable of "serving the most ambitious film production."

The size of Mel's Cité du Cinéma's stages was a key factor in bringing Roland Emmerich's *The Day after Tomorrow* and Martin Scorsese's *The Aviator* to Montreal. With the acquisition of its principal competitor, Ciné Cité Montreal, in late 2003, Mel's Cité du Cinéma added a further ten soundstages, giving it control of twenty-three soundstages.

Ciné Cité Montreal

Ciné Cité Montreal is Montreal's second major studio space. Situated as so many other major facilities have been, in refurbished hangars on a former airport site—in this case a military air base in the suburb of Saint Hubert—the studio required extensive soundproofing to be serviceable. However, the convenience of proximity to air services became a selling point for the facility. The hangars were used by numerous productions before the refurbished and renamed Ciné Cité Montreal officially opened in 2000. The owner's plan in 1999 was to invest C$25.5 million in the conversion of former hangars into stages and a new building. Its creation was seen as decisively addressing the problem of a lack of film production infrastructure in the city.

There was significant government involvement in the site's refurbishment. The cultural agency, SODEC (Société de développement des entreprises culturelles), and the economic agency, SGF (Société générale du financement du Québec), cocontributed to this public-private partnership. SODEC guaranteed a C$4 million loan, while SGF made an initial C$5 million investment in the company. The cultural agency's involvement was part of a panoply of "tools for intervention" in its support "for the growth of cultural enterprises"; while the economic development agency's support was part of the C$250 million it was making available in the recreation and tourism sectors in Quebec for "partnerships based on the usual terms and conditions of profitability of business." By the time the project went into receivership in late 2003, SGF had invested C$6 million since 1999 and had taken a 40 percent share of the limited partnership. It had also made an additional, nonsecured loan to the company of C$500,000. SODEC had co-invested C$1 million. At the time of the project's collapse, it owed creditors C$23.4 million.[63]

A month after going into receivership, the site was acquired by its major competitor, Mel's Cité du Cinéma, which also acquired the smaller Ice Storm Studio nearby—giving Cité du Cinéma ten additional soundstages. Various reasons were advanced for its problems, ranging from a downturn of local French-language production in the wake of cutbacks to the Canadian Television Fund to difficulties associated with drawing production to its suburban location—unlike its principal competitor, it was not an innercity studio but located on "the unfashionable side of the river."[64] Upon acquisition, Michel Trudel suggested that the site could find its niche in long-term TV shoots rather than for feature production. At the time of its receivership, its six stages totaled 159,350 square feet, and the studio had recently hosted shoots for *Timeline*, *Galidor: Defenders of the Outer Dimension*, and *Rollerball*.[65]

Conclusion

This chapter has outlined the variety of location interest strategies pursued by the three major film production locations in Canada. Studios have been an important part of the pitch by Vancouver, Toronto, and Montreal film commissions and service providers for production. Each place has sought to enhance its position within Canada and within a larger North American audiovisual space. Studios have become increasingly important parts of this competition for Montreal and then Toronto in the wake of the success of the Vancouver model. These studio developments have largely been undertaken in the contemporary period and have coincided with the consistent and sizable growth in the Canadian share of location production.

This growth needs to be understood in terms of what Canada affords the design interest. First, Canada has become significant precisely because its location interests have been able to offer more than one thing. The three major film cities are identifiably different places offering a range of stages, permanent sets, urban and natural environments, and production competences.

It is, therefore, not so many interchangeable studios as so many different spaces in different filmmaking milieus and film location matrices. So while these locations are sometimes in competition with each other—particularly Toronto and Montreal—they are also, for a substantial portion of their production slates, more in competition with other places in the United States and Europe than with each other. This makes them able to fulfill and pitch for quite different production needs.

A critical advantage for Canadian studios and locations in this pitching has been their continental geography and shared North American culture. This has meant that Vancouver, Montreal, and Toronto have been able to manage split location production almost as easily and sometimes more easily than it is possible to manage two locations *within* the United States. This has encouraged productions and parts of production to be either partially or wholly completed in Canada.

Another important but scarcely recognized factor has been the importance of Canada to the design interest. This can be the Hollywood activities of the Canadian mini-major Lions Gate—a company large enough to bankroll a slate of twenty blockbuster feature films in the 2000s. It can be the many Canadian cable companies that initiated and then brought in U.S. partners for their productions or came on board to make U.S.-based productions possible—these Canadian companies were fundamental to the business model of pay-TV in the United States, with as much as 30 percent of production for cable in the early 1990s sourced from Canada. It can be the design activities of Stephen J. Cannell, cofounder and majority shareholder of North Shore Studios (now Lions Gate), and minority shareholder, Canadian film services provider Paul Bronfman, over the 1990s, who from this studio's inception ensured that it was much more than just a rental facility for runaway production. And it can be the recently wound-up Canadian tax-shelter financing that provided between 6 and 8 percent of the budgets for so many Hollywood productions.

While the recent circumstances of this growth, coupled with the inherent vulnerabilities associated with "foreign location production," has ensured that there is ongoing Canadian concern for the continuing viability of these operations, there are not the kinds of further non-Hollywood options available to Canadians as to U.K. locations and facilities providers. Canadian operations have naturally tended to see their future as tied up with more of the same—their response has been one of promoting further integration and seeking to remain ahead of the game, with studios being an important part of this competition. And this has become more, not less, the case with the contraction in domestic Canadian production for film and television in the wake of market fragmentation, multichannel marketplaces, and declining support for Canadian domestic production as the various provincial and national governments move toward film services orientations in their film policy. Acutely conscious of the cyclical nature of the film business and therefore the studio business, Canadian facilities providers and personnel work to become more integrated and more ensconced in North American production networks—and one of the ways they have done so is through their studios. From Vancouver Film Studios to Mel's Cité du Cinéma to the proposed Great Lakes Studio and the Port Lands complex, Canadian studio complexes promote their facilities as state-of-the-art, leading-edge, and technologically sophisticated in their orientation. It really does seem in these circumstances that a measure of a city is the quality of its studios.

Canadian studios can not afford complacency: The very circumstances of globally dispersed production that made their spectacular participation possible in the first place means that any number of places within North America can emulate these cities. So "while it may currently be convenient to shoot here, the fact that Vancouver can play New York means Houston, Texas can probably do it as well."[66] Canadian studios need to be innovative in their strategies and business practices.

Canada has an important place in the theorization of the globalizing dynamics in film and television production. This is not just because it is an example of the intersection of the global and the local, but because it is an instance where the local is implicated in the global—where Canada and Canadians are the "same but different." And it is here, more than anywhere else apart from the United States itself, where the design and location interests are so intimately and integrally entangled.

Notes

1. BC Pavilion Corporation, "The Bridge Studios," available at www.bridgestudios.com/ (7 September 2004).

2. For an Australian report discussing its position with respect to Canada, see Malcolm Long Associates, *A Bigger Slice of the Pie: Policy Options for a More Competitive International Film & Television Production Industry in Australia—A Report for AusFILM International Inc.* (Sydney: Malcolm Long Associates, 2000), 3.

3. Martha Jones, *Motion Picture Production in California* (Los Angeles: California Research Bureau, 2002), 48.

4. Canadian Film and Television Production Association (CFTPA), *Profile 2004: An Economic Report on the Canadian Film and Television Production Industry* (Toronto, Ottawa, and Vancouver: CFTPA in association with L'Association des producteurs de films et de télévision du Québec [L'APFTQ] and Canadian Heritage, 2004), 11.

5. Jones, *Motion Picture Production in California*, 30.

6. Jones, *Motion Picture Production in California*, 30. The figures quoted for 1999 and 2000 are (1) Los Angeles, $29.4 billion and $31.0 billion; (2) New York, $2.5 billion and $2.45 billion; (3) British Columbia, $1.1 billion and $1.18 billion; (4) Toronto, $834.5 million and $1.01 billion; (5) Orlando, Florida, $390 million and $432 million; (6) North Carolina, $300.2 million and $250 million; (7) Chicago, $124 million and $84 million; (8) Miami, $31 million and $160 million.

7. Paul Attallah, "Canadian Television Exported: Into the Mainstream," in *New Patterns in Global Television: Peripheral Vision*, ed. John Sinclair, Elizabeth Jacka, and Stuart Cunningham (Oxford: Oxford University Press, 1996), 166.

8. Jason Kirby, "Starr Power: If You Think No One Makes Money in the Canadian Film Industry, You've Never Met Don Starr, a Tax Lawyer Who's Loopholed His Way to Making Millions," *Canadian Business* 75, no. 17 (September 2002).

9. Karen Murray, "Local Fare Finds Hungrier Palates South of the Border," *Variety*, 16 November 1992, 41.

10. Attallah, "Canadian Television Exported."

11. Brendan Kelly, "Shoots Rediscover City's Charms," *Variety*, 25–31 August 2003, 35.

12. Mike Gasher, *Hollywood North: The Feature Film Industry in British Columbia* (Vancouver: University of British Columbia Press, 2002), 31.

13. Gasher, *Hollywood North*, 24.

14. Denis Seguin, "The Battle for Hollywood North: Vancouver, Montreal and Toronto are Each Leading the Charge to Be Canada's Capital of Movie Production; Big-name Stars and Big-money Budgets Are the Coveted Prize," *Canadian Business* 76, no. 17 (September 2003): 55.

15. Martha Jones, *Motion Picture Production in California*, 27.

16. Susan Christopherson, "The Limits to 'New Regionalism,'" *Geoforum* 34, no. 4 (2003): 414.

17. Katrina Onstad, "Cut to the Cash: They're Making More Than Most Bank Managers," *Canadian Business* 70, no. 7 (June 1997): 36–43.

18. Entertainment Industry Development Corporation (EIDC), *MOWs—A Three Year Study: An Analysis of Television Movies of the Week 1997–1998, 1998–1999, 1999–2000* (Hollywood: EIDC, 2001), 4.

19. Denis Seguin, "Hawking Hogtown," *Canadian Business* 76, no. 10 (May 2003): 112.

20. Gasher, *Hollywood North*, 105.

21. Gasher, *Hollywood North*, 105.

22. Seguin, "The Battle for Hollywood North," 55.

23. CFTPA, *Profile 2004*, 26.

24. Onstad, "Cut to the Cash," 36–43.

25. Doris Toumarkine, "Canadian Attraction: Busy Film Commissions Continue to Lure Big Productions," *Film Journal International*, 1 May 2004, available at http://filmjournal.com/filmjournal/search/search_display.jsp?vnu_content_id=10006922699 (12 August 2004).

26. Brendan Kelly, "Few Projects Migrate North," *Variety*, 2–8 September 2002, A8.

27. Dave McNary, Tamsen Tillson, and Don Townson, "Vancouver Vexed as Regional Rivals Rally," *Variety*, 2–8 December 2002, 4.

28. Etan Vlessing and Adele Weder, "Rising Canada $ Seen as Slowing US Production," *Hollywood Reporter*, 13–19 May 2003, 65.

29. Seguin, "The Battle for Hollywood North," 55.

30. Kelly, "Shoots Rediscover City's Charms," 35.

31. Toronto Economic Development Corporation (TEDCO), "Backgrounder: Toronto Film/Media Complex," July 2003, available at www.tedco.ca/backgrouder.html (13 September 2003).

32. "Control Freak: Scully, Mulder and Their Creepy Enemies May Get All the Limelight, but Canuck Producer JP Finn Makes *The X-Files* Happen," *BC Business* 24, no. 11 (November 1996): 84–87.

33. Jonathan Kandell, "Vaunted Vancouver," *Smithsonian* 35, no. 1 (April 2004), 84–93.

34. Gordon Hardwick, location manager for the series, quoted in John Calhoun, "Vancouver," *TCI* 31, no. 4 (April 1997): 36–41.

35. BC Film Commissioner Susan Croome, quoted in Toumarkine, "Canadian Attraction."

36. John Calhoun, "Bridge Studios," *TCI* 31, no. 4 (April 1997): 41.

37. John Harding, Chief Financial Officer of the BC Pavilion Corporation, quoted in Adele Weder, "Rival Said to Bid on Bridge Studio," *Hollywood Reporter*, 5 December 2002, 39.

38. James Careless, "What's Shooting on Canuck Stages: The Bridge Studios Fills Gap with Spots," *Playback*, 21 July 2003, 21.

39. Peter Leitch, studio manager vice president, quoted in Careless, "What's Shooting on Canuck Stages," 21.

40. Randall Mang, "Dialed In: Bell Sweeps into the West," *BC Business* 31, no. 5 (May 2003): 103–4,106.

41. Mang, "Dialed In," 103–4, 106.

42. Careless, "What's Shooting on Canuck Stages," 21.

43. TEDCO, "Backgrounder."

44. Toumarkine, "Canadian Attraction."

45. "Lights, Action, Canada! (Toronto Has Staged a Spectacular Comeback, Turning Entertainment into a Hot New $2b Industry)," *Canadian Business* 67, no. 8 (August 1994): 58–65.

46. TEDCO, "Backgrounder."

47. Tamsen Tillson, "Quality Not Quantity for Local News," *Variety*, 25 February–3 March 2002, 67.

48. TEDCO, "Backgrounder."

49. All previous quotations in this paragraph are taken from TEDCO, "Backgrounder."

50. James Adams, "Megastudio Nears Port: Project Aimed at Bringing 'Hollywood North' Back to Toronto," *Globe and Mail*, 29 June 2004, R3.

51. Seguin, "The Battle for Hollywood North."

52. Seguin, "The Battle for Hollywood North."

53. Rhonda Silverstone, film commissioner, Toronto Film and Television Office, quoted in Toumarkine, "Canadian Attraction."

54. Kirby, "Starr Power."

55. Cinespace Studios, "Cinespace Studios," available at www.cinespace.com (12 August 2004).

56. Toronto Film Studios, "Company Background," available at www.torontofilmstudios .com/company_background.php (12 August 2004).

57. Toronto Film Studios, "Company Background."

58. Adams, "Megastudio Nears Port."

59. Bissonnette in Toumarkine, "Canadian Attraction."

60. Toumarkine, "Canadian Attraction."

61. Norma Reveler, "Runaway Competition," *Hollywood Reporter*, 2–8 September 2003, 66.

62. Bissonnette, quoted in Reveler, "Runaway Competition," 66.

63. Leo Rice-Barker, "Moliflex-White Assets on the Auction Block," *Playback*, 24 November 2003, 1.

64. Paul Bronfman, the Chair of the Board of Ciné Cité Montreal and one of the founders of North Shore Studios in Vancouver, claimed that the problem of not being downtown was exaggerated. After the first two years, North Shore Studios did not have a problem with being twenty to thirty minutes from downtown.

65. Rice-Barker, "Moliflex-White Assets on the Auction Block," 1.

66. Brant Drewery, "The Chameleon Coast: On Location with *The X-Files* in Anyplace, USA. Otherwise Known as Vancouver, Canada," *BC Business* 25, no. 5 (May 1997): 44–50.

CHAPTER NINE

Still the Center

Studios and the United States

Governor Arnold Schwarzenegger promises to bring Hollywood home to Californian soundstages. A succession of studies, including the U.S. Commerce Department's *The Migration of U.S. Film and Television Production* (2001), have endorsed the view that Hollywood and American production and U.S. advantage is being hollowed out by "runaway" production. From all this anxiety about the loss of film industry jobs, especially to Canada but also to the United Kingdom, Ireland, Australia, New Zealand, and a resurgent Europe, it would seem that Hollywood's geographic base in Los Angeles and U.S. global centrality in film and television production are under threat in an era of globally dispersed production. With political pressure being placed on Hollywood producers to shoot in California and on legislatures to "protect" American cultural patrimony and jobs, U.S.-based film interests—particularly those in Los Angeles—are, like their counterparts internationally, using the political means available to them to promote their particular location interests.

While these controversies and campaigns show that at the hub of international production, location and design interests do not always coincide, what is more important for our purposes here is that they point to the centrality of the relation between location and design interests in an era of globally dispersed production. Indeed, these controversies might be best thought of as signs of the difficult adjustment by American-based production to the circumstance of an increasingly globalized design and production regime in which Los Angeles—and America more generally—are simply other possible locations pitching for production.

Such globally dispersed production systems both privilege and expand the Hollywood design interest as dynamics of globally dispersed production require substantial concentration of the design and coordination functions of film and television production in one or two global media cities to be effective. For Saskia Sassen, this kind of dynamic in the allied fields of financial and producer services has generated "new forms of locational concentration."[1] There is considerable evidence that Los Angeles has been a significant beneficiary of this locational concentration with benefits not only to the design but also to the production segments in the city. At the same time, the geographic dispersal of production has encouraged the formation and growth of various location interests that have built facilities and infrastructures like studios within the United States to take advantage of these opportunities. As we have seen, places like Orlando, Florida, and Wilmington, North Carolina, have over the 1980s and 1990s developed substantial production capacity with the building of large studios—and an increasing number of new U.S. locations are likewise seeking to participate as locations for dispersed production. This is an expansion that precedes and is in substantial continuity with similar developments discussed in earlier chapters. If we only focus on the geographic dispersal of production outside the United States without recognizing the simultaneous dispersal within the United States and the substantial agglomeration of film industry services, facilities, and capacity in Los Angeles, we miss the interconnectedness of these agglomeration and dispersal dynamics and consequently misunderstand the nature and benefits of this global production system to U.S.-based design and location interests.

What is particularly striking about this global dispersal of production is that it has both connected and cohered the international production system to an unprecedented degree. Sassen is again helpful here in that she stresses that these new forms of locational concentration of financial and producer services sectors in a select few global cities have been "fed by the globalization and dispersal of economic activity that . . . telecommunications capability makes feasible." This has created the paradoxical situation where there is "consolidation in fewer major centers across and within countries" accompanied by "a sharp growth in the number of centers that become part of the global network as countries deregulate their economies."[2]

This theme of increased locational participation in globalizing networks generating ever-greater centralization of activity in core locations is particularly apposite for thinking about international film and television production. The sharp growth in participation in international production by countries, cities, and regions around the world has served—just as it has in finance and producer services—to bring an increasing number of places into Hollywood's global production net. But, at the same time, Los Angeles and New York have benefited from the significant centralization and "agglomeration"[3] of activities and facilities that have accompanied and been an entailment of these patterns of decentralization and dispersal. The system of location production characteristic of so much contemporary Hollywood production supports Los Angelean–centricity in a context of global production. Los Angeles is, as Allen Scott shows in *On Hollywood: The Place, The Industry*, "one of the most remarkable examples of a successful industrial agglomeration anywhere in the world."[4]

In our terms, the combination of the design interest of the Hollywood majors in developing projects and the location interest of places in securing projects has given rise to interrelated dynamics of global geographic dispersal at the level of the production shoot and concentration in Los Angeles at the level of production design. The very project-based form of production requires an increasingly sophisticated "back room" to facilitate the governing of productions at a distance. In circumstances of project-based forms of contemporary Hollywood production where each film is approached as an individual project, a design center is an essential feature as it supplies the enduring institutions and skills needed for the successful packaging of projects. Los Angeles provides this global creative and deal-making hub through which increasing amounts of production, including production generated and financed elsewhere, passes through.

With Hollywood producers now routinely deciding among a number of competing locations for a film including Los Angeles itself, Los Angeles is just another location for production. But it is a privileged production location with Los Angeles location interests benefiting from both their collocation with the headquarters of Hollywood's design interests and the unprecedented range, depth, and scale of Los Angeles's production facilities, infrastructures, and skills base. The great surge in the construction of studio complexes globally was matched over the 1990s in Los Angeles with a similar surge in the construction of new soundstages and renovation of existing facilities.[5] At the same time, the potential for noncoincidence between the design interest and location interests is now built into the mind-set of Los Angeles location interests as securing Hollywood productions for Los Angeles and California has become a priority of private consortia, labor, and city and state governments alike, just as it has in Vancouver, Prague, London, New York, Sydney, and Berlin.

Regimes of dispersed production have also substantially cohered and rendered interoperable participating locations putting location interests and their associated studio infrastructures inside and outside the United States on a similar footing. Here U.S.-derived and -generated common "rules of the game" have diffused throughout the system and become increasingly shared among actors within and outside the United States. Our example of Los Angeles facilities providers and crews behaving as just another (albeit privileged) location interest provides one instance of this. Another is provided by the rising number of film and television offices and film commissions involved in pitching for international production which are spinging up both in the United States and internationally. Forms of dispersal of production infrastructure to "extreme places" might have arguably began as a North American process in the 1980s with the building of greenfields studio infrastructures in Wilmington, Vancouver, and Orlando[6] but became quickly extended internationally to the Gold Coast and beyond in the late 1980s.

As the form of location interests has stabilized, locations have become so many interchangeable packages of facilities, services (including postproduction, which has also become more globally distributed), incentives, and natural and built environments. A common, increasingly global market for international footloose productions has emerged, with producers now not only taking advantage of subsidies to production provided by U.S. cities and states but also those provided internationally by Canadian, Australian, Irish, and British governments, among others. In becoming competitive and pitching professionally for international production, the rest of the world learned from America and adopted "American" forms of organization. Now the onus is being placed on the innovators—the U.S. locations, infrastructures, and service providers—to continue to innovate their approaches to split location production and competitive advantage in the pursuit of globally dispersed production. As Morty Dubin of the New York Production Alliance puts it, "[t]he rest of the world is becoming better at what we're doing; therefore, it gets back to the fact that we must promote our advantages and uniqueness— and we must be as cost-competitive as possible."[7]

While the political rhetoric of banding together within the United States to ensure that "our" production does not continue to go "offshore" certainly constructs something of a sense of common purpose and identity of interest among U.S. locations, there are, nonetheless, enduring differences among production centers within the United States reflecting not only their uniqueness and advantages in Dubin's formulation but the distinct location (and design) interests of cities, states, and regions in an era of globally dispersed production. Consequently, the challenges and opportunities facing film production locations in the United States are best thought as a relation between a regional—place-based—scale and global scales.

American Production Locations

Los Angeles is the premier design center and production location. In its co-ordinating and designing functions for the global film and television indus-try, Los Angeles has unequal but collaborative relationships with other loca-tions inside and outside the United States. Here the design interest of the Los Angeles–based Hollywood majors to package, finance, and promote film production productively intersect with the location interest of cities, states, and regions within and outside the United States to shoot films in their ter-ritory.

After Los Angeles is New York, which shares some design and production characteristics with Los Angeles but is also a production shoot rather than postproduction location for the many film and television stories set in New York. New York has much in common with its counterpart global media city of London in that it is both a design center and a privileged production lo-cation and the second film and television production center in North Amer-ica, with long-standing and deep connections with Los Angeles.

Another rung down are the states of North Carolina and Florida, which vie for the status of the third production center after Los Angeles and New York. Miami has some of the characteristics of New York in that it is a pro-duction shoot location for advertising, features, and television series and is also a Spanish-language production center in its own right. Orlando is like its North Carolinean counterparts in Wilmington and Raleigh in that it is a satellite film production location dependent on externally generated film and television production to fill the large studios at these locations. (Raleigh may be emerging as a more fully fledged media city courtesy of the larger Raleigh-Durham mix of universities and high-tech and creative industries.) Satellite production centers like Wilmington and Orlando without a sub-stantial local production base are in cutthroat competition with places inside and outside the United States for such production.

On the rung below Florida and North Carolina is Chicago, which hosted more film production than Miami in 1999 (US$124 million vs. $30 million)[8] and is a historically important production center, always hosting some film and television production courtesy of its size and importance as a film and television market. After Chicago are various places such as New Orleans, which is growing rapidly as a film production destination courtesy of the mix of soundstages and locations, and Savannah, Georgia, which is famous for its hosting of one film, *Midnight in the Garden of Good and Evil* (1997).

We will now examine in more detail the intersection of location and de-sign interests in shaping studio and related location infrastructure through particular case studies of Los Angeles, New York, Miami, Wilmington, and Orlando.

Los Angeles: The Design and Production Center

There is still some truth to the notion of Hollywood as a place located in southern California. The district of Hollywood is still more or less the geographic center of a cluster of production facilities, soundstages, office buildings, and studio ranches, stretching from Culver City, Venice, and Santa Monica in the south to Glendale, Burbank, North Hollywood, and even the Simi Valley in the north. The dozen or so companies that control more than half of the world's entertainment have headquarters in Los Angeles, within a thirty-mile radius of Hollywood. The executives, agents, producers, actors, and directors are there. The meetings to decide what movies will be made are held there. At some point, every major figure in world entertainment has to come to Hollywood, if only to accept an Academy Award.[9]

As Christopher Vogler observes here, Los Angeles effectively combines in this era of globalization its status as a design center with its status as a formidable production location for international production. These advantages are reflected in selected statistics: 581 feature films were made in Los Angeles in 2000. The city is the continuing site for higher-cost and therefore more profitable production. In March 2003, for instance, of the twenty-one major studio films in production at the time, fourteen were being shot at least in part in Los Angeles.[10] To put its dominance into perspective, the spending on production in Los Angeles is ten times larger than New York and thirty times larger than either Vancouver or Toronto. Between 1993 and 2000, the total number of film production days in Los Angeles actually increased from 26,640 to 46,808.[11] The extent of Los Angeles's preeminence in design and coordination functions is also found in the employment figures for the statistical category motion picture and video distribution where in 1999 Los Angeles had 22,399 of the 27,669 employees in distribution in the United States.[12] Los Angeles accounted in 1997 for some 61.4 percent of production employment within the United States[13]; in 1999, California's share expressed in dollars of motion picture production was 54 percent[14] (Los Angeles dominates Californian figures.) Los Angeles is then not only the design center necessary to support, facilitate, and integrate increasingly dispersed nodes of international production but also the place in which most of the high-value-added and high-waged areas of pre- and postproduction are carried out. With the range and depth of its studios, its prop houses, and its concentration of digital visual effects, it is, unsurprisingly, a preferred destination for high-budget blockbuster production and high-budget international television series production.

Allen J. Scott's discussion of Los Angeles's unrivaled infrastructural, technical and organizational capacities is instructive here. He notes that Los Angeles has some 5 million square feet of soundstages covering 72 different studios and 369 soundstages. It clearly dwarfs its closest U.S. competitor, New York, which has an estimated 740,000 square feet of studio space.[15] The figures confirm the sheer scale of Los Angeles in comparison to any of its competitor locations within the United States. Scott estimates that Los Angeles has almost three times the combined capacity of its four main location competitors of New York, North Carolina, Miami/Orlando, and Chicago,[16] and as noted in the previous chapter, it dwarfs the studio space available in Canada. It has a dense regional cluster of specialized and complementary producers and a unique pool of talent drawn from many different countries.[17] And Los Angeles has witnessed a tremendous growth in employment in production and service activities, with Scott noting a 194 percent growth in employment and 284 percent growth in establishments over the period from 1980 to 1997.[18] It also gains from what could be termed headquarter advantages that ensure that critical areas like postproduction can be carried out close to the customer—the media conglomerate distributor or advertising agencies—with these critical areas being responsible for much of the employment growth in the period.

Scott also points to the continuing involvement of the Hollywood majors and U.S. broadcast networks in the control of studios, with majors controlling 40 percent of the total square footage available in the city; while the American networks—CBS, ABC, and NBC—control "about 10 percent" of the total square footage.[19] This continuing and substantial control of half of the available studio space by majors and broadcast networks points to the continuing importance of directly connecting location and design interests within Los Angeles just as it points to the continuing importance of vertical integration within the one company as a continuing source of competitive advantage. These figures underscore not only the continuing infrastructural capacity maintained by the majors and broadcast networks in Los Angeles but the importance of this control in circumstances where the "in-house studio represent[s] an independent profit center whose mandate is simply to treat other divisions of the parent company on a par with all other potential lessors."[20]

Los Angeles provides every imaginable permutation and combination of studios and facilities—inner-city and edge city, clear-span effects to smaller digital studios, permanent sets, costumes and props, backlots, and facilities.

Rather than trying to provide an exhaustive list, we will focus here on two studios—Warner Bros. Burbank and LA Center Studios—which Scott sees as representative of some key patterns in studio development in Los Angeles.

Like its counterparts in Sydney, Melbourne, and Montreal, LA Center Studios is an inner-city studio located closed to the central business district. It is one of the many new studios constructed in Los Angeles over the past decade. It has over one hundred thousand square feet of studio space compressed onto a small piece of land. At its core is a converted high-rise office building. As Scott notes, this is seen as a "unique asset in terms of the opportunities that it offers for filming special scenes and backgrounds."[21] It also has on-site what is seen as an innovative mix of its own services and services provided by outside companies.

Warner Bros.' Burbank studios is, in comparison to most of the studio complexes we have examined so far in this study, a studio on an extraordinary scale. On 110 acres, it includes 28 soundstages ranging from 10,000 to 30,000 square feet and two water tanks. It also has a large range of permanent sets. It has a "jungle" and an associated lagoon, and archetypal streetscapes of New York (New York Street and Brownstone Street), Europe (French Street), and the American Midwest (Midwestern Street). It maintains a costume department and has a designated building for physical special effects and set construction. The site also offers postproduction services ranging from screening and cutting rooms to editing suites, musical scoring, and dubbing, to sound-transfer facilities. Both Warner Bros. Records and Warner Bros. Television headquarters are also on-site. It provides equipment rental and a great many production offices. It has as complete a range of facilities as can be found on any film studio lot anywhere.[22]

In addition to the remarkable range of facilities and services available in Hollywood, which are clustered in a number of districts in the city, Hollywood also has a number of continuing location advantages over rival locations. It does not have the same weather problems as does New York (cold in winter, hot in summer) or Florida (hot in summer and wet). It also has a variety of proximate natural locations that attracted production in the first place and allow it—like Vancouver—to stand in for a variety of natural environments, although with urban infill, it now takes longer to reach these locations. Los Angeles service providers have also built up unparalleled expertise in dressing locations and sets to stand in for other locations anywhere in the world. While locations around the world are now participating in Hollywood's longstanding re-creation of existing, future, and fantasy worlds, the studios, Hollywood backlots, and the built and natural environments in the vicinity of Los Angeles continue to stand in for the rest of America and the rest of the world.

And while "elsewhere in the world"—particularly Canadian—locations are standing in for U.S. locations, including Los Angeles itself, Los Angeles still plays itself consistently and evidently week in, week out.

Los Angeles is, in fact, a different kind of city than either New York or Miami in that it is the "generic city" rather than a distinctive place in its own right. As Norman Klein puts it, Los Angeles "is the most photographed and least remembered city in the world, and will most likely stay that way."[23] This is a consequence of not only Los Angeles standing in for everywhere else in the world but also the many ways in which Los Angeles is the modern city. This aspect of Los Angeles owes itself to the constantly changing built environment and landscapes of the city that mean that built signature landmarks such as those available in New York are simply not available. It is also a city that it is marked less by the life of its streets and the continuity these streets might provide through enduring structures such as the Empire State Building than by its multiple centers decentralized along freeway axes. Its history of constantly destroying and remaking itself ensures that it is not marked by continuity so much as permanent change. If this allows Los Angeles to be "replaceable" and "imitable" in ways in which New York is not, it also means that Los Angeles has become the default, generic, modern city with all of the benefits and drawbacks ensuing from this.

So for all the global dispersal of international production and the growing trend for films to be produced in English within Europe and financed without reference to the Hollywood majors, the command and control center for international production remains firmly in Los Angeles. With Los Angeles also remaining the preeminent production center, the interrelated dynamics of global geographic dispersal in the production shoot aid concentration in Los Angeles in production design. As Clough argues, "expanding production outside of Southern California need not depress activity within the region—much as the Silicon Valley high-tech economy expands even as production facilities move elsewhere."[24] Los Angeles also benefits at times of uncertainty—in the wake of the war in Iraq, a production boom was sparked in the city attributed to "potential threats to film crews overseas."[25]

New York: Center and Satellite

New York is one of the big three cities historically involved in Hollywood production both in terms of production and design. Like London, it is both a satellite of Hollywood and a significant production center in its own right. The analogy with London can be taken further. New York functions like London did in the 1950s and 1960s in that it is at arm's length from the Los

Angeles–based majors so providing a certain degree of creative independence from them.[26] It also has considerable lifestyle benefits not available in Los Angeles, and unlike London it still permits people to remain in the United States.

New York is the center of U.S. independent film production, with one-third of all independent films produced in New York. The New York City Economic Development Corporation claims New York has 145 studios and stages comprising 740,000 square feet of production space.[27] It shoots and produces over one hundred national television shows; New York locales are used in "a dozen primetime series," and four of the "biggest daytime TV soaps" are produced in New York. Moreover, twenty-seven of the top thirty-six advertising agencies are located in New York. And New York is the home of national television news and current affairs. In 2000, it had 201 feature film starts.[28]

New York has a considerable pool in terms of both expertise and depth of actors, crews, film services providers, and above-the-line creative and craft communities available for film and television production work. As an international production center, it has significant creative and crafts communities, production facilities, and technological infrastructure to draw upon. The concentrated presence of headquarters in advertising, finance, publishing, and broadcast television further underscores the advantages available to New York as a production location.[29]

New York has several other advantages over other locations. The steady stream of film and television programs set in New York provide a continuing interest in the city. As Whoopi Goldberg notes, "You can't mistake Canada, anywhere in Canada, for New York. New York on the other hand, has elements of every city in the world in it."[30] This suggests that New York locations are not as imitable as are Los Angeles locations. And unlike Los Angeles locations, "New Yorkness" is defined in the life of the street and its enduring spaces. New York can also stand in for other cities and its hinterland provides a wide range of locations in ready proximity. While the prevalence of New York story settings ensures that New York is the most copied U.S. location inside and outside the United States (with backlots of New York a feature in, for instance, Orlando, Los Angeles, and Toronto studios), it also builds a floor under production shoots in New York. At the same time, the New York domicile of so much of the talent involved in film and television production ensures that pressure is continually exerted on producers to film close to home.

It should come as no surprise that in its survey of "traditional media" production location decision making (for film, TV, commercials) the Boston

Consulting Group found that script requirements and talent demands were the first (27 percent) and third (18 percent) most important considerations in considering New York locations, with costs of labor (24 percent), government policies and incentives (10 percent), and industry cooperation (7 percent) making up the remaining important factors. If this survey points to the natural advantages that location and domicile of key creatives provide, it also highlights some of the disadvantages of New York as a production location.

In "the absence of unique script or talent situation, cost will be [the] main driver of decision[s]" on location.[31] While the existence of so much film and television production activity ensures a competitive market for crew and significant crew depth and quality across the board, it is difficult for New York to compete on cost. The cost of living in New York is higher than in Los Angeles and is among the highest in the world.[32] And in New York, affordable space—for production offices, postproduction, and space-consuming film and television production (principal photography)—is an ongoing challenge.[33] At the same time, with so much production seeking access to premier shooting locations such as the Empire State Building, there is considerable pressure upon and competition for these shooting locations. New York also has another problem: As Ric Wolfe, Sony Studios' stage manager, puts it, "we don't have weather in Los Angeles . . . with you it's cold, snowy, and nasty, and in the summer, it's hot and unbelievably humid. The [New York facilities] better buy good air conditioning."[34]

The costs associated with filming in New York mean that it is common for filmmakers to shoot on location in New York and then do soundstage/indoor and postproduction work elsewhere, "in Los Angeles or increasingly in Canada, where costs are lower than in New York or Los Angeles."[35] This means that while Miramax may have considered filming *Chicago* in New York because the majority of the people involved in the film's development lived there, the "savings in Toronto were so substantial that the studio couldn't make the case for New York."[36] In 2002, for instance, more than 90 percent of films that used New York as a location went elsewhere for soundstages and postproduction.[37] In these circumstances, New York film providers tend to make the "value proposition" argument contending that New York–based film workers compete on quality, which can cost less in the long run than shooting elsewhere with less experienced and competitive crew.

Some of this cost dynamic is reflected in the relative expenditures in New York on each part of the production value chain—preproduction, production, and postproduction. Overall spending on production is dominated by the "production shoot." Boston Consulting Group estimates that production accounts for 80 percent of spending while preproduction and postproduction account for 10 percent each.[38] Of this, "traditional media" expenditure television accounted for 42 percent; features, 40 percent; commercials production, 16 percent; and other, 2 percent (student films, industrial films, music videos, and documentaries).

It should come as no surprise that New York's Mayor's Film Office, film service providers, and economic agencies are oriented to maintaining this existing production shoot orientation while seeking ways to extend New York's share of both the production shoot and postproduction. As Andrew Stern of the New York City Economic Development Corporation (EDC) puts it, "Locations bring people to New York—I want them to stay. . . . If I can keep 1 percent (more of the films) here, I can fill another facility—and we can definitely keep more than 1 percent."[39] The measures to maintain the existing production shoot include free permits, free locations, free police assistance and zero sales tax, online shooting permit approval processes, discounts for hotels and parking, efforts to make "difficult locations like the Empire State Building more film friendly," a marketing campaign including a short film, a plaque program "to recognize historically significant locations,"[40] and attention to the development of neighborhood incentives to "encourage greater availability of film-ready, film-friendly production locations."[41]

In terms of facilities, the city's mix of soundstages continues to be a hotly contested topic. On the one hand, independent and commercial producers who may have little use for large soundstages tend to see new tax incentives as being of greater assistance to production than more studio spaces.[42] On the other hand, advocates for more soundstages, particularly large, competitively priced soundstages in studio complexes with backlots, are looking to secure Hollywood blockbuster production for New York. But this would require, given New York land prices and the shortage of space, the making available of publicly owned land at low cost to studio complex promoters. As Michael Steed, senior vice president of Union Life in Washington, put the issue: "It's clear that New York doesn't have enough studios to handle both television and film production that could take there. What's unclear to us is exactly what types of studios should be there—film or television—and where they should be."[43]

This debate over studio space, which uncannily echoes that observed for its "double," Toronto, turns on New York's production aspiration. Should it aspire to participate in areas where it has not previously—such as hosting the whole production needs of studio-based blockbusters like *Spider-Man*, requiring gated soundstages and extensive backlots? Or should it be oriented rather to servicing existing feature, television, and commercials production needs with studio spaces providing an option alongside the location shoot?

Two studio complexes—the Steiner Studios currently being built in the former Brooklyn Navy Yard site and the Kaufman-Astoria studios—represent these two different aspirations. The Steiner Studios contain huge "lock-up," gated, weather-proofed studio space of sufficient height to handle "a Godzilla or simulated skyscraper."[44] It has ample parking and will permit the one-stop shop clustering of firms and companies. It also has provision for a substantial backlot. Built by shopping center tycoons used to the small margins and fixed costs of shopping malls, it encompasses the aim of hosting complete productions. It aims to fill what is perceived to be a gap in New York infrastructure: "large, modern, purpose-built stages—meaning stages built from scratch to be soundstages."[45] By contrast, when the Kaufman-Astoria added another medium-sized stage, it was doing so to create space "big enough for a movie that is not *Jurassic Park* or *Spider-Man*, but small enough not to frighten away television." Television is important to both Kaufman-Astoria and Silvercup Studios on Long Island, with the former having hosted television series such as *The Cosby Show* and *Sesame Street*, while the latter has hosted *Sex in the City* and *The Sopranos*. Commercials production is also important to these studios.

Unsurprisingly, production activity in New York has tended to be cyclical. Levels of production surged from 1993, peaking in 1998 and 1999. Since then, there has been a leveling back—a phenomenon compounded by the events of 9/11, with production not returning to previous highs. At the time of writing (late 2004), industry commentary was still suggesting that any "renewed threat of terrorism could further drive production away from the city," with New York not benefiting from trends to more U.S.-based production as Hollywood fears of terrorism disrupting film shoots in overseas markets took hold.[46] Hal Rosenbluth, president of Kaufman-Astoria Studios Inc., was reported as saying, "We have to rebuild the confidence in coming to New York."[47] In reaction to competition for production from within the United States and outside it, the solution becomes one of promoting advantages and uniqueness while remaining as cost-competitive as possible.

Miami: Gateway City, Latino Center, Hollywood Satellite

The most disappointing thing about the rest of the US was that it did not look like Miami. . . . Movie-made America was splendid and it was that Hollywood splendor that differentiated this country from mine, where except for the modern sectors of Havana nothing glittered like those American cities of the movies. Nothing glittered like that in the US either. Except Miami. It was this silver-screen-come-to-life quality that made Miami magical for me then, as it still does today, when with a veteran movie-goer's eye I survey a skyline that seems more painted on a backdrop than built out of glass and steel.[48]

Miami bears some resemblance to New York in that over the past twenty years it has become a "center" in its own right albeit on a smaller scale. In Miami's case it is, increasingly, the international center for Hispanic cultural production—particularly in the television and music industries. It is variously called the "capital of Latin media,"[49] the "Hollywood of Latin America,"[50] and the "center of the entertainment industry for all of Latin America."[51] With Miami-based TV networks Univision and Telemundo producing Spanish-language programming for U.S. and Spanish-speaking outlets worldwide, and with the Spanish-language divisions of Discovery Networks, MTV, HBO, Disney, and Universal working out of Miami and the Latin music divisions of international recording labels such as Sony, the conditions for ongoing levels of screen, particularly TV, production are present irrespective of whether Hollywood producers bring English-language film and television production to Miami.[52] Like Los Angeles and New York, Miami is increasingly involved in initiating production. While other, larger U.S. cities such as Chicago maintain a substantial film television production infrastructure, only Los Angeles and New York have the same born "global" and "international orientation" in their everyday operations.

This production and design center status for Latin production has grown out of Miami's status as a gateway city for Latin America and Spanish-language tourists, refugees, actors and performers, and film workers. It is a gateway both into the United States and the English-language territories and to the rest of Latin America. George Yudice usefully describes it as a "transnational" cultural corridor in that it functions not only as a Spanish-language production and distribution center but also as a crossover space for Spanish-language stars, performers, and directors into English.[53]

Miami is also a satellite location for English-language production. In the late 1980s and 1990s, Florida and North Carolina "benefited the most from production that ran away from Los Angeles."[54] Like New York, Hollywood producers come to shoot in Miami because it is Miami—because of the particular look and feel that Enriques Fernandez describes and that is present in movies such as *The Birdcage*. Miami is a place that plays itself—represents itself and projects its own aesthetic and distinctiveness.

While this capacity to represent itself in an international economy of representation makes it akin to other cities with strong and enduring identities, it is probably only in the past twenty years that Miami has been projected with such regularity as a production location. This design center status and signifying location status is an emerging phenomenon and still very much a work in progress. So while production industry and infrastructure is growing significantly in Miami and has helped Florida to become a film and television production powerhouse, this growth needs to be put into perspective. Florida is still the fourth production region in the United States behind North Carolina (third), New York (second), and California (first) in shares of film and television drama production. While this in itself is a considerable achievement given the low base the location started from, it still points to the many ways in which the combination of Hollywood runaway production and an embryonic Hispanic Hollywood makes Miami, and Florida generally, a "work in progress."

Miami has a network of soundstages and facilities developed from the mid-1980s to service the needs of commercials, split location feature production, higher-budgeted television programming (in English), and low-cost television programming in Spanish. While none of these facilities approaches the scale of the studios provided upstate in Orlando, they do provide complementary spaces for the kinds of film and television productions Miami attracts, much as New York does for the film and television production industry located there.

While Miami has routinely featured in film and television production slates over the twentieth century, two production events seem to have been significant in reshaping Miami's status as a premier production location. The first was the 1986 advertising shoot for Calvin Klein underwear and the second the production of the hit 1980s TV series *Miami Vice*. The first represented the "high-profile" start of Miami as a fashion photography advertising production center, leading to the establishment of advertising, modeling, and talent agencies and production agencies and studio facilities servicing the commercial production industry.[55] The second, *Miami Vice*, provided a contemporary narrative image of Miami as a modern, interesting, gateway city in a hit television series. This extended Miami's range beyond intermittent feature production and commercial production into television. This popularity as a story setting has created for Miami some of the same problems New York faces in that it runs the risk of being represented elsewhere. Like New York, it now needs to work at keeping the settings in the story lines in the local place. And like all production locations, it has to work to secure productions, ensure its "film friendliness," and manage its national and international reputation. Industry reports suggested that by the late 1990s to early 2000s, Florida had "lost out on a number of major motion picture productions" owing to its "tarnished reputation." The state was seen as "antagonistic to the movie industry" and expensive, with Florida's marketing claims being "far rosier than the reality of filming here."[56]

Miami—and southeast Florida more generally—have benefited from glob-alization and the dispersal of production and stand to benefit still further. In-deed, Economic Research Associates' analysis for the Governor of Florida's Office suggests that it has the opportunity to become "a leading center for motion picture distribution, finance and other higher order activities within the industry."[57] Miami and Florida's larger ambition is, in the words of Gov-ernor Jeb Bush, to build more of an "indigenous industry" particularly in the area of postproduction and design.[58] An important part of this opportunity turns on its "transnational cultural corridor" status, which has created op-portunities for Miami as an apparently neutral space from which to organize and coordinate the limited internationalization of Latin media and to organ-ize "crossovers" of performers, properties, and personnel between Spanish- and English-language production, distribution, and exhibition. Miami also had the advantage of being a crossover place for performers, cultural prod-ucts, and creative personnel into English. The Miami Film Festival was thus able to introduce Antonio Banderas and Pedro Almodovar to American au-diences.[59]

Miami started to have this gateway function for a number of reasons. It was a neutral international space that could transcend the "host of tradi-tional jealousies and rivalries" of the "more than 20 countries in Latin Amer-ica."[60] Functioning as an "entertainment Switzerland," in the words of Richard Arroyo, first managing director of MTV Latino,[61] it was possible to "avoid a lot of political baggage," as Tom Hunter, Arroyo's successor, put it. It was also politically and economically stable, giving it business advantages over other, Latin American locations in that risks and uncertainty were min-imized. As Frank Welzer, president of Sony Discos, told Rohter, "You don't have to worry you're going to wake up some morning to find that the banks want to seize your accounts or that the currency has been devalued." This stability also counted for Miami as a secure production location. Several celebrities told Rohter that one of Miami's attractions was that one did not need to "fear that guerrillas are going to kidnap your child."[62]

Like Los Angeles, Miami was ideally placed to play this coordinating role for Latin America and this crossover and integrating role with respect to English-language production (Hollywood). It was already a meeting space where wealthy Latin Americans including celebrities would holiday, visit, immigrate to, or just regularly perform in. It was also an intermittent pro-duction location for Mexican, Brazilian, and Venezuela *telenovelas* whose rat-ings apparently "automatically soar" whenever they include episodes set in Miami.[63] Miami arguably had a gatekeeping role as a performance center for Latin music with its facilities filling some of the same functions as Madison

Square Garden and Radio City Music Hall within English-language music. As Mario Kreutzberger notes, "the big dreams of Latin artists are here, because whatever they do in Miami has impact in their homelands."[64] This meant that Miami was ideally situated to deliver "a truly Latin American program and reach an international audience."[65] It also ensured that Miami was in a position to "influence what goes on in Latin America."[66] In the words of Sergio Rozenblat, WEA Latina, "Miami is what Rio de Janeiro is to non-Latins, a city that has a magical name, an aura."[67] Something of this status is captured in Mexican actor Lucia Mendez's comment that "Miami is 'a Caribbean paradise full of talented Latin Americans' who have 'a vision of the world with more reach' than those who have chosen to remain in their homelands."[68]

These "international" advantages were coupled with sophisticated business and services infrastructure courtesy of the tourism industry and its large Hispanic population base. Television networks Univision and Telemundo decided to locate their operations in Miami for a variety of additional reasons, including its proximity to Latin America and Miami's well-educated, bilingual workforce.[69] Another factor was the "efficiency and professionalism of the United States" when compared with their Latin counterparts.[70] Miami also benefited from its "cosmopolitan dynamic" that allowed producers to "test among different Hispanics." Unlike in other competitor locations in Latin America, in Miami "you can find an Argentinian, a Bolivian, a Chilean, without ever leaving the country."[71] In this context, the demography of Miami and South Florida's population, with its mix of nationalities and its roughly split Hispanic and English-speaking populations, provided "the ability to create and service a programming mix that you can't get in other places."[72] This made it an especially effective location for production to service the heterogenous and growing Latino U.S. populations and media outlets.

In this context, being based in Miami allowed Latino producers to address if not the most populous then certainly the most wealthy Spanish-speaking population in the Americas—in the United States. The very substantial base of this Hispanic film and television production industry in its turn provided opportunities for established names such as Cristina Saralegui, who had worked as a talk show host in Miami for fifteen years and was billed as the "Latin Oprah Winfrey," was "offered a development deal with Disney . . . to create an English-language sitcom based on her life, in which she would star."[73]

With respect to the rest of Latin America, Miami does not and cannot compete on costs. It will always be more expensive to produce TV shows and movies in Miami than it is in the rest of Latin America. Rather, Miami competes through its "gateway" and coordinating functions.

Wilmington and Orlando: Greenfields Sites, Satellite Production Centers

A number of important locations for film and TV production in the United States have emerged over the last twenty-five years in Wilmington, North Carolina, and Orlando, Florida. These are satellite locations that provide plug-in production infrastructures and services for Hollywood production. Unlike New York and Miami, these places are not capable of sustaining production in their own right and are explicitly designed to take advantage of location production and various locational, labor, and other advantages in the sites in question. Unsurprisingly there is a great deal of continuity between the American greenfields sites and the commensurate sites that developed in the Gold Coast in Australia and Vancouver in Canada. This should not be surprising, as Dino de Laurentiis was a key figure in the development of the Wilmington and Gold Coast studios, with the North Carolina studio model replicated to some extent on the Gold Coast.

As satellites, these greenfields sites do not seek or aspire to alternative center status. Rather, they seek to become "at a distance" appendages imitating, simulating, and complementing the resources at the center. These places pride themselves on being at the service of the center and able to match this center in the limited ways they have staked out for themselves in the production shoot and aspects of postproduction. They not only accept their satellite status but glory in it. They work within its limits and explore these to secure areas of local advantage and benefit. In this sense these greenfields sites are the purest expression of internationally networked and integrated production. As they are entirely dependent on this production, they work for and underwrite the system of networked and split location in important ways.

Wilmington, North Carolina

On some counts, North Carolina is the third-largest production center in the United States and the second-largest production center on the East Coast behind New York, although this point is disputed by Florida. There are significant studio complexes in both Wilmington and Raleigh. There are twenty-nine soundstages in North Carolina, a state-sponsored film school in Winston-Salem, and "a large pool of well-trained technicians and crewmembers."[74] North Carolina is a classic production services location, competing on cost and the "business friendliness" of the location. Working in its favor have been the state's "right-to-work status, its non-union labor, and its business incentives packages."[75]

North Carolina has remained a production services precinct and has not developed its own local film production capacity. It aims to provide facilities and services that become an extension of what is available at the center in Los Angeles—they are a part of the center available elsewhere. As Frank Capra Jr. of Wilmington's Screen Gems studio puts it, 'When people get here they realize that it really operates very much like a Los Angeles studio, with support facilities like on an LA lot. They feel at home." He adds that this normalization extends to the "the townspeople let[ting] the stars relax."[76] As the quote on the front page of his studio's website (screengemsstudios.com) proclaims, "If you can do it there, we can do it here!"

North Carolina has been able to capitalize on the initial development of a studio complex, with lower wage rates and right–to-work provisions ensuring levels of flexibility not possible in Los Angeles. While Wilmington is not close to Los Angeles, it is in functional proximity to major East Coast locations. It is also able to provide what it claims as the largest soundstages east of Los Angeles, making it an ideal location for studio soundstage-intensive blockbuster productions. Wilmington was also advantaged in comparison to other low-cost locations internationally in that producers would not have to leave the United States. Finally, there was the entrepreneurial, collaborative activity of local agents and a sympathetic government in providing incentives and investing in infrastructure. Like their Canadian counterparts in Vancouver, the North Carolineans understood the need to maintain a collaborative and entrepreneurial approach to ensure their continuing international competitiveness, profile, and reputation as a center for international production.

The story of North Carolina's participation in securing Hollywood production shoots begins with Dino de Laurentiis constructing what is now the Screen Gems studio in Wilmington in 1984 to make the film *Firestarter* and take advantage of its right-to-work status. This studio gave rise to the development of subsequent soundstages. Since 1980, North Carolina has attracted nearly six hundred feature films; six network television series; and more than US$5.5 billion in production revenue. Of this amount, Wilmington's production spend over Screen Gem studio's life was put at just under half—US$2.6 billion with notable feature productions such as *Blue Velvet* and *Sleeping with the Enemy* and network television series such as *Dawson's Creek* made in the studios.[77] Other notable feature film credits from the Screen Gems studios include *Divine Secrets of the Ya-Ya Sisterhood*, *28 Days*, *Lolita*, *The Crow*, and *The Hudsucker Proxy*.

The increasing globalization of film and television production both created and benefited Wilmington but also leaves it vulnerable as a film and television production location. It is in direct competition particularly with low-cost Canadian locations and facilities. Here Wilmington's traditional competition on the basis of price might put it at some disadvantage.

Orlando, Florida

Orlando is going Hollywood. You're going to have all these Ferraris, Porsches, great guys with sunglasses and open-buttoned shirts. The tourists will mingle and dine with Mickey Mouse and Burt Reynolds.[78]

Another example of a greenfields site that did not exist as a space for film and television production twenty years ago is Orlando in Florida, touted in some of its publicity as "Hollywood East." Once an interstate bus stop en route to Miami, Orlando has developed into an important satellite film and television space, growing from a US$2.5 million film and television production market in 1988 to a US$402 million market in 2003. In 2000, fifteen feature films were made there. The catalyst for this development was the establishment of two film studios—Universal Studios Orlando and Disney-MGM Studios in 1988. These studios were created in two of Orlando's three major theme parks, Walt Disney World and Universal Studios Orlando. Metro Orlando promotes itself at the time of writing in mid-2004 as having ten state-of-the-art soundstages.

Locating film studios in such an obviously greenfields site was an intrinsically risky operation as the absence of any sustained film and television production capacity would leave the region particularly susceptible to industry downturns and the likelihood of the studio being empty for long periods. The colocation of the studios with a theme park precinct provided a means of addressing this difficulty. This relationship is worth exploring here as it has very much defined Orlando as a production space.

The existence of an on-site film studio helped these theme park franchises in that it made real their claims to "movie world" status. Publicity for Orlando describes them as "much like" their counterpart parks in California in that tours of "an actual TV and film studio and backlot" are attractions. The production of high-profile movies like *Waterboy* (1998) served both the studio's reputation as a production space, the theme park's need to sell itself as a "movie location," as well as providing a ready and willing pool of extras for the film. So there were good "theme park" reasons for having a film studio as a loss leader for the core business of these two massive and self-contained theme parks with their own hotel precincts offering the complete family holiday appropriate to the "Family Entertainment Capital of the World" as the *Scottish Daily Record* claimed.[79]

The theme park also helped the new studio's reputation by giving it "cachet"—associating it with leading names in the film and television production industry in Disney and Universal. Theme park operations could also assist in defraying running costs associated with servicing and maintaining the studio space (grounds, security, commissary, accounts, etc.) as these could be rolled into larger theme park operations. From the media conglomerate's standpoint, "theme parks offer a good source of diversification for the inherently risky motion-picture business"[80]—theme parks have been thought to "complement" media conglomerates "by pumping out steadier cash flow than film and TV," and "they also help studios extend public awareness of film franchises though movie-themed attractions."[81]

There are also useful connections and synergies between the theme park and studio complex. At the level of physical infrastructure, there is the possibility of using each other's physical plant and facilities with productions sometimes using the theme parks as locations for production and the theme parks using the studio and its facilities. For instance, the theme park version of the television variety show *Who Wants to Be a Millionaire?* was in mid-2003 taking up three soundstages with "occasional working visits by the real show."[82] This enabled it to take up some of the slack when there was not the production work available. In addition, soundstages with their height, size, soundproofing and fittings can be repurposed for film rides.

These operations are, however, vulnerable. By May 2003, Ellen Forman in *Hollywood Reporter* was claiming that the days when "sparkling new soundstages . . . promised to make the area a full-fledged film-making center" were "long gone." She argued that the Hollywood majors did not send their big films to shoot in these facilities (which is debatable) and that the soundstages were underutilized with only "small indie features" occasionally using them. These circumstances had driven their "morphing" into attractions for the theme park business. Disney closed its Orlando animation studio in January 2004, leaving most of its 260 employees out of work.[83]

In a study prepared by Economic Research Associates for the Governor's Office of Film and Entertainment, mid-Florida (which includes Orlando) was ranked second with 18 percent and Tampa Bay third with 16 percent of the region's motion picture production in 2001.[84] By contrast, southeast

Florida, which includes Miami, had 56 percent of the state's motion picture employment. Mid-Florida also seems to have been more affected by trends toward shooting offshore in that any cost advantages that it may have had have been eroded. This points to the wider set of problems with Orlando that were identified at the start.

> Many film industry people and analysts say Orlando has too many deficiencies that will prevent it from becoming an industry hub. Egon Stephan, a noted cinematographer and president of Video Tech Inc., a Miami Panavision dealership, believes Orlando's ordinariness and J.C. Penney style culture bores writers, talented performers and many of the creative people upon whom the industry depends.[85]

Conclusion

This chapter has argued that we are seeing the American adjustment to the circumstances of an increasingly globalized design and production regime in which Los Angeles is simultaneously the design center and, like the rest of America and the many other places in the world discussed in this book, a location pitching for production. As Scott shows, there is an unprecedented industrial agglomeration of distribution and production infrastructure, facilities, and related services in Los Angeles, making it not less but more of a *global media city*. This ensures that there is, to a significant extent, a happy coincidence of design and location interests in Los Angeles, with location interests in preproduction, production, and postproduction being able to take advantage of their proximity to the design center. But even with agglomeration and the immense privilege it provides location interests based in Los Angeles, the circumstances of globally dispersed production also bring with them competitive pressures and anxieties about remaining competitive as a production location with respect to locations elsewhere in the United States and beyond.

Another component of our argument has been that there has been a dispersal of production locations *within* the United States that parallels the similar dispersal to production locations *outside* the States that we have observed in previous chapters. And we have seen in this American situation the reality of a globally dispersed production system that does not simply include the lower-cost productions that have been a staple in Toronto and Wilmington but also include now high-budget television series and also mid- to high-budget blockbuster productions.

The story that emerges in this chapter turns out to be not one of American exceptionalism but a variant on a theme found in previous chapters in this book. Other places like Canada, Australia, and the Czech Republic have been likewise making this difficult adjustment—and each has found that this system of globally dispersed production carries great risks and vulnerabilities as much as benefits. U.S. governments—at a city, state, and even federal level—have, like their counterparts elsewhere in the world, been embracing film services approaches to the development of film policy. This embrace of film services approaches is a part of the larger services orientation of governments to facilitate global interconnectedness and secure place-based benefits from globalizing dynamics. Studios have been identified as key strategic assets alongside the natural and built environment and the related film services available in a location. The studio and increasingly the megastudio amplify a location's attraction for international production and are critical to securing ongoing production over the long term. Studios and facilities in Los Angeles and other American cities have become part of a global network of places and spaces for production. The result is a mixed blessing for American locations as it is elsewhere. International production supported over the 1990s significant increases in jobs and income in the United States, but in the late 1990s and early 2000s there has been a downturn in American fortunes due in no small part to the increasing competition from other international locations and facilities providers. The more extensive and global location interests have become, the greater the competition between international and American locations for production—and the more vulnerable they all become. The construction of state-of-the-art studios in Montreal, Toronto, or Alicante is part and parcel of an escalation of the location interest game that began with development of state-of-the-art facilities in North America.

In this study, we have used the studio to illuminate the complex relation between international production and location. Many of the studios we have discussed in this book both have been supported by and form major parts of the location interest of particular places. Changing film policy formations and a turn to film services frameworks have undergirded both studio development and the promotion of location interests, and in the process these factors increased the competition among places for international production. Through the optic of the film studio, we have shown that the global dispersal of production and the location strategies and policy frameworks that have both enabled and responded to this dispersal are best understood in terms of an unstable and unequal but symbiotic relationship between the design interest and the location interest. The existing literature on international production tends to overlook the development of studios and other situated infrastructure and tends to concentrate instead on the economic and strategic factors driving this global dispersion of production. By contrast, our focus on the studio highlights, first, the range of infrastructure, services, and support mechanisms necessary to attract international production to a place; second, the transformations enabled by the provision of this infrastructure; and third, why places are competing so vigorously for international production. In the process, we recognize that studios are not simply interchangeable locations but are rooted in particular local circumstances and, like the film and television production they enable, are in a constant negotiation with the place in which they are situated.

Notes

1. Saskia Sassen, *The Global City: New York, London, Tokyo* (Princeton, N.J.: Princeton University Press, 2001), 34.

2. Sassen, *The Global City*, 118.

3. UCLA Anderson School of Management, "UCLA's Anderson Forecast Conference Examines the Forces Altering the Business of Hollywood," *UCLA Anderson School of Management*, 27 March 2002, available at www.anderson.ucla.edu/x4495.xml (25 February 2004).

4. Allen J. Scott, *On Hollywood: The Place, The Industry* (Princeton, N.J.: Princeton University Press, 2005), 58.

5. Scott, *On Hollywood*, 80.

6. In the mid-1980s, the Los Angeles unions and film services providers' concern about "runaway production" was with location production in other, lower-cost U.S. locations who were competing strongly with Hollywood and Southern California for both blockbuster and television series production.

7. Cited in Ian Mohr, "Bright Lights, Big City," *New York Production Alliance*, 23 September 2003, available at www.nypa.org (27 February 2004).

8. Martha Jones, *Motion Picture Production in California* (Sacramento: California Resource Bureau, 2002), 30.

9. Christopher Vogler, cited in Janet Wasko, *How Hollywood Works* (London: Sage, 2003), 40.

10. Miriam Kreinin Souccar, "Film Production Hits Break in Action," *Crain's New York Business* 19, no. 13 (31 March 2003): 3.

11. Jones, *Motion Picture Production in California*, 53.

12. Allen J. Scott, "A New Map of Hollywood: The Production and Distribution of American Motion Pictures," *Regional Studies* 36, no. 9 (2002): 969.

13. Scott, "A New Map of Hollywood," 966.

14. Jones, *Motion Picture Production in California*, 6.

15. Peter Applebome, "Hopes and Doubts Greet a Plan for Sound Stages at the Brooklyn Navy Yard," *New York Times*, 22 June 1999, E1.

16. Scott, *On Hollywood*, 84.

17. Allen J. Scott, *The Cultural Economy of Cities: Essays on the Geography of Image-producing Industries* (London: Sage, 2000).

18. Scott, "A New Map of Hollywood," 965; for a further discussion of this growth, see Jones, *Motion Picture Production in California*.

19. Scott, *On Hollywood*, 85.

20. Scott, *On Hollywood*, 44.

21. Scott, *On Hollywood*, 88.

22. For a further discussion of Burbank as a representative megastudio, see Scott, *On Hollywood*, 82–83.

23. Norman Klein, *The History of Forgetting: Los Angeles and the Erasure of Memory* (London: Verso, 1997), 250.

24. Clough, cited in Jones, *Motion Picture Production in California*, 53.

25. Souccar, "Film Production Hits Break in Action."

26. However, it should be remembered that one of the reasons for the establishment of the film industry in Hollywood was a desire to be at arm's length from New York.

27. New York City Economic Development Corporation, "Media and Entertainment," available at www.newyorkbiz.com/Industries/Entertainment/index.html (27 February 2004). Reference to 600,000 square feet in 1999, Peter Applebome, "Hopes and Doubts Greet a Plan for Sound Stages at the Brooklyn Navy Yard," *New York Times,* 22 June 1999, E1.

28. See New York State Governor's Office, "About Production in New York," New York State Governor's Office for Motion Picture and Television Development, www.nylovesfilm.com/prodinny.asp (27 February 2004).

29. Boston Consulting Group, *Building New York's Visual Media Industry for the Digital Age: Findings and Recommendations* (Boston: Boston Consulting Group, June 2000).

30. Whoopi Goldberg, cited in "Beyond the Skyline," The City of New York Mayor's Office of Film, Theatre, and Broadcasting, 29 April 2003, available at www.nyc.gov/html/film/html/home/beyond_skyline_384kqt.shtml (27 February 2004).

31. Boston Consulting Group, *Building New York's Visual Media Industry for the Digital Age*, 16.

32. The Internal Revenue Service's guidelines for daily living and meal allowance rate New York at $254 per day, with Los Angeles at $155 per day (see Souccar, "Film Production Hits Break in Action," 3).

33. Boston Consulting Group, *Building New York's Visual Media Industry for the Digital Age*, 15.

34. Anthony Kaufman, "Backlot Dreams," *Village Voice* 48, no. 12 (19–25 March 2003): 53.

35. Applebome, "Hopes and Doubts Greet a Plan for Sound Stages at the Brooklyn Navy Yard," E1.

36. Souccar, "Film Production Hits Break in Action," 3.

37. Randee Dawn, "Production Junction," *Hollywood Reporter* 379 (June 2003): 8.

38. Boston Consulting Group, *Building New York's Visual Media Industry for the Digital Age*, 12.

39. Dawn, "Production Junction," 8.

40. Dawn, "Production Junction," 8.

41. Boston Consulting Group, *Building New York's Visual Media Industry for the Digital Age*, 26.

42. Dawn, "Production Junction," 8.

43. Charles Bagli, "De Niro and Miramax Plan a Film Studio at the Brooklyn Navy Yard," *New York Times,* 29 April 1999, B1.

44. Kaufman, "Backlot Dreams."

45. Stern, quoted in Christine Champagne, "Setting the Stage at the Navy Yard," *New York Production Alliance,* available at www.nypa.org (27 February 2004).

46. Souccar, "Film Production Hits Break in Action."

47. Souccar, "Film Production Hits Break in Action."

48. Enrique Fernandez, "Critique: Finding Greater Havana in Dade County, Florida," *Wall Street Journal,* 21 July 1987, 1.

49. Deborah Wilker, "Miami Nice for Hispanic TV Surge," *Hollywood Reporter*, 6–12 January 2004, 30.

50. Larry Rohter, "Miami, the Hollywood of Latin America," *New York Times*, 18 August 1996, 1.

51. Lindy Zesch, "Miami's Theatrical Cache," *American Theatre* 13, no. 9 (November 1996): 26.

52. See Wilker, "Miami Nice for Hispanic TV Surge," 30.

53. George Yudice, *The Expediency of Culture: Uses of Culture in the Global Era* (Durham, N.C.: Duke University Press, 2004).

54. Jones, *Motion Picture Production in California*, 46.

55. Felicia Levine, "The 'Hispanic Hollywood' Works to Keep Show Business Here to Stay," *South Florida Business Journal*, 18 October 1996, 1.

56. Cynthia Barnett, "Action," *Florida Trend* 42, no. 9 (1 January 2000): 112.

57. Economic Research Associates (ERA), *Project Report Assessment of the Florida Motion Picture Industry*, prepared for the Governor's Office of Film & Entertainment, February 2003.

58. Deborah Wilker, "Head of State: Dialogue with Jeb Bush," *Hollywood Reporter* 380, 21–27 October 2003, 18.

59. Larry Rohter, "Miami, the Hollywood of Latin America," 1.

60. Rohter, "Miami, the Hollywood of Latin America."

61. Richard Arroyo, first managing director of MTV Latino, quoted in Rohter, "Miami, the Hollywood of Latin America."

62. Rohter, "Miami, the Hollywood of Latin America."

63. Rohter, "Miami, the Hollywood of Latin America," 1.

64. Mario Kreutzberger, quoted in Rohter, "Miami, the Hollywood of Latin America," 1.

65. Rohter, "Miami, the Hollywood of Latin America," 1.

66. Sergio Rozenblat, WEA Latino, quoted in Rohter, "Miami, the Hollywood of Latin America," 1.

67. Sergio Rozenblat, quoted in Rohter, "Miami, the Hollywood of Latin America," 1.

68. Lucia Mendez, quoted in Rohter, "Miami, the Hollywood of Latin America."

69. Rohter, "Miami, the Hollywood of Latin America," 1.

70. Lucia Mendez, quoted in Rohter, "Miami, the Hollywood of Latin America."

71. Luis Villanueva, President of Venevision International, cited in Daniel Chang, "Spanish-Language TV Production Firm Aims to Make Miami 'Hispanic Hollywood,'" *Knight Ridder Tribune Business News*, 11 May 2002, 1.

72. Jeff Peel, Miami-Dade film commissioner, quoted in Wilker, "Miami Nice for Hispanic TV Surge," 30.

73. Wilker, "Miami Nice for Hispanic TV Surge," 30.

74. Jones, *Motion Picture Production in California*, 46.

75. Jones, *Motion Picture Production in California*, 46.

76. Tim W. Ferguson and William Heuslein, "Cape Dear," *Forbes*, 28 May 2001, 132–46.

77. Ferguson and Heuslein, "Cape Dear," 132–46.

78. Real estate man, quoted in Paul Sweeney, "Studio Wars," *Florida Trend* 31, no. 3 (July 1988): 40.

79. "World—Destination Florida—Get in a Right State," *Scottish Daily Record*, 31 January 2004, 4.

80. Sweeney, "Studio Wars," 40.

81. Carl DiOrio, "Theme Parks a Bumpy Ride for Congloms," *Variety*, 6–23 June 2003, 5.

82. Ellen Forman, "Backlot Bounty," *Hollywood Reporter*, 20–26 May 2003, F6.

83. Greg Hernandez, "Disney Dismantles Animation Facility," *Los Angeles Daily*, 13 January 2004, B1.

84. Economic Research Associates (ERA), *Project Report*.

85. Sweeney, "Studio Wars," 40.

Bibliography

Unauthored Works

"Babelsburg [sic] Opens 'Biggest' Euro Film Studio." *Pro Sound News Europe* (January 1994): 1.

"Barrandov Film Studio Expects CZK 100 mln Drop in Revenues in 2001." *Interfax Czech Republic Business News Service*, 24 November 2001. Available at http://global.factiva.com (21 September 2004).

"Barrandov Laboratories Have World-Parameters Equipment." *CTK Business News*, 16 November 2001. Available at http://global.factiva.com (21 September 2004).

"Board of Ente Cinema Approves Three-Year Relaunch Plan," *Il Sole 24 Ore*, 6 July 1994, 16.

"British Ealing Eyes Bulgaria's Boyana Film Studios." *SeeNews*, 25 June 2004. www.see-news.com (21 September 2004).

"Bulgaria Offers Boyana Film Studios for Sale." *SeeNews*, 15 June 2004. Available at www.see-news.com (21 September 2004).

"The Business." *Sight and Sound* 5, no. 11 (November 1995): 5.

"Cinecittà." *Unesco Courier*, July 1995, 68.

"Cinecittà Prepares for Relaunch with New Agreements," *Il Sole 24 Ore*, 4 July 1995, 9.

"Cinespace Studios." Cinespace Studios. www.cinespace.com (12 August 2004).

"Company Background." Toronto Film Studios. Available at www.torontofilmstudios.com/company_background.php (12 August 2004).

"Control Freak: Scully, Mulder and Their Creepy Enemies May Get All the Limelight, but Canuck Producer JP Finn Makes *The X-Files* Happen. *BC Business* 24, no. 11 (November 1996): 84–87.

"Culture Minister Sues AB Barrandov." *CTK Business News*, 23 April 1998. Available at http://global.factiva.com (28 May 2002).

"Czech Barrandov Studios Sold." *Hollywood Reporter*, 26 June 1992, 4.

"Czech Films to Receive State Subsidies Again." *Reuters News*, 3 April 1991. Available at http://global.factiva.com (28 May 2002).

"Czech Republic: Take One: Prague," *Newsweek International*, 19 March 2001, 84–85.

"Czech Studio Landed with Copyright Bill." *Screen Digest*, 1 June 1998, 126.

"'Disgraceful' Waste." *This Is Local London*, 19 May 2004. Available at www.thisislocallondon.co.uk/search/display.var.491044.0.disgraceful_waste.php (21 September 2004).

"Ealing Creative Links: Outline Strategy for the Creative Industries in Ealing." Era Ltd, 2003. Available at www.era-ltd.com/strategic_work/EalingCreativeLinks.pdf (15 September 2004).

"EC Approves $1.6 mil in Babelsberg Studios Aid." *Hollywood Reporter*, 2 November 1993, I2.

"Elstree in Need of £20m." *The Stage*. 13 May 2004, 3.

"Ente Cinema Reports Losses in 1993, Draws up Relaunch Plan." *Corriere della Sera*, 6 March 1994, 19.

"Ente Cinema's Three-Year Plan Proposes Creation of Communications Centre in Rome." *Il Sole 24 Ore*, 7 December 1994, 9.

"Epic Fade-Out in Rome." *Financial Times*, 12 October 1996, 1.

"Europe: Cooperation between Studios." *Media Monitor*, 18 March 1994, 4.

"Fishermen Try to Hook *Titanic*." *Variety*, 3 March 1997, 67.

"Fish Story." *Hollywood Reporter*, 3 February 1998, 12.

The Focal Encyclopedia of Film and Television Techniques. London: Focal, 1969.

"The Fox Baja Studios." Available at www.titanicmovie.com/present/mi_prodnote_6.html (15 December 2003).

"Frodo Economy rings up the dollars for New Zealand." *ABC Online*, 30 November 2003. Available at www.abc.net.au/news/newsitems/200311/s1000231.htm (23 February 2004).

"German Studio Launches Production Outfit." *Screen Digest* (October 1998): 218.

"Germany: Extra Cash for Babelsberg." *Media Monitor*, 12 November 1993, 4.

"Government Stresses Desire to Maintain DEFA." *Sueddeutsche Zeitung*, 21 February 1991, 31.

"Italian Film Studio Going into Tour Business." *Variety*, 5 July 1994, B-7.

"Kodak, New Image Join Efforts for Boyana Film." *Pari Daily*, 13 July 2004. Available at www.news.pari.bg/cgi-bin/pari-eng.home.cgi (15 July 2004).

"Lights, Action, Canada! (Toronto Has Staged a Spectacular Comeback, Turning Entertainment into a Hot New $2b Industry)." *Canadian Business* 67, no. 8 (August 1994): 58–65.

"Movie Makers Create Environmental Ending." *In Business* 24, no. 2 (2002): 4.

"Movie Mecca." *Telegraph-Mirror* (Sydney), 19 October 1994, 4.

"New Zealand Home of Middle-earth: Services and Partners." Available at www.filmnz.com/middleearth/partners/index.html (20 February 2004).

"Prague Film Studio Incurs Losses on Czech-Language Films." *Pravo*, 15 January 1996, 1, 4.

"Search on for Film Studios Big Spender." *This is Local London*, 15 May 2004. Available at www.thisislocallondon.co.uk/search/display.var.490200.0.search_on_for_film_studios_big_spender.php (21 September 2004).

"Structural Funds: The Commission Approves the Community Support Framework for Germany 1994–99." IP/94/564, 21 June 1994; European Union. Available at http://europa.eu.int/ (26 February 2003).

"UCLA's Anderson Forecast Conference Examines the Forces Altering the Business of Hollywood." UCLA Anderson School of Management. Available at www.anderson.ucla.edu/x4495.xml (25 February 2004).

"UK Studios: Watch This Space." *Televisual*, 2 June 2004, 30.

"When Film-makers Seek Workspace." *The Times* [London], 14 May 1999, 33.

"World All-Time Box Office Chart." Internet Movie Database, 24 February 2004. Available at www.imdb.com/Charts/worldtopmovies (24 February 2004).

"World—Destination Florida—Get in a Right State." *Scottish Daily Record*, 31 January 2004, 4.

Authored Works

Acheson, Keith, and Christopher Maule. "Shadows behind the Scenes: Political Exchange and the Film Industry." *Millennium Journal of International Studies* 20, no. 2 (1991): 287–307.

Adams, James. "Megastudio Nears Port: Project Aimed at Bringing 'Hollywood North' Back to Toronto." *Globe and Mail*, 29 June 2004, R3.

Aksoy, Asu, and Kevin Robins. "Hollywood for the 21st Century: Global Competition for Critical Mass in Image Markets." *Cambridge Journal of Economics* 16 (1992): 1–22.

Applebome, Peter. "Hopes and Doubts Greet a Plan for Sound Stages at the Brooklyn Navy Yard." *New York Times*, 22 June 1999, E1.

Attallah, Paul. "Canadian Television Exported: Into the Mainstream." Pp. 161–91 in *New Patterns in Global Television: Peripheral Vision*, ed. John Sinclair, Elizabeth Jacka and Stuart Cunningham. Oxford: Oxford University Press, 1996.

Audit Office of New South Wales. *Performance Audit Report: Sydney Showground, Moore Park, Lease to Fox Studios Australia.* Sydney: Auditor-General Victoria, 1997.

Auditor-General Victoria. *Report on Public Sector Agencies.* Melbourne: Auditor-General Victoria, 2003.

Australian Film Commission. *Get the Picture: Essential Data on Australian Film, Television, Video and New Media.* 4th ed. Sydney: Australian Film Commission, 1996.

———. "Get the Picture Online." Available at www.afc.gov.au/gtp/index.html (22 September 2004).

———. *National Survey of Feature Film and TV Drama Production 2002/2003.* Sydney: Australian Film Commission, 2004.

———. "Value and Share of All Drama Production Activity (Feature Films and TV Drama; Australian, Co-production and Foreign) by Location of Spending in Australia, 1994/95–2002/03." *Get the Picture Online*, 2004. Available at www.afc.gov.au/gtp/mpvaluexspending.html (21 September 2004).

Bagli, Charles V. "A New Idea of 'Get Me the Coast': Hollywood's Major Competition is Western Queens." *New York Times*, 5 August 1999, B1.

———. "De Niro and Miramax Plan a Film Studio at the Brooklyn Navy Yard." *New York Times*, 29 April 1999, B1.

Balio, Tino. "Hollywood Production Trends in the Era of Globalisation, 1990–99." Pp. 165–84 in *Genre and Contemporary Hollywood*, ed. Steve Neale. London: British Film Institute, 2002.

———. *United Artists: The Company That Changed the Film Industry.* Madison: University of Wisconsin Press, 1987.

Ball, Deborah. "Film: Privatization May Spur Lethargic Cinecittà—Storied Studio Refocuses on International Filmmakers." *Wall Street Journal Europe*, 9 December 1997, 4.

Barnett, Cynthia. "Action." *Florida Trend* 42, no. 9 (January 2000): 112.

Barr, Charles, ed. *All Our Yesterdays: 90 Years of British Cinema.* London: British Film Institute, 1986.

Bateman, Louise. "*Star Wars* Casting Its Lot with Leavesden." *Hollywood Reporter*, 9 September 1996.

Bell, Desmond. "Communications, Corporatism, and Dependent Development in Ireland." *Journal of Communication* 45, no. 4 (1995): 70–88.

Bensinger, Ken, and Pat Saperstein. "Filmmaker Plans Lavish Studio." *Variety*, 5–11 April 2004, 13.

Blair, Helen, and Al Rainnie. "Flexible Films?" *Media, Culture & Society* 22, no. 2 (March 2000): 187-204.

Blaney, Martin. "Babelsberg Workforce Protest at Takeover." *Screen Daily*, 16 July 2004. Available at www.screendaily.com/story.asp?storyid=18426 (6 September 2004).
———. "New Babelsberg Chiefs Outline Studio Strategy." *Screen Daily*, 22 July 2004. Available at www.screendaily.com/story.asp?storyid=18494 (6 September 2004).
———. "Vivendi Universal Sells Babelsberg Studios." *Screen Daily*, 14 July 2004. Available at www.screendaily.com/story.asp?storyid=18410 (6 September 2004).
Bondanella, Peter. "From Italian Neorealism to the Golden Age of Cinecittà." Pp.119–38 in *European Cinema*, ed. Elizabeth Ezra. Oxford: Oxford University Press, 2004.
———. *Italian Cinema: From Neorealism to the Present*. 3d ed. New York: Continuum, 2001.
Bordwell, David. "The Classical Hollywood Style, 1917–1960." Pp. 3–84 in *The Classical Hollywood Cinema: Film Style & Mode of Production to 1960*, ed. David Bordwell, Kristin Thompson, and Janet Staiger. London: Routledge, 1996.
Bordwell, David, Janet Staiger, and Kristin Thompson, eds. *The Classical Hollywood Cinema: Film Style and Model of Production to 1960*. 2d ed. London: Routledge, 1985.
Boston Consulting Group. *Building New York's Visual Media Industry for the Digital Age: Findings and Recommendations*. Boston: Boston Consulting Group, June 2000.
Braczyk, Hans-Joachim, Gerhard Fuchs, and Hans-Georg Wolf, eds. *Multimedia and Regional Economic Restructuring*. London: Routledge, 1999.
Brennan, Steve. "Galway Getaway." *Hollywood Reporter*, 5 September 2000, 18.
Bringas-Rábago, Nora L. "Baja California and California's Merging Tourist Corridors: The Influence of Mexican Government Policies." *Journal of Environment & Development* 11, no. 3 (September 2002): 267–96.
Brinsley, John. "Hollywood's Obsession Over Runaway Production: Eyes Wide Shut." *Los Angeles Business Journal*, 2 August 1999, 1.
British Columbia Pavilion Corporation. "The Bridge Studios." Available at www.bridgestudios.com/ (7 September 2004).
Browne, Stephen E. *Film-Video Terms and Concepts*. Stoneham, Mass.: Focal, 1992.
Brož, Jaroslav. *The Path of Fame of the Czechoslovak Film: A Short Outline of its History from the Early Beginning to the Stream of Recent International Successes*. Prague: Československý Filmexport Press Department, 1967.
Calhoun, John. "Bridge Studios." *TCI* 31, no. 4 (April 1997): 36–41.
———. "Vancouver." *TCI* 31, no. 4 (April 1997): 36–41.
Canadian Film and Television Production Association (CFTPA). *Profile 2004: An Economic Report on the Canadian Film and Television Production Industry*. Toronto, Ottawa, and Vancouver: CFTPA in association with L'Association des producteurs de films et de télévision du Québec (L'APFTQ) and Canadian Heritage, 2004.
Careless, James. "What's Shooting on Canuck Stages: The Bridge Studios Fills Gap with Spots." *Playback*, 21 July 2003, 21.
Carrillo, Jorge. "Foreign Direct Investment and Local Linkages: Experiences and the Role of Policies: The Case of the Mexican Television Industry in Tijuana." Paper presented at XV World Congress of Sociology, Brisbane, Australia, July 2002.
Champagne, Christine. "Setting the Stage at the Navy Yard." *New York Production Alliance*. Available at www.nypa.org (27 February 2004).
Chang, Daniel, "Spanish-Language TV Production Firm Aims to Make Miami 'Hispanic Hollywood.'" *Knight Ridder Tribune Business News*, 11 May 2002: 1.
Choi, Audrey. "Filmmakers Adjusting Focus for the Future." *Wall Street Journal Europe*, 31 January 1994, 38.

Chrisafis, Angelique. "Ealing on a Roll as Deal Revives Studios." *The Guardian*, 24 May 2002, 9.

Christopherson, Susan. "Flexibility and Integration in Industrial Relations: The Exceptional Case of the US Media Entertainment Industries." Pp. 86–112 in *Under the Stars: Essays on Labor Relations in the Arts and Entertainment*, ed. Lois S. Gray and Ronald L. Seeber. Ithaca, N.Y.: ILR Press/Cornell University Press, 1996.

———. "The Limits to 'New Regionalism': (Re)Learning from the Media Industries." *Geoforum* 34, no. 4 (2003): 413–15.

Christopherson, Susan, and Michael Storper. "The City as Studio, the World as Backlot: The Impact of Vertical Disintegration on the Location of the Motion Picture Industry." *Environment and Planning D: Society and Space* 4 (1986): 305–20.

City of New York Mayor's Office of Film, Theatre, and Broadcasting. "Beyond the Skyline." 29 April 2003. Available at www.nyc.gov/html/film/html/home/beyond_skyline_384kqt.shtml (27 February 2004).

Clapp, Cristina. "Digital Cinecittà—How Two Innovators Using Quantel and Other Leading-edge Technologies Are Advancing the Science of Digital Intermediates." *Digital Cinema*, 1 December 2002, 20.

Cochrane, Allan, and Andrew Jonas. "Reimagining Berlin: World City, National Capital or Ordinary Place?" *European Urban and Regional Studies* 6, no. 2 (1999): 145–64.

Coe, Neil M. "A Hybrid Agglomeration? The Development of a Satellite-Marshallian Industrial District in Vancouver's Film Industry." *Urban Studies* 38, no. 10 (2001): 1753–75.

———. "The View from Out West: Embeddedness, Inter-personal Relations and the Development of an Indigenous Film Industry in Vancouver." *Geoforum* 31 (2000): 391–407.

Coletti, Elisabetta Anna. "'Made in Italy' Label Gains Celluloid Cachet." *Christian Science Monitor* 92, no. 220 (4 October 2000). Available at http://csmonitor.com/cgi-bin/durable Redirect.pl?/durable/2000/10/04/p1s4.htm (3 September 2004).

Comer, Brooke. "Production Incentives." *Louisiana Film Commission* (2003). Available at www.lafilm.org/media/index.cfm?id=29 (20 April 2004).

Connolly, Kate. "Bridge for Hire—$7,000 a Morning." *The Guardian*, 12 April 2002, 8

Cooke, Phil. "New Media and New Economy Cluster Dynamics." Pp. 287–303 in *The Handbook of New Media*, ed. Leah Lievrouw and Sonia Livingstone. London: Sage, 2002.

Cox, Alex. "Britain is Big Enough." *Sight and Sound* 13, no. 1 (January 2003): 6–7.

Creative Industries Research and Applications Centre. *Creative Cities: Cinema and the Built Environment*. Brisbane: Creative Industries Research and Applications Centre, 2004.

Cuff, Martin. *Business Plan 2003/04 Including Industry Growth Strategy, Marketing Strategy, Film Development Strategy*. Cape Town: Cape Film Commission, June 2003.

Davis, Susan G. "Space Jam: Media Conglomerates Build the Entertainment City." *European Journal of Communication* 14, no. 4 (1999): 435–59.

Dawn, Randee. "Production Junction." *Hollywood Reporter*, June 2003, 8.

De Castella, Tom. "Way Out West," *Sight and Sound* 14, no. 1 (January 2004): 9.

Department of Communications, Information Technology and the Arts (DCITA), Australia. *Creative Industries Cluster Study: Stage One Report*. Canberra: DCITA, 2002.

Dezzani, Mark. "RAI Gets More Domesticated," *Broadcast*, 17 February 1995. Available at http://global.factiva.com (21 September 2004).

DiOrio, Carl. "Theme Parks a Bumpy Ride for Congloms." *Variety*, 23–29 June 2003, 5.

Drewery, Brant. "The Chameleon Coast: On Location with *The X-Files* in Anyplace, USA. Otherwise Known as Vancouver, Canada." *BC Business* 25, no. 5 (May 1997): 44–50.

Ealing Council. *Report on a Strategy for Creative and Media Industries in Ealing.* Ealing: Ealing Council, 2003.

Economic Research Associates (ERA). *Project Report Assessment of the Florida Motion Picture Industry.* Prepared for the Governor's Office of Film & Entertainment, Los Angeles, February 2003.

Entertainment Industry Development Corporation (EIDC). *MOWs—A Three Year Study: An Analysis of Television Movies of the Week 1997–1998, 1998–1999, 1999–2000.* Hollywood: EIDC, 2001.

Ferguson, Tim W., and William Heuslein. "Cape Dear." *Forbes,* 28 May 2001, 132–46.

Fernandez, Enrique. "Critique: Finding Greater Havana in Dade County, Florida." *Wall Street Journal,* 21 July 1987, 1.

Fernett, Gene. *American Film Studios: An Historical Encyclopedia.* Jefferson, N.C.: McFarland, 1988.

Fisher, Ian. "On Dracula's Terrain, an Infusion of New Blood." *New York Times,* 22 July 2003, A4.

Forman, Ellen. "Backlot Bounty." *Hollywood Reporter,* 20–26 May 2003, F6.

Foroohar, Rana, Alexandra Seno, and Stefan Theil. "Hurray for Globowood: As Motion-Picture Funding, Talent and Audiences Go Global, Hollywood Is No Longer a Place, but a State of Mind." *Newsweek International,* 27 May 2002, 51.

Frayling, Christopher. *The Spaghetti Western: Cowboys and Europeans from Karl May to Sergio Leone.* London: Routledge & Kegan Paul, 1981.

Freestone, Robert, ed. *The Twentieth Century Planning Experience.* Sydney: University of New South Wales, 1998.

Garry, Patrick. "A Different Voice: An Industry Is Born." *Commonweal* 122, no. 6 (1995): 17.

Gasher, Mike. *Hollywood North: The Feature Film Industry in British Columbia.* Vancouver: University of British Columbia Press, 2002.

Gill, Alexandra. "End of BC Film Seed Money Decried." *The Globe and Mail,* 7 April 2004, R2.

Goldman, Michael. "Set Incentives." *Millimeter* 29, no. 11 (1 November 2001): 9.

Goldsmith, Ben. "From the Ruins of Berlin: Imagining the Postmodern City." In *Passionate City Symposium Proceedings* [online]. Melbourne: RMIT, 2004. Available at www.rmitpublishing .com.au/products.asp?type=il (22 November 2004).

Goldsmith, Ben, and Tom O'Regan. *Cinema Cities, Media Cities: The Contemporary International Studio Complex.* Sydney: Australian Film Commission, 2003.

———. "Locomotives and Stargates: Inner-city Studio Complexes in Sydney, Melbourne and Toronto." *International Journal of Cultural Policy* 10, no. 1 (March 2004): 29–46.

Goldsmith, Jill. "Ahoy, Busy Producers." *Variety,* 26 January–1 February 2004, 9.

Grabher, Gernot. "Cool Projects, Boring Institutions: Temporary Collaboration in Social Context." *Regional Studies* 36, no. 3 (2002): 205–14.

Grassi, Giovanni. "Italy to Privatize Cinecittà." *Hollywood Reporter,* 6 September 1994, 1.

Gray, Lois S., and Ronald L. Seeber, eds. *Under the Stars: Essays on Labor Relations in the Arts and Entertainment.* Ithaca, N.Y.: ILR Press/Cornell University Press, 1996.

Guback, Thomas. *The International Film Industry: Western Europe and America since 1945.* Bloomington: Indiana University Press, 1969.

Hall, Peter. *Cities in Civilization.* London: Weidenfeld & Nicolson, 1998.

———. *Cities of Tomorrow.* 3d ed. Oxford: Blackwell, 2002.

———. "The Future of Cities." *Computers, Environments and Urban Systems* 23 (1999): 173–85.

Hall, Sandra. "Queensland Takes the Plunge." *Bulletin*, 18 December 1979, 65.

Hamnett, Stephen. "The Late 1990s: Competitive versus Sustainable Cities." Pp. 168–88 in *The Australian Metropolis: A Planning History*, ed. Stephen Hamnett and Robert Freestone. Crows Nest, Australia: Allen & Unwin, 2000.

Hamnett, Stephen, and Robert Freestone, eds. *The Australian Metropolis: A Planning History*. Crows Nest, Australia: Allen & Unwin, 2000.

Hancock, David. *Film Production in Europe: A Comparative Study of Film Production Costs in Five European Territories: France, Germany, Italy, Spain, UK*. Strasbourg: European Audiovisual Observatory, 1999.

Hannigan, John. "Cities as the Physical Site of the Global Entertainment Economy." Pp. 181–95 in *Global Media Policy in the New Millennium*, ed. Marc Raboy. Luton: University of Luton Press, 2002.

Harvey, David. *Spaces of Capital: Towards a Critical Geography*. Edinburgh: Edinburgh University Press, 2001.

Heinrich, Mark. "East German State Film Studio Feels Cold Wind of Capitalism." *Reuters News*, 25 April 1990. Available at http://global.factiva.com (21 September 2004).

Hernandez, Greg. "Disney Dismantles Animation Facility." *Los Angeles Daily*, 13 January 2004, B1.

Hopewell, John, and Emiliano de Pablos. "Gov't Backs Top Studio Complex." *Variety*, 19–25 January 2004, 10.

Horst, Carole. "Winter Games, Lumiq Studios bring Northern Region an Edge." *Variety*, 27 October 2003, B2.

House of Commons Culture, Media and Sport Committee [United Kingdom]. *The British Film Industry*, Sixth Report of Session 2002–2003, vol. 1. London: House of Commons Culture, Media and Sport Committee, 2003.

House of Representatives Standing Committee on Communications, Information Technology and the Arts. *From Reel to Unreal: Future Opportunities for Australia's Film, Animation, Special Effects and Electronic Games Industries: Inquiry into the Future Opportunities for Australia's Film, Animation, Special Effects and Electronic Games Industries*. Canberra: Commonwealth of Australia, 2004. Available at www.aph.gov.au/house/committee/cita/film/report.htm (20 August 2004).

Hozic, Aida. *Hollyworld: Space, Power and Fantasy in American Cinema*. Ithaca, N.Y.: Cornell University Press, 2001.

———. "The Political Economy of Global Culture: A Case Study of the Film Industry." Pp. 55–78 in *Culture, Politics, and Nationalism in the Age of Globalization*, ed. Renéo Lukic and Michael Brint. Aldershot, U.K.: Ashgate, 2001.

Hughes, Helen, and Martin Brady. "German Film after the *Wende*." Pp. 276–96 in *The New Germany: Social, Political and Cultural Challenges of Unification*, ed. Derek Lewis and John R. P. McKenzie. Exeter: University of Exeter Press, 1995.

Iordanova, Dina. "East Europe's Cinema Industries since 1989." *Media Development* 3 (1999): 13–17.

Johnson, Louise, William S. Logan, and Colin Long. "Jeff Kennett's Melbourne: Postmodern City, Planning and Politics." Pp. 436–41 in *The Twentieth Century Planning Experience*, ed. Robert Freestone. Sydney: University of New South Wales, 1998.

Johnson, Mark R., and Vanessa Liertz. "German Studio Transforms Itself into a Co-producer." *Asian Wall Street Journal*, 21 March 2001, N5.

Jones, Martha. *Motion Picture Production in California*. Sacramento: California Research Bureau, 2002.

Kandell, Jonathan. "Vaunted Vancouver." *Smithsonian* 35, no. 1 (April 2004): 84–93.

Katz, Ian. "The Tread of a Velvet Tightrope." *The Guardian*, 4 June 1992, 24.

Katz, Stephen. *The Migration of Feature Film Production from the US to Canada and Beyond: Year 2001 Production Report*. Los Angeles: Center for Entertainment Industry Data and Research (CEIDR), 2002.

Kaufman, Anthony. "Backlot Dreams." *Village Voice* 48, no. 12 (19–25 March 2003): 53.

Kay, Jeremy. "Eliasoph Named Head of New Warner China." *Screen Daily*, 24 June 2003. Available at www.screendaily.com (15 July 2003).

Kelly, Brendan. "Few Projects Migrate North." *Variety*, 2–8 September 2002, A8.

———. "Shoots Rediscover City's Charms." *Variety*, 25–31 August 2003, 35.

Kiefer, Peter. "Runaway Roadblocking: Do Industry and Political Leaders Have the Power and the Will to Protect Hollywood?" *Hollywood Reporter*, 20 November 2002, 44.

Kirby, Jason. "Starr Power: If You Think No One Makes Money in the Canadian Film Industry, You've Never Met Don Starr, a Tax Lawyer Who's Loopholed His Way to Making Millions." *Canadian Business* 75, no. 17 (September 2002).

Klein, Norman M. *The History of Forgetting: Los Angeles and the Erasure of Memory*. London: Verso, 1997.

Kracauer, Siegfried. "Calico World: The Ufa City in Neubabelsberg." Pp. 191–93 in *Film Architecture: Set Designs from* Metropolis *to* Blade Runner, trans. and ed. Dietrich Neumann. Munich: Prestel, 1999.

Krätke, Stefan. "Global Media Cities in a Worldwide Urban Network." *Globalization and World Cities Study Group and Network Research Bulletin* 80 (March 2002). Available at www.lboro.ac.uk/gawc/rb/rb80.html (6 August 2003).

———. "Network Analysis of Production Clusters: The Potsdam/Babelsberg Film Industry as an Example." *European Planning Studies* 10, no. 1 (2002): 27–54.

Kreimeier, Klaus. *The UFA Story: A History of Germany's Greatest Film Company, 1918–1945*. Berkeley: University of California Press, 1999.

Lehrer, Jeremy. "Brooklyn Navy Yard Deck Is Reshuffled—Development into a Movie Studio." *Shoot* 22 (October 1999). Available at www.findarticles.com/p/articles/mi_m0DUO/is_42_40/ai_57796020/print (13 September 2004).

Levine, Felicia. "The 'Hispanic Hollywood' Works to Keep Show Business Here to Stay." *South Florida Business Journal*, 18 October 1996, 1

Levitt, Joshua. "Cameras, Sound, Money, Action . . . : Critics Are Asking If Investments in Film Studios May Not Be Enough to Bring in the Scale of Film-making the City Needs," *Financial Times*, 31 October 2002, 3.

Liehm, Antonín J. *Closely Watched Films: The Czechoslovak Experience*. White Plains, N.Y.: International Arts and Sciences Press, 1974.

Lievrouw, Leah, and Sonia Livingstone. *The Handbook of New Media*. London: Sage, 2002.

Linehan, Hugh. "Corman Uncovered." *Irish Times*, 22 August 1997, 13.

McAleer, Phelim. "Hollywood's Finest Flock to Romania: Cost Savings and Varied Scenery Make the Former Communist State a Hot Destination for Filmmakers." *Financial Times* 25 June 2003, 10.

———. "Where Stars Stroll in the Streets: The Film Industry: Producers Are Flocking In, Attracted by Cheap, Skilled Labour." *Financial Times*, 14 October 2003, 2.

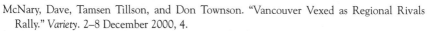

McNary, Dave, Tamsen Tillson, and Don Townson. "Vancouver Vexed as Regional Rivals Rally." *Variety*. 2–8 December 2000, 4.

McNary, Dave. "Runaway Relief on Hold as Gov. Battles Budget." *Variety*, 1–7 December 2003, 6.

Maher, Sean. *The Internationalisation of Australian Film and Television Through the 1990s*. Sydney: Australian Film Commission, 2004.

Malcolm Long Associates. *A Bigger Slice of the Pie: Policy Options for a More Competitive International Film & Television Production Industry in Australia—A Report for AusFILM International Inc*. Sydney: Malcolm Long Associates, 2000.

Mang, Randall. "Dialed In: Bell Sweeps into the West." *BC Business* 31, no. 5 (May 2003): 103–4, 106.

Marsh, Ed W. *James Cameron's* Titanic. New York: HarperCollins, 1997.

Meza, Ed. "Film-Rich Region Targets More Prod'n." *Variety*, 2 February 2004, B8.

———. "Studio Exex Allay Worries." *Variety*, 26 July 2004, 15.

Miller, Danny, and Jamal Shamsie. "The Resource-Based View of the Film in Two Environments: The Hollywood Film Studios from 1936 to 1965." *Academy of Management Journal* 39, no. 3 (1996): 519–43.

Miller, Toby, Nitin Govil, John McMurria, and Richard Maxwell, *Global Hollywood*. London: British Film Institute, 2001.

Miller, Toby. *Technologies of Truth: Cultural Citizenship and the Popular Media*. Minneapolis: University of Minnesota Press, 1998.

Ministry of Culture of the Czech Republic. *Report on the State of Czech Cinematography in 2000*. Prague: Ministry of Culture of the Czech Republic, 2001.

Minns, Adam. "Pinewood-Shepperton Eyes European Expansion." *Screen Daily*, 12 February 2001. Available at www.screendaily.com/story.asp?storyid=3994 (28 February 2003).

———. "UK's Ealing Studios Set for $100m Revamp." *Screen Daily*, 14 June 2001. Available at www.screendaily.com/story.asp?storyid=4966 (28 February 2003).

Mohr, Ian. "Bright Lights, Big City." New York Production Alliance, 23 September 2003. Available at www.nypa.org (27 February 2004).

Moran, Albert. "A State Government Business Venture: The South Australian Film Corporation." Pp. 252–63 in *An Australian Film Reader*, ed. Albert Moran and Tom O'Regan. Sydney: Currency Press, 1985.

Murphy, David G. "The Entrepreneurial Role of Organized Labour in the British Columbia Motion Picture Industry." *Relations Industrielles/Industrial Relations* 52, no. 3 (1997): 531–53.

Murphy, Robert. "Under the Shadow of Hollywood." Pp. 47–71 in *All Our Yesterdays: 90 Years of British Cinema*, ed. Charles Barr. London: British Film Institute, 1986.

Murray, Karen. "Local Fare Finds Hungrier Palates South of the Border." *Variety*, 16 November 1992, 41.

Naughton, Leonie. "That Was the Wild East: Filmpolitik and the 'New' Germany." Paper presented at History and Film Conference, Brisbane, November 1998.

Nauman, Talli. "*Titanic* Prompts Pollution Study." United Press International, 6 April 1998.

Neale, Steve, ed. *Genre and Contemporary Hollywood*. London: British Film Institute, 2002.

Neumann, Dietrich, ed. *Film Architecture: Set Designs from* Metropolis *to* Blade Runner. Munich: Prestel, 1999.

New York City Economic Development Corporation. "Media and Entertainment." Available at www.newyorkbiz.com/Industries/Entertainment/index.html (27 February 2004).

New York State Governor's Office. "About Production in New York." New York State Governor's Office for Motion Picture and Television Development. Available at www.nylovesfilm.com/prodinny.asp (27 February 2004).

Nowell-Smith, Geoffrey. "Cities: Real and Imagined." Pp. 99–108 in *Cinema and the City: Film and Urban Societies in a Global Context*, ed. Mark Shiel and Tony Fitzmaurice. London: Blackwell, 2001.

Oakley, Kate. "Not So Cool Britannia: The Role of the Creative Industries in Economic Development." *International Journal of Cultural Studies* 7, no. 1 (2004): 67–77.

Onstad, Katrina. "Cut to the Cash: They're Making More Than Most Bank Managers." *Canadian Business* 70, no. 7 (June 1997): 36–43.

Osborne, Helen. "Studio in the Frame." *Estates Gazette*, 18 March 2000, 84.

Parisi, Paula. *Titanic and the Making of James Cameron: The Inside Story of the Three-Year Adventure That Rewrote Motion Picture History*. London: Orion, 1998.

Parker, Sir Alan. "Building a Sustainable UK Film Industry: A Presentation to the UK Film Industry." UK Film Council, 5 November 2003. Available at www.ukfilmcouncil.org.uk/usr/downloads/BaSFI.pdf (20 February 2004).

Parkes, Christopher. "Farewell, My Lovely: Hollywood Is Hollowing Out as Global Competition and Digital Technology Take Hold." *Financial Times*, 4 April 2002, 25.

Pavasaris, Sue. "Lights, Camera, Ahern! Queensland Film Gets a New Start." *Filmnews* 18, no. 9 (1988): 3.

Pettitt, Lance. *Screening Ireland: Film and Television Representation*. Manchester: Manchester University Press, 2000.

Phillips, John. "Italy Sells Off Dream Factory on the Tiber—Cinecittà Film Studios." *The Times*, 27 August 1994, 12.

Pratt, Andy C. "The Cultural Economy: A Call for Spatialized 'Production of Culture' Perspectives." *International Journal of Cultural Studies* 7, no. 1 (2004): 117–28.

Rawsthorn, Alice. "Film Industry Searches for a Second Take on Success: The Sector May Face Trouble if Another Blockbuster is Not Found." *Financial Times*, 27 August 1998, 7.

Reveler, Norma. "Runaway Competition." *Hollywood Reporter*, 2–8 September 2003, 66.

Rice-Barker, Leo. "Moliflex-White Assets on the Auction Block." *Playback*, 24 November 2003, 1.

Rockett, Kevin. "Irish Cinema: The National in the International." *Cineaste* 24, nos. 2–3 (1999): 23.

———. "Phases of the Moon: A Short History of Cinema in Ireland." *Film Comment* 30, no. 3 (1994): 25–28.

Rohter, Larry. "Miami, the Hollywood of Latin America." *New York Times*, 18 August 1996, 1.

Rose, Nikolas. *Powers of Freedom: Reframing Political Thought*. Cambridge: Cambridge University Press, 1999.

Rosenbaum, Jonathan. "Multinational Pest Control: Does American Cinema Still Exist?" Pp. 217–29 in *Film and Nationalism*, ed. and with an introduction by Alan Williams. New Brunswick, N.J.: Rutgers University Press, 2002.

Rowe, David, and Pauline McGuirk. "Drunk for Three Weeks: Sporting Success and City Image." *International Review for the Sociology of Sport* 34, no. 2 (1999): 125–41.

Sassen, Saskia. *The Global City: New York, London, Tokyo*. Princeton, N.J.: Princeton University Press, 2001.

Schatz, Thomas. "The Return of the Hollywood Studio System." Pp. 73–106 in *Conglomerates and the Media*, ed. Patricia Aufderheide, Erik Barnouw, Richard M. Cohen, Thomas Frank,

Todd Gitlin, David Lieberman, Mark Crispin Miller, Gene Robers, and Thomas Schatz. New York: New Press, 1997.

Schulze, Laurie. "The Made-for-TV Movie: Industrial Practice, Cultural Form, Popular Reception." Pp. 155–75 in *Television: The Critical View*, 5th ed., ed. Horace Newcomb. New York: Oxford University Press, 1994.

Scott, Allen J. "The Cultural Economy: Geography and the Creative Field." *Media, Culture and Society* 21, no. 6 (1999): 807–17.

——. *The Cultural Economy of Cities: Essays on the Geography of Image-producing Industries.* London: Sage, 2000.

——. "Cultural Products Industries and Urban Economic Development: Prospects for Growth and Market Contestation in Global Context." *Urban Affairs Review* 39, no. 4 (March 2004): 461–90.

——. "A New Map of Hollywood: The Production and Distribution of American Motion Pictures." *Regional Studies* 36, no. 9 (2002): 957–75.

——. *On Hollywood: The Place, The Industry.* Princeton, N.J.: Princeton University Press, 2005.

——. "The Other Hollywood: The Organizational and Geographic Bases of Television-Program Production." *Media, Culture & Society* 26, no. 2 (2004): 183–205.

Seguin, Denis. "The Battle for Hollywood North: Vancouver, Montreal and Toronto Are Each Leading the Charge to Be Canada's Capital of Movie Production; Big-name Stars and Big-money Budgets Are the Coveted Prize." *Canadian Business* 76, no. 17 (September 2003): 55.

——. "Hawking Hogtown." *Canadian Business* 76, no. 10 (May 2003): 112.

Shiel, Mark. "A Nostalgia for Modernity: New York, Los Angeles, and American Cinema in the 1970s." Pp. 160–79 in *Screening the City*, ed. Mark Shiel and Tony Fitzmaurice. London: Verso, 2003.

Shiel, Mark, and Tony Fitzmaurice, eds. *Cinema and the City: Film and Urban Societies in a Global Context.* London: Blackwell, 2001.

——. *Screening the City.* London: Verso, 2003.

Simpson, Victor L. "Liz's Queenly Bed Snapped Up for $4,500: Huge Italian Film Studio, Cinecittà, Auctions Off Thousands of Props." *The Globe and Mail*, 2 June 1993, C3.

Sinclair, John. "'The Hollywood of Latin America': Miami as Regional Center in Television Trade." *Television and New Media* 4, no. 3 (August 2003): 211–29.

Souccar, Miriam Kreinin. "Film Production Hits Break in Action." *Crain's New York Business* 19, no. 13 (31 March 2003): 3

Staiger, Janet. "The Hollywood Mode of Production to 1930." Pp. 85–153 in *The Classical Hollywood Cinema: Film Style and Model of Production to 1960*, 2d ed., ed. David Bordwell, Janet Staiger, and Kristin Thompson. London: Routledge, 1985.

——. "The Hollywood Mode of Production, 1930–60." Pp. 309–37 in *The Classical Hollywood Cinema: Film Style and Model of Production to 1960*, 2d ed., ed. David Bordwell, Janet Staiger, and Kristin Thompson. London: Routledge, 1985.

Storper, Michael. "The Transition to Flexible Specialisation in the US Film Industry: External Economies, the Division of Labor, and the Crossing of Industrial Divides." *Cambridge Journal of Economics* 13 (1989): 273–305.

Studnickova, Lenka. "Barrandov Deal Off Due to a Lack of Capital." *Prague Business Journal*, 27 November 2000. Available at http://global.factiva.com (28 May 2002).

Sussman, Gerald, and John A. Lent, eds. *Global Productions: Labor in the Making of the "Information Society."* Cresskill, N.J.: Hampton, 1998.

Sweeney, Paul. "Studio Wars." *Florida Trend* 13, no. 3 (July 1988).

Terezono, Emiko, Peter Hudson, Amy Kazmin, Ian Bickerton, and John Reed. "Creative Minnows Hunt Big Fish: Rich Imaginations and Inspirational Settings are Helping Advertising Backwaters Emerge in to the Mainstream." *Financial Times*, 18 November 2003, 10.

Tillson, Tamsen. "Quality Not Quantity for Local News." *Variety*, 25 February–3 March 2002, 67.

Toronto Economic Development Corporation (TEDCO). "Backgrounder: Toronto Film/Media Complex." 2003. Available at www.tedco.ca/backgrounder.html (13 September 2003).

Toscano, John. "Astoria Studios to Build 7th Sound Stage." *Western Queens Gazette*, 11 August 1999. Available at www.qgazette.com/NEWS/1999/0811/Front_Page_Folder/ (21 September 2004).

Toumarkine, Doris. "Canadian Attraction: Busy Film Commissions Continue to Lure Big Productions." *Film Journal International*, 1 May 2004. Available at http://filmjournal.com/film journal/search/search_display.jsp?vnu_content_id=1000692699 (22 November 2004).

Tunstall, Jeremy, and David Walker. *Media Made in California: Hollywood, Politics and the News.* New York: Oxford University Press, 1981.

Unger, Craig. "Prague's Velvet Hangover after Their Revolution." *Los Angeles Times*, 12 May 1991, 20.

United States International Trade Administration. *The Migration of US Film and Television Production: Impact of "Runaways" on Workers and Small Business in the US Film Industry.* Washington, D.C.: U.S. Department of Commerce, 2001.

Victorian Film and Television Industry Task Force. *The Film and Television Production Industry in Victoria.* Report to Minister for the Arts. Melbourne: Victorian Film and Television Industry Task Force, September 2000.

Vlessing, Etan, and Adele Weder. "Rising Canada $ Seen as Slowing US Production." *Hollywood Reporter*, 13–19 May 2003, 65.

Wakin, Daniel J. "Even in Death, Fellini Assumes Epic Proportions: All-Night Wake Held at Rome Studio." *New Orleans Times-Picayune*, 2 November 1993, A11.

Walker, Alexander. *Hollywood UK: the British Film Industry in the Sixties.* New York: Stein & Day, 1974.

Ward, Janet. "Berlin, the Virtual Global City." *Visual Culture* 3, no. 2 (2004): 239–56.

Warner Roadshow Studios. *The Economic Effect of Warner Roadshow Movie World Studios on the Film and Television Industry in Queensland.* Gold Coast, Australia: Warner Roadshow Studios, May 1992.

Wasko, Janet. *How Hollywood Works.* London: Sage, 2003.

Watson, Stuart. "The Dream Crashes." *Estates Gazette*, 12 October 2002, 106.

Weder, Adele. "Rival Said to Bid on Bridge Studio." *Hollywood Reporter*, 5 December 2002, 39.

Weinstein, Bernard L., and Terry L. Clower. "Filmed Entertainment and Local Economic Development: Texas as a Case Study." *Economic Development Quarterly* 14, no. 4 (November 2000): 384–94.

Wilker, Deborah. "Head of State: Dialogue with Jeb Bush." *Hollywood Reporter* 380 (21–27 October 2003): 18.

———. "Miami Nice for Hispanic TV Surge." *Hollywood Reporter*, 6–12 January 2004, 30.

Willey, David. "The End as Lights Fade Forever at Italy's Hollywood." *The Observer*, 23 May 1993.

Williams, Alan, ed. *Film and Nationalism.* New Brunswick, N.J.: Rutgers University Press, 2002.

Yudice, George. *The Expediency of Culture: Uses of Culture in a Global Era.* Durham, N.C.: Duke University Press, 2004.

Zesch, Lindy. "Miami's Theatrical Cache." *American Theatre* 13, no. 9 (November 1996): 26–27.

Index

217

About the Authors

Ben Goldsmith recently took up the position of head of the Centre for Screen Studies and Research at the Australian Film, Television, and Radio School in Sydney. From 2001 to 2004, he held an Australian Research Council postdoctoral fellowship at Griffith University, Brisbane, Australia, to investigate the new ecology of English-language feature film production, focusing on the development and renovation of film studios, the phenomenon of footloose or "runaway" production, and the increasing incidence of coproduction as an industry norm. Goldsmith coauthored (with Tom O'Regan) a report for the Australian Film Commission on the contemporary studio complex entitled *Cinema Cities/Media Cities* (2003) and has published a number of journal articles and book chapters on studio developments in recent years.

Tom O'Regan is professor of media and cultural studies in the School of English, Media Studies, and Art History at the University of Queensland. He is the author of *Australian National Cinema* (1996) and *Australian Television Culture* (1992) and the coauthor of the reports *Cinema Cities/Media Cities* (2003 with Goldsmith) and *The Future for Local Content* (2001 with Goldsmith, Cunningham, and Thomas). He is also the coeditor of a book on audience development strategies in the arts and media sectors, *Mobilising the Audience* (2002). In 2002, he was elected a fellow of the Australian Academy of the Humanities. O'Regan was the director of the Australian Key Centre for Cultural and Media Policy (CMP) from 1999 through 2002 and was integrally involved in developing media and cultural studies in Australia and internationally. He cofounded the cultural and media studies journal *Continuum* (1987–1995).